The
Work/Life
Collision

The
Work/Life
Collision

What work is doing to Australians
and what to do about it

Barbara Pocock

THE FEDERATION PRESS
2003

Published in Sydney by:
    The Federation Press
    PO Box 45, Annandale, NSW, 2038
    71 John St, Leichhardt, NSW, 2040
    Ph (02) 9552 2200 Fax (02) 9552 1681
    E-mail: info@federationpress.com.au
    Website: http://www.federationpress.com.au

National Library of Australia
Cataloguing-in-Publication entry

    Pocock, Barbara
    The work-life collision : what work is doing to
    Australians and what to do about it.

    Bibliography
    Includes index.
    ISBN 1 86287 475 1

    1. Hours of labour – Australia. 2. Work and family – Australia.
    3. Work design – Australia. I. Title.

331.2570994

Typeset by The Federation Press, Leichhardt, NSW.
    Printed by Ligare Pty Ltd, Riverwood NSW.

Table of Contents

For Jake and Indi

About the Author

Associate Professor Barbara Pocock is Director of the Centre for Labour Research at Adelaide University, where she is a Research Fellow in social science and labour studies.

She has worked in several industries and advised a range of governments and political parties. During 2001-2002 she was seconded to work for the former Leader of the Australian Democrats, Senator Natasha Stott Despoja, to advise on work, industrial, family and women's issues.

Barbara Pocock's publications include *Demanding Skill: Women and technical education in Australia* (1988) and *Strife: sex and politics in Australia* (1997) which she edited.

Acknowledgments

I have benefited from the support of many people on the road to, and through, this book. My greatest debt is to those who joined focus groups or allowed themselves to be interviewed in the qualitative studies that partially underpin this book. I thank them for their time, thoughtfulness and generous honesty.

I thank the researchers who worked with me to conduct focus groups and interviews during 2000. Jane Clark and Robyn Ressom set up and ran focus groups with me amidst South Australians. They talked through many of the ideas that found their way into the discussion of those interviews and focus groups. I was lucky to work with such creative and efficient friends. This work was assisted by the Office of Status of Women in South Australia and the Australian Research Council.

I worked with Brigid van Wonrooy (then at the Australian Centre for Industrial Relations Research and Training), and Stefani Strazzari and Ken Bridge (from the Centre for Labour Research, University of Adelaide) conducting interviews with long-hours workers and their partners across Australia in 2001. John Buchanan helped design this study. Once again, I was lucky to work with a team of creative, flexible and very effective researchers. This research was funded by the Australian Council of Trade Unions and I thank the union affiliates, officers and staff at the ACTU. Like so many others, I have been the beneficiary of the Australian Bureau of Statistics' many years of statistical collection and their increasing accessibility, at least to academics.

Through this study I have benefited from the friendship and collegiality of Dr John Buchanan at the Australian Centre for Industrial Relations Research and Training, Sydney University,. Iain Campbell of the Royal Melbourne Institute of Technology and Susan Oakley at the University of Adelaide. They each live a generous practice of research cooperation, for which I am very grateful. I may not have read everything they have pointed me to, but I have benefited in many ways from their ideas, corrections, reading lists, comments, and research and policy creativity.

Richard Dennis and John Wishart also read chapters in the book and I thank them for their comments and discussions.

Students, friends and colleagues at the Centre for Labour Research, and the University of Adelaide itself, have been generous in supporting my research, and my erratic work, mothering and leave patterns for a decade and a half. In recent times, Sharon Lewis, Sonya Mezinec, Kathie Muir, Thalia Palmer, Margie Ripper and Pat Wright have helped me out in many ways.

Senator Natasha Stott Despoja gave me an opportunity to see the inside workings of parliamentary policy and law making up close for 14 months during 2001 and 2002 while I was her advisor on industrial relations, work, family and women's issues. I didn't always savour the parliamentary experience and its disembodied life, but I was lucky to have such a good boss – committed to improving the terms of life in Australia. I enjoyed working with a staff who knew how to keep perspective in the rough and rocky terrain of political life. I thank them all, and especially Richard Dennis and Alison Rogers.

At Federation Press, Margaret Farmer and Clare Moss have efficiently supported the book and its production.

Thank you Sue Outram, Cathie Murray, Helen Willoughby, Susan Lane, Janet Giles, Collette Snowden, Maureen Gallagher, Pam Schofield, Maureen Grainey, Jane Clark, Robyn Ressom, Margaret Hallock, Jane Flohr, Jane Tassie, Kay Pocock, Claire Pocock and Mary Yeates for your various acts of friendship and support. Special thanks to Marie and Jim Pocock for your many years of work and care. I also thank my other neighbours, friends and family who have been vital supports to me at many points and made up a community that I am lucky to live amidst.

Thank you John Wishart for your generous partnership and for continuing to make your way with me. Thank you Jake and Indiana for taking the ride, for supporting me, and for regularly debunking public life. This book is for you.

Abbreviations

ABS	Australian Bureau of Statistics
ACIRRT	Australian Centre for Industrial Relations Research and Training
ACTU	Australian Council for Trade Unions
AWIRS	Australian Workplace Industrial Relations Survey
HILDA	Household, Income and Labour Dynamics in Australia
HREOC	Human Rights and Equal Opportunity Commission
IsssA	International Social Science Surveys Australia
LSL	Long Service Leave
NPEC	National Pay Equity Coalition
OECD	Organisation for Economic Cooperation and Development
PML	Paid Maternity Leave
RDOs	Rostered Days Off
SNAGs	Sensitive New Age Guys

CHAPTER 1

The work/life collision

This book is about the collision between work and care and its consequences for life in Australia It is about *the interactions between the spheres of work, gender relations, consumption, community and family.*

Household patterns in Australia are changing. A quarter are now single person households, and this has steadily risen over the last decade. The majority of Australian households are families, and in more and more of them, couples work while they have dependants at home. Changes occurring in workplaces have reduced the number of hours we have available to spend on our homes, communities and care. Activities that were once mostly the province of women at home – cooking and care of small children, for example – are increasingly provided by the market. In contrast, some forms of market work are now being done at home, or in new ways. Accompanying these shifts has been a steady decline in men's participation in market work, as women's participation has steadily risen. This long-term, secular shift in men's and women's market work rates has given rise to, and reflects, very significant social change.

However, all this change is not mirrored in compensating changes in the key cultures and institutions that shape behaviours at work, at home and in the market. Australian households reveal not only unchanging patterns of domestic and care work that remain largely the work of women, but also unrenovated models of motherhood and fatherhood, and workplaces that still have at their centre an 'ideal-worker' who is care-less.

Workplaces, and the other institutions that frame them like the law, the labour market, schools, preschools and the institutions of care, have changed all too little. The 'ideal worker' (with a wife at home) now forms the minority of those participating in the Australian labour market at any particular point in time.

Care – care of ourselves, each other, our households, families and communities, and our quality of life, care in childhood, old age, sickness and death, and our efforts to live well and to reproduce – these are the casualties of the collision between the changing and the unchanging spheres.

A model of the Work/Life Collision: A map of this book

Figure 1.1 opposite provides a visual key to the argument presented in this book, It represents the collision of the Australian 'Work/Care' regime – a moving vehicle of change in work patterns and in family structures, meeting a solid wall of relatively unchanging labour market institutions, culture and practice.

Chapter 2 introduces a model of total labour, and of 'Work/Care' regimes, through which we can analyse work and care outcomes. The importance of transitions in increasingly dynamic labour markets is also discussed. The chapter maps significant social and labour market behaviours that are reshaping work, households, the gender composition (and, consequently, care-loads) of the labour market, and the market exchange of goods and services for earned income.

Chapter 3 considers the impact of these collisions and changes upon our community fabric. The location of community has increasingly shifted from the neighbourhood to the workplace, with important implications for carers at home, and for the overall health of our communities and neighbourhoods and social capital.

Chapter 4 discusses many of our cultural habits and embodied history. The ideas and practices of motherhood and fatherhood are just one part of this embodied historical and social apparatus. The cultural constructions of 'proper mothers', and 'proper carers' have not changed commensurate with change in their roles in paid work. Many still think of a good mother as an ever-available generous carer – exactly what the worker-mother finds

Figure 1.1 The Collision: A Model

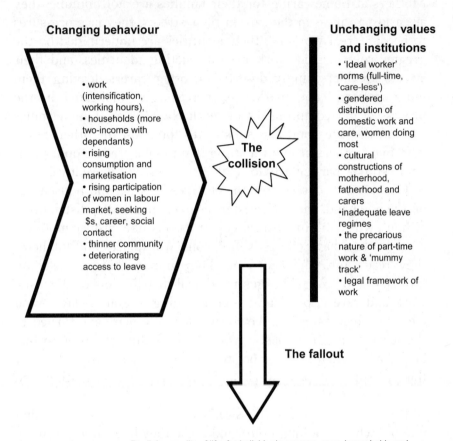

Changing behaviour

• work (intensification, working hours),
• households (more two-income with dependants)
• rising consumption and marketisation
• rising participation of women in labour market, seeking $s, career, social contact
• thinner community
• deteriorating access to leave

The collision

Unchanging values and institutions

• 'Ideal worker' norms (full-time, 'care-less')
• gendered distribution of domestic work and care, women doing most
• cultural constructions of motherhood, fatherhood and carers
•inadequate leave regimes
• the precarious nature of part-time work & 'mummy track'
• legal framework of work

The fallout

• Declining quality of life, for individuals, women, men, households and children
• Loss of community. Shift of community from street to workplace
• Rising levels of guilt, especially for mothers and carers
• Erosion of relationships and intimacy
• Pressure on those carers still at home, and on grandparents. Resentment.
•Marketisation of care and love as market goods and services replace relationships, care and time

it hardest to be. More than most, working mothers must elaborately plan and adapt, and they privately experience guilt. Mothers at home caring for their families are not immune: they are asked to pick up the care in their streets, they face pressures to become 'real workers', their identities are undermined by the greater role of paid work in constructing identities, and their streets are increasingly deserted of other carers, leaving them more isolated. The market is increasingly implicated in the processes and compromises of motherhood – as it undermines care on the one hand and substitutes for it on the other. Some working mothers attempt a straight symbolic trade, hoping that 'more stuff' – particularly for children – conveys 'more love'.

Chapter 5 discusses how the changes in work and households on the one hand, and the resistances to change in the distribution of housework and in cultural constructions like 'proper mothers' on the other, have effects well beyond workplaces and kitchens: they reach into the bedroom. They impose hidden costs on intimacy and love. The gendered mal-distribution of domestic work and care is persistent – entrenching a 'double-day' – and affects an increasing number of women. Women have turned to the market to get domestic work done, finding it easier to buy help than to change men's behaviour. Intimacy is crowded out by the pressures of paid work and the strain of navigating and negotiating workloads.

Chapter 6 considers the significant costs on the increasing number who work long hours and those they live among or work alongside, as the regulatory regime which controlled hours and effort, has eroded.

The failure of workplace and labour market institutions to keep up with the changing care loads of Australian workers is nowhere better reflected than in relation to part-time work, discussed in Chapter 7. Those who voluntarily work part-time seek paid jobs that sit more comfortably with their larger lives. However, many find themselves paying a big price for their adaptation. The Australian 'mummy track' of part-time work – with its poor job security and lower rate of benefits relative to full-time work – has entrenched the peripheral status of carers in many workplaces. The price of their care is marginal labour market status.

Chapter 8 considers how we are caring for those who depend upon us. There are particular, repetitive crisis points in the lives of many: not least in the event of sick dependants. Institutions have struggled to meet new needs and some workplaces, for example, respond much better than others. Care institutions – like child care centres – have strained to support new care demands, while in other households informal care creates new demands – and sometimes pleasures – for grandparents and the extended family.

Chapter 9 considers the critical issue of leave from work for men, women and carers who hold down jobs. The amount of paid leave – in all its forms – has barely changed in its formal provision over the past 30 years despite the transformation of work and household. However, access to many forms of leave has eroded with rising rates of casual work.

The rigidity of market work patterns, domestic workloads and some social and cultural beliefs, contribute to important phenomena like our falling birth rate. Women and carers know most intimately the ways in which market work is squeezing care. If women believe that they must have their working lives on track before they have children, or see that the current terms of parenting will overload them, they delay birth and reduce the desired size of their family. As they age, their fertility options narrow. The work/life collision has important effects beyond how we *feel*: it affects vital economic and demographic trends.

Meeting these problems is not a trivial task. It is not a matter of tweaking the workplace, or the home. Nor is it a matter of adopting the Swedish model of care, or the French model of hours – or any other country's solution. In the middle of the 19th century, Australia led the world on fair wages (for men) and reductions in working time through a unique industrial system. We must again find our own approaches for our own time and place. These are in the final chapter.

Unpacking the cover stories

There are a range of 'cover stories' that obscure the complexities and compromises that arise from the work/life collision. These include the cover stories that domestic work is now shared and the egalitarian household has arrived; that paid work has meant liberation and equality for women; that 'family friendly' workplaces now smooth the way for parents; and that flexible work practices now facilitate flexible parents. The cover stories obscure the truth. We must get beneath them to garner a more accurate picture of experience and improve the terms of work/life in Australia.

Pressure is not new to Australian households. The work-time squeeze is not new. Households with dependants, where single parents or both adults work, have always existed and always been time pressured. However, the long-term rise in the proportion of children being raised in such households, and the growing proportion of couple families where adults are in the labour market, means that the problem is now much larger. And as more people experience it, our communities are affected more broadly. When ten per cent of a school's parents all work, sport coaching and classroom reading is easily accommodated. When 60 per cent are in paid work, the squeeze is on.

Social commentators have long pointed to the effect of new labour market patterns on Australians: Hugh Mackay drew attention to the exhaustion and guilt of Australian working mothers in 1993. In the UK, Patricia Hewitt proposed radical reforms to working time in 1993 and is now part of the Blair Government which is implementing change in the slip stream of European reform (1993). In the US, American sociologist Juliet Schor has documented the phenomena of 'overwork' and 'overspend', while Arlie Russell Hochschild has documented the double shift worked by women and that society's 'time bind' (1997). There are those who speak of an *intersection* of paid work and home life, while Lisa Belkin, the work and family writer for the *New York Times*, more accurately refers to these as 'the collisions that happen daily at that intersection' (2002).

Some labour market changes in Australia bear close parallel with those in the US and the UK. The remarkable thing about the work/life collision in Australia, however, is not its existence, but the lack of analysis of its broad effects on our public and private lives, and – most surprising of all – *the persistence of the collision and lack of real response to pressures that are reverberating in more and more households.*

The effects of this collision are now obvious in any newspaper on many days of the week in Australia, with stories of growing hours of work, jobs hungry for the unpaid overtime of employees, and families and carers under pressure. Some of its effects cause bitter division. Lively 'mother wars' are underway in the letters pages, as mothers are pitted against non-mothers, and 'mothers at home' are pitted against – or attack – 'mothers at work'. The 'types' are set in opposition to each other. While this makes a fascinating fight for some, we might ask where do these wars get mothers? We might also ask: where are the 'father wars'?

Other divisions are also incited by the work/care collision. Phoney wars are provoked between those who 'selfishly' choose not to have children, against those who 'selfishly' do. The gender struggle between women and men is sharpened by the squeeze of work on households and care. While the paid workplace is increasingly occupied by both sexes, the unpaid work of care and home still falls mostly to women, but not without cost to relationships and families. Overshadowing these clashes is the larger collision between the market – with its logics of self-interest and cost-benefit calculation – and the logic of care, especially selfless mothering.

The work/care collision also raises questions about some of feminism's legacies and its future prospects. Any claim that women's liberation lies down the road of paid work has unravelled as the super-woman myth has soured in the face of unchanging work practices, an unchanging burden of domestic work, and the model of the care-free worker that squats at the centre of the factory or legal firm. Of course feminism's claims – always diverse – cannot be reduced to a narrow claim to paid work. That goal always sat (and sits) beside other claims, including the redistribution of work and care at home, and changes in the paid workplace. However, a key goal for feminists has been women's entry to public life through paid work, and much progress has been made towards it. This goal has found its happy co-conspirator in a market greedy for women's labour, its 'flexibility', and enthusiastic for the spending power of women's earnings. Of all feminism's goals, entry to paid work has been the most compatible with the globalising market.

However, access to paid work was always, at best, only half the change sought. This book confirms that this advance is seriously undermined by society's inattention to the questions of care, its redistribution, its powerful role as an engine of community, and its (in)compatibility with market work as it is currently organised. While some delight in the failure of a 'feminist' strategy of entry to paid work – a straw feminist figure if ever there was one – the failures of policy and our established institutions are greater. It is not feminism that has let women down, but the institutions that are our workplaces, families, markets, governments and methods of organising work and care. Ironically, feminism's 'failure' lies in its success in winning the right to a job and significant individual equality in paid work, while essential accompanying changes on the household, personal and institutional front have been puny, fragile and energetically resisted.

The key question now is what goals are appropriate for those who want to see a fairer world, with less disadvantage and damage to women, children and men, and a more robust community?

The inadequacy of special 'family friendly' measures

Much of the public discussion to date about dealing with this fundamental shift in men's and women's participation in home and work has focused on changing the workplace through special 'family friendly' measures – or increasingly 'Work/Life balance' initiatives. These include supportive statements by senior managers, employee counselling, flexible start and finishing times, sick leave to care for sick children, middle manager and supervisor training, job-sharing, telecommuting, and part-time work (Spearritt and Edgar 1994, Russell et al 1992). These programs are significant. They have been widely celebrated and publicised through government reports and national annual work and family awards. In a growing number of larger companies and the public sector, carers have access to special arrangements that are designed to help bridge their roles. One 2002 Australian survey of 195 workplaces (including members of CCH Australia and others who volunteered to participate) showed that around 60 per cent of employees in these workplaces had access to part-time work and to flexible start and finish times, with just over half having access to paid parental leave of some kind. The top quartile of surveyed companies (with a high incidence of 'work/life' measures that are used) have lowered their employee turnover by an average of 3.7 per cent, their absenteeism by an average of 3 per cent, and increased the return rate from parental leave by an average of 23 per cent (Managing Work/Life Balance 2003). However, such measures exist in only a small minority of Australian workplaces. The 'enterprise as island' approach – which relies on individual workplaces adopting changes as they wish – cannot deliver for most (Buchanan and Thornthwaite 2001: 3).

The celebrations of these islands of change and innovation have been accompanied by changes in work organisation – rarely marked – that have moved in the opposite direction, complicating the business of work and care, and causing many to experience a deterioration in their quality of work and family life. Even 15 per cent of the 'best of the best-practice' companies included in the 2002 'Work/Life' survey (the top quartile) report an average increase in stress related absence in 2002, and 8 per cent report increases in labour turnover 'due to the 'long hours' culture' (Managing Work/Life Balance 2003: 2). 'Special measures' are not enough – alone – to combat the hidden changes in work/life that contradict the more visible initiatives mostly in larger companies. We can think of these as the concealed bulk of the 'family friendly' iceberg as in Figure 1.2, with the innovative measures adopted in a minority of workplaces – the visible and energetically promulgated tip of the iceberg – outweighed by significant changes in the nature of work itself, along with care and community. As long as the lower bulk of this iceberg remains invisible, many workplaces, families and individuals will founder upon it. And as long as innovative examples are publicised in ways that obscure the experience of the majority, that majority cannot advance. Our task is to make the invisible obvious and clearer, and to consider ways to respond to its bulk and effects.

Figure 1.2 The Family Friendly/Unfriendly Iceberg

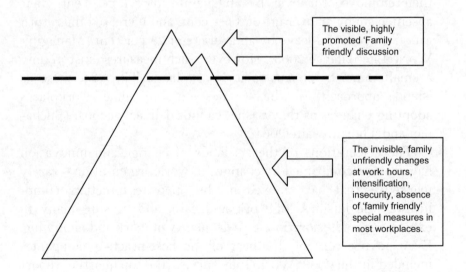

The visible, highly promoted 'Family friendly' discussion

The invisible, family unfriendly changes at work: hours, intensification, insecurity, absence of 'family friendly' special measures in most workplaces.

The evidence: Who speaks?

Fifty years ago, C Wright Mills argued for a social science that helped make sense of 'personal troubles' by illuminating the larger social and historical context in which they occur, to understand 'the intimate realities of ourselves in connexion with larger social realities' (1959: 22). This study is in that tradition, attempting to link personal experience with larger issues, to link the public and the private, and to build upon a range of concepts arising from the analysis of gender and the analysis of labour markets in recent decades.

The book analyses a wide variety of information (the Appendix discusses these in more detail). These include a range of ABS surveys about work and households, data arising from the Australian Workplace Industrial Relations Survey (AWIRS) and the Household, Income and Labour Dynamics in Australia (HILDA) Survey (Melbourne Institute, 2002). Large surveys can tell us a great deal about what is happening in our community. They have an important role to play, especially where they are longitudinal in nature like AWIRS and HILDA. However, it is also useful to look beneath the statistics about issues like family structure and working hours, to reach a deeper understanding. Surveys have limitations when it comes to discussion of complex issues like values and motivation: *why* people do things, or the *effects* of their situations, or what people might *prefer*. So this book draws on the voices of a number of Australians as they talk about the effects of work on their lives, to put flesh on the bones of quantitative data.

I rely on two main sources of qualitative evidence. The first arises from a series of focus groups and interviews among 163 mainly women living in South Australia. These investigated how work – broadly defined to include market and non-market work – is affecting people. The second source is a set of interviews of workers in 12 industries or occupations across Australia, and their partners, investigating the effects of long hours of work on individuals, families and the community. These qualitative materials draw on relatively small, non-random samples and do not carry the weight of large randomised surveys in terms of providing indicators of population behaviour (Evans and Kelley 2002: 56). However, in many cases it is difficult to structure large, randomised surveys in ways that allow people to discuss their thinking in an open-ended way, as opposed to 'ticking the box' among a set of pre-selected closed options. The latter approach generally does not capture complex motivations, beliefs and actions and their intersections with the cultural and institutional realities that condition them. And it cannot capture discussion between people, as some qualitative data does. Where it exists, the qualitative sources relied on in this book are supplemented by larger survey data about labour market behaviour and so on. Ambivalence and complexity characterise much work/care behaviour and a combination of methods has better hope of illuminating this. The combination of quantitative and qualitative data gives us important insights into what is changing, what is unchanging, and the consequences of the two, for life, care and community.

Some will find the concentration upon households with dependants, and the primary focus on the relations between work and care, too narrow – missing an analysis of the diversity of household types, for example, beyond heterosexual and conventional family norms. This may be so. There are examples of homosexual parents in the qualitative study groups, along with male and female single-headed households. These differences are not the main focus of the study, however, which takes as its primary analysis the complex relations between life, care and work across a range of households. Class factors also differentiate experience: households with different levels of wealth and income experience the work/life squeeze in significantly different ways. The voices of workers in low-income and high-income households are present in the qualitative studies which draw out commonalities as well as difference. While these are important, the primary focus here is upon the impact of work on care and vice versa.

Building a better 'Work/Care' regime in Australia

There are those who think these issues – love, relationships, family – are personal and private, that there is no role for government or public action in these realms, given the private nature of decisions about work, family, relationships, spending, love and money. There is certainly a role for private decisions about these issues, perhaps most importantly in relation to consumption and the substitution of products for relationships. However, it is a core contention of this book that governments affect these spheres, as do employers, unions and community organisations – even where they attempt to declare themselves absent from the bedrooms, workplaces and households where personal decisions are made. Institutions play a powerful role in our lives. They affect the conditions and hours of our work though law; they affect our patterns of consumption through their construction of care regimes for children, the aged, the sick; and they shape our patterns of earnings, benefits and taxation. Governments, the media, employers, unions and community organisations powerfully affect the economic, social and cultural frameworks that naturalise, or makes strange, our ways of being at work, at home, and in our households.

Falling birth rates are increasingly a focus of public concern, given the problems they create for the social and economic base of industrialised societies (McDonald, 2001a). Who will pay to care for the sick and aged when the population base – and its taxpayers – shrinks? As long as industrialised countries adopt a restrictive approach to the free-flow of immigrant labour across national boundaries (and there is little sign of this relaxing, indeed the reverse is more common), then an Australian 'fertility crisis' looms. It is clear that 'Work/Care' regimes affect fertility outcomes though the *extent* of this effect is not so obvious. The key question is, however, what regimes of work and care result in a steady birth rate, fair gender outcomes, an efficient use of our resources and a good life?

Even those who have no interest in fairness or equality in society, and who believe that all social outcomes should be the 'natural' outcome of pure individual choice, must recognise that the nature of choices is constructed in significant part by governments, public institutions, law and social convention. If mothers do not, for example, have access to paid leave when they have a baby because governments will not ensure paid maternity leave, or there is little support for extended periods of parental leave, the bedrooms and households of Australia – and perhaps our birth rate – reflect the consequences.

For those of us who believe that fair outcomes for *all* women and men, as well as for those on lower incomes and the disadvantaged, are worth striving for, government, employer, union and community action is essential. Without it, the penalties of the mismatch of public working life with private home and reproductive life will erode further, and the private costs rise and overflow into degraded communities, workplaces, households and life.

CHAPTER 2

Mapping labour,
households and care

What conceptual tools help us make sense of the intersection of care and market work and their implications for our lives, and how have patterns of work changed over recent years? This chapter explores these through consideration of the ways in which we think about 'labour' and the relationship between market work and care. These relationships have changed in recent decades with fewer people at home to support those in paid work. A model of total labour is proposed, with changing boundaries of marketisation and of care, and attention to the moments of transition in labour markets where risks are high and institutions weak. We review who works at home and outside it, how patterns of labour have changed (or not) in recent decades, and analyse these using a model of Work/Care regimes which shape outcomes and change over time.

An economy of care underpins an economy of production and consumption

Many Australians live within a complex web of working and home life, where caring, reproduction and paid work jostle alongside each other in their demands for time, energy and money. 'Home' and 'work' cannot be separated into a neat binary, into neatly gendered jobs. They cannot be 'balanced', since they are part of a seamless, messy whole: a conglomerate. Conventional categories of labour and economic analysis, which treat paid work as separate from home, life and the care that essentially underpins work, are hopelessly inadequate to the task of understanding this whole. Labour market economists have not successfully integrated the analysis of the spheres of caring, home and workplace when they analyse 'labour'. Indeed, neo-classical economists (who dominate the teaching and profession of economics) barely recognise the issue, with a myopic focus on market relations where the paid workplace and its entire product actually swims unconsciously atop, and totally dependent upon, an unrecognised world of the unpaid – where workers, and their managers and employers are reproduced and sustained. These economists generally recognise only the superficial skin of this life, the part that is in the market – where profits are made and money is exchanged. When 'caring' or reproductive work enters the market and becomes the subject of monetary exchange it is recognised – but only then. Typically, such work is the shadowy ghost that is essential to the superficial market exchange economy, but rarely counted, as many feminist economists and sociologists have long pointed out (Folbre 2001a, Waring 1988). This unpaid sphere is far from inconsequential: it amounted to 48 per cent of total Gross Domestic Product in 1997 in Australia (ABS Cat No 5240.)

The basic assumptions of neoclassical economics – of 'Economic Man', weighing economic costs and benefits and making choices which maximise his utility based on perfect information – are fatally contradicted by most caring decisions which rely upon altruism and the sacrifice of personal interests to the interests of another. Adam Smith, one of the fathers of modern economics, is a case in point: in 1776, he described children in the US as 'a source of opulence and prosperity' to the parents: 'The labour of each child, before it can leave their house, is computed to be worth a hundred pounds clear gain to them' (1776, 1952: 30). Smith saw a straightforward functional, market relationship between rates of reproduction and wage rewards: 'the demand for men, like that for any other commodity, necessarily regulates the production of men; quickens it when it goes on too slowly, and stops it when it advances too fast. It is this demand which regulates and determines the state of propagation in all the different countries of the world' (1776, 1952: 34). However, narrowly *economic* explanations of care and reproduction have severe limitations. Today, even with widespread contraceptive control in many industrialised countries which at least makes 'choice' feasible, having a child makes little *economic* sense to individuals. Parents cannot necessarily depend upon their children in old age, are unlikely to benefit from their earnings, and the costs of rearing a child are now very large, as are the foregone earnings of main carers. The balance of economic costs has moved dramatically against children – indeed, against any care including aged parents, a disabled child or a sick neighbour.

The economy of care which underpins the economy of paid work and production has its own laws and circulations, but its guiding principles contradict the founding assumptions of neoclassical economics: rational man who maximises his private utility. Carers make decisions that shape labour market participation, production and consumption – indeed, which shape the official economy – based on motivations where costs are a minor player. These decisions are instead related to love, reciprocity and a complex economy of relationships, community and family where 'gain' derives not narrowly from *individual utility* but also from obligations, love and responsibility that cannot be measured in dollars or individually, and often cannot be predicted. Perfect knowledge about effects, events, costs and benefits rarely accompanies care decisions.

A model of total labour – and how it has changed in Australia

Any account of Australian work and care cannot accurately represent experiences of 'work' without reference to a broader definition of labour, and consideration of its relationships with care and households, and with our drive to live in healthy households and relationships where 'care' – of ourselves, our children, our friends and our community – is possible. An inclusive analysis of all forms of labour must capture both the spheres of production and reproduction (Glucksmann 1995), including analysis of voluntary work, paid work and unpaid household work. Clearly, the composition of total labour is highly gendered in Australia – and around the world. Women are under-represented in the paid work sector, and over-represented in the sectors that are unpaid. Figure 2.1 represents the notion of total labour, which occurs within a more or less marketised system, and given social and cultural milieu and institutions. The market boundary between paid and unpaid work is changing significantly at present in Australia, as households make greater use of food, clothing, care and services produced and sold by others. The reach of the market – or the boundary of commodification – expands as more labour enters the market economy.

Figure 2.1 A Model of Total Labour

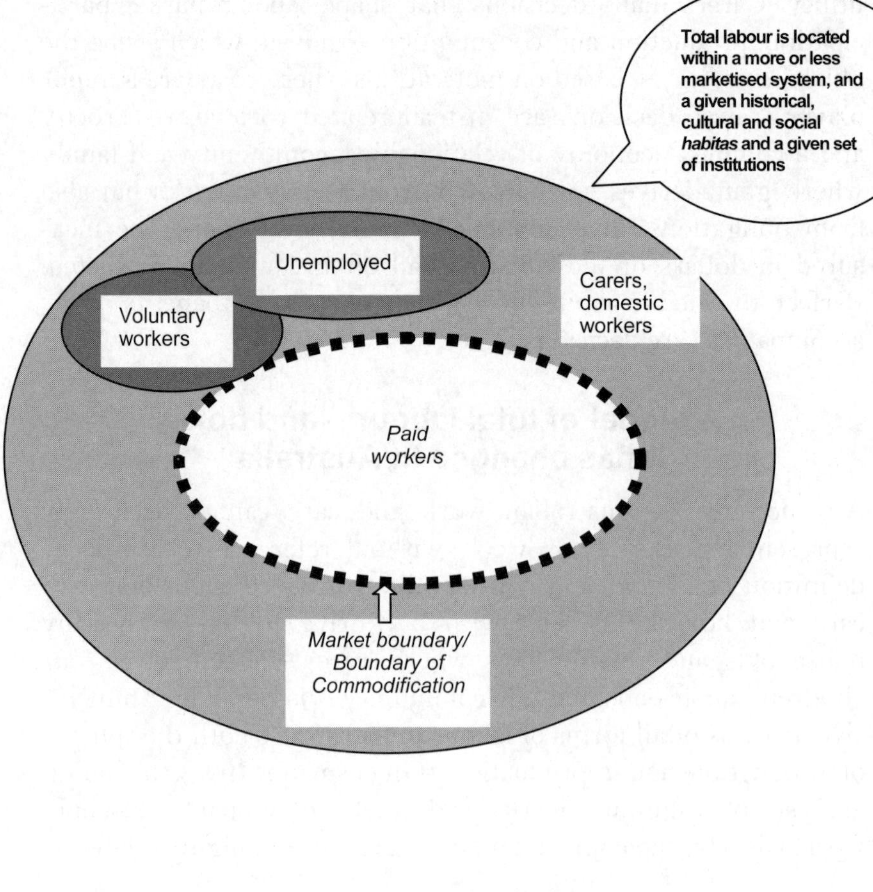

Total labour is located within a more or less marketised system, and a given historical, cultural and social *habitas* and a given set of institutions

Unemployed

Voluntary workers

Carers, domestic workers

Paid workers

Market boundary/ Boundary of Commodification

Changes in women's and men's participation in the labour market over recent decades have fundamentally changed the relationship between work and care, with a contraction in the proportion of women undertaking care outside the labour market, and an increase in their participation in paid work. In 1966, 36 per cent of women were in the labour market, leaving 64 per cent outside it participating in various forms of care and home life. By mid-2002, the situation is reversed with over half of women – 55 per cent – in the labour market and 45 per cent outside it (AIFS 1997: 83, ABS Cat No 6203.0). In 35 years, the participation rate of women has grown by 19 percentage points, while men's has fallen by 12 percentage points. If the same proportion of women were in the labour market in 2002 as in 1966, there would be 1.5 million less women in the labour market, and almost one million more men – or one third fewer women and 16 per cent more men. In a labour force of around 10 million in 2002 these gender shifts are very sizeable. The shrinkage in those outside the labour market who can undertake unpaid work must be met either through intensification among traditional unpaid labourers, or contraction in the amount of unpaid care and work that is done, or its redistribution to others.

In the 20 years since 1982, women's participation has grown within a growing overall labour market, as Figure 2.2 shows. The growth in women's participation has been especially pronounced among those aged between 20 and 54, when their responsibility for dependants is most intense. Accompanying the growth in women's overall participation has been a growth in part-time jobs, three quarters of which are held by women. Forty-four per cent of women in paid jobs work part-time in Australia – a high proportion by international standards. The average level of part-time employment among women in the OECD countries is 26 per cent (OECD 2002b: 43).

The proportion of men working part-time has doubled over the same period but remains much lower, at about 14 per cent of all men in paid work (ABS Cat No 6203.0). Part-time work in Australia has some unique characteristics: two thirds of it is

Figure 2.2 Men and Women in the Labour Force,
1982 and 2003 (000)

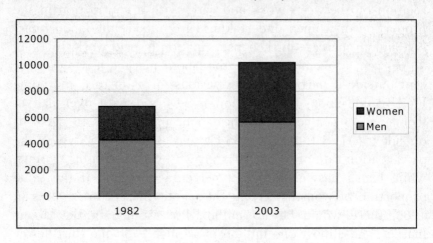

Source: ABS Cat No 6203.0, 1982 and February 2003

casual, with very restricted rights and entitlements, and no job security. The degraded nature of part-time jobs in Australia, their sizeable and growing proportion of total paid employment, and their use by carers as a main vehicle of juggling paid jobs and care, create particular Australian challenges which we explore in Chapter 7.

The rate of participation in the labour market tells only part of the story about changes in work. Australia has also witnessed a growth in paid working hours that is well in excess of the growth in our working age population over the same period. Between 1982 and 2001, the working age population (15-70 years) in Australia grew by 31 per cent (ABS Cat No 3210.0). However, the size of the *labour force* grew by 45 per cent in this period (ABS Cat No 6202), while the aggregate hours from this paid workforce grew by 37 per cent (ABS Cat No 6291.0). In other words, a growing proportion of Australians are working, and the total hours we put into paid work are rising faster than the growth in the size of the working age population.

Figure 2.3 shows the change in aggregate hours worked in Australian between 1982 and 2002. This Labour Force Survey measure is based on actual hours worked by employees (including the self-employed), rather than 'usual' hours worked (which is generally higher, given that in any period a proportion of employees is on leave or not working for some reason), and may be different from hours *paid* for (given that it includes unpaid time) (ABS Cat No 6203.0). It shows that full-time women and men contribute a growing proportion of aggregate hours. Overall, women's share of aggregate hours has risen from 30 per cent in 1982 to 36 per cent in 2002.

The largest growth has occurred among married (including *de facto*) women, whose aggregate hours have grown by 76 per cent in the past 20 years, while men's have increased by only 26 per cent (ABS Cat No 6291.0.40.001).

Figure 2.3 Aggregate Hours of Part-time and Full-time Workers, by Sex, 1982 and 2002 ('000 hrs)

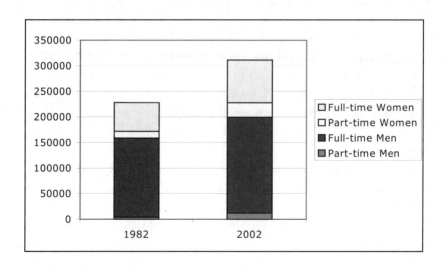

Source: ABS Cat No 6291.0.40.001

Average hours of work per worker have also changed over the last 20 years, especially among full-time male employees while the average of part-timers has stayed fairly steady at around 16 per week (ABS Cat No 6203.0; ABS Cat No 4102.0). The weekly hours of full-time employees increased from an average of 38.2 hours per week in 1982 to 41.3 in 2001, or 3.1 hours (Campbell, 2002a: 93). Campbell has described the growth in average weekly hours worked by full-time employees as 'dramatic', placing Australia at the long hours end of the international spectrum of working hours. What is more, as he points out, our average full-time hours continue to grow while those in many other countries are declining. Much of the growth in working time in Australia is unpaid: as much as two thirds of all overtime worked (Campbell 2002b). The proportion of all employees working more than 45 hours a week has increased from 18 per cent in 1985 to 26 per cent in 2001, and growth is especially strong among those working fifty hours or more (Campbell 2002a: 94).

Growth in hours at work is compounded by more travelling time. Total travel has multiplied nine-fold over the past fifty years in metropolitan Australia, congesting roads and increasing the average commute-time to paid jobs (*The Weekend Australian Magazine*, 14–15 September, 2002: 9). For men who travel to work, it rose by six minutes a day between 1992 and 1997 to reach 60 minutes in total, and by eight minutes a day for women to 53 minutes in total (ABS Cat No 4153.0). This means that those who travel five days a week are spending around five hours a week on work transport, and this grew by half an hour in the five years to 1997.

For many Australians, work has not only increased in hours and travel demands, or in household density; it has also increased in *intensity*. In the 1995 Australian Workplace Industrial Relations Survey over half of employees (59 per cent) said that their work effort had increased over the previous 12 months, 50 per cent said that stress was higher, and 46 per cent said that the pace of work was faster (Morehead et al 1997: 274). More recent evidence of intensification is explored in other Australian studies

– among nurses through increased workloads and understaffing (Allen, O'Donnell and Peetz 1999, Considine and Buchanan 2000), medical scientists (Weekes, Peterson and Stanton 2001), teachers and finance sector workers (Probert, Ewer and Whiting 2000), and a broad range of industries and occupations (ACTU 1999; Pocock, van Wanrooy, Strazzari and Bridge 2001; 1999; Probert, Ewer and Whiting 2000). The links to a deteriorating work/family balance are clear, with Allen et al concluding that 'broad intensification', which they find across a wide range of workplaces, creates 'patterns of dysfunctional behaviour in workers' personal lives, which affect the quality of their interactions with their families and friends' (1999: 531). Intensification takes different forms in different industries. Research technicians must do a broader range of tasks, carry their own equipment, work harder, and be individually available for more unpredictable emergencies and repairs. Paramedics have a greater proportion of more acute cases in their workload. Teachers' class sizes are larger. Postal workers describe new management systems that fine-tune staffing levels to business load. Public sector workers describe work design that minimises staff 'until the system screams'. People in these work situations are 'managed' to high levels of stress, and they in turn 'manage' by working harder and working long hours.

Along with a growing proportion of women in paid work, more travel time, increasing numbers working long hours and growing intensification, the *pattern* of hours in paid work has also shifted so that there is greater variance in the structure of the working week, with more people working on weekends, and at unsocial times of the day (Bittman and Mahmud Rice, 2002: 21). This change in the timing of work, assaults common family and recreational time and has been accelerated by enterprise agreements with a quarter of agreements current in late 2002 extending ordinary hours into the weekend (ACIRRT 2002). This means that employees covered by these agreements can be called into work on weekends without receiving penalty rates that recognise the unsocial nature of their working hours.

While the reach of paid work into households has been increasing on all of these fronts over the past 20 years, what of unpaid work? The value of unpaid work rose by 15 per cent between 1992 and 1997, applying the conservative market replacement approach to all forms of unpaid work, including services undertaken in homes like meal preparation, cleaning, home maintenance, and unpaid services performed outside the home like voluntary work, care of aged relatives and other work performed free of charge (ABS Cat No 5240.0). In 1997 unpaid work amounted to 48 per cent of the value of total measured Gross Domestic Product. Unpaid domestic household work makes up most of this work, with community and voluntary work contributing only ten per cent of the 1997 total.

Table 2.1 Unpaid Work,
Market Replacement Value, 1992 and 1997

	1992	1997	Per cent Change
Unpaid household work	$210 bn	$236 bn	12
Unpaid voluntary and community work	$18 bn	$25 bn	39
All unpaid work	$228 bn	$261 bn	15
Women's contribution	65 per cent	64 per cent	
Men's contribution	35 per cent	36 per cent	

Source: ABS Cat No 5240.0. This source uses time-use data, and imputed value based on cost of employing replacement workers at wage rates appropriate to the task ('individual function method' and person age rates) to calculate market replacement rate.

As is well known, women do the majority of unpaid work: in 1997, women undertook almost twice as much domestic and caring work as men. They completed, on average, 33 hours a week of housework, child care and shopping compared to men's 17 hours a week (this counts only the main activities and excludes secondary activities like caring for children while cooking) (ABS Cat No 4153.0). This imbalance has barely changed between 1992 and 1997 and the segmentation of unpaid tasks remains highly gendered (Bittman and Pixley 1997). A review of the gender distribution of housework between 1986 and 1997 found that men's contribution had not increased, though women were spending less time on some tasks so that the gender gap is declining a little 'mainly because women are doing much less, rather than men doing much more' (Baxter 2002: 420).

Figure 2.4 Men's and Women's Paid and Unpaid Hours of Work, 1992, 1997

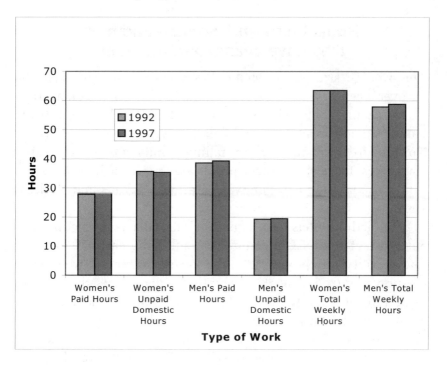

Source: Computed from data in ABS Cat No 4153.0 and 6291.0.40.001(June 1992 and 1997) applying average male and female patterns of working hours. Unpaid work includes domestic work, childcare, shopping and voluntary work and care.

In 1997, despite changes in women's share of paid work, they continued to undertake 65 per cent of unpaid household work, and do more of all kinds of household activities than men, with the exceptions of gardening, lawn and pool care and home maintenance. Women undertake around three quarters of unpaid childcare work, and two thirds of housework. Women in couples or single parents do much more domestic work than men, *regardless of their participation in paid work* (ABS 5240.0: 7). Women also do more volunteer and community work than men. The combination of unpaid workloads, and average paid working hours means that women are shouldering a greater overall work burden than men, as set out in Figure 2.4.

Households and labour – and how they have changed in Australia

The average size of households has steadily fallen in Australia for over a century. In 1911, households were made up on average of 4.6 people. This fell to 3.0 in 2001 (ABS Cat No 4102.0). Families made up 71 per cent of all households in 2001 (ABS Cat No 4102.0). Explanations for falling family size lie in falling birth rates, more single older people staying in their own homes, delays in marriage and family separation (de Vaus and Wolcott 1997: 5).

The birth rate has been falling in Australia as it has throughout most of the OECD community since the early 1960s. The total fertility rate is now 1.73, the lowest on record, well below the previous trough in the early 1930s, and below the replacement rate of 2.1 (OECD 2001: 24; ABS 3301.0 2001: 6). This falling rate is the consequence of three demographic changes: rising levels of childlessness, delayed first births, and the fact that there are fewer births overall (McDonald, 2001a). In 2001, there were 246,400 births in Australia, 1 per cent down on 2000 (ABS Cat No 3301.0 2001: 6). These babies are increasingly born to older women, who have less of them. The median age of Australian mothers on their first birth was 23 years in 1966 but reached 30 in 2001 (de Vaus and Wolcott 1997: 50; ABS Cat No 3301.0 2001: 6).

The rate of childlessness has also increased. At present about one in four Australian women is likely to remain childless. A high 33 per cent of women in the ACT and 31 per cent in Victoria are likely to remain so (ABS Cat No 3301.0 2000: 38). A relatively small slice of this childlessness is explained by natural infertility, although this rises with age. There are significant differences in childlessness according to cultural background and childlessness is particularly associated with higher qualifications. In 1996, 20 per cent of women with a bachelor degree or higher were childless, compared to only nine per cent of those with no post-school qualification. Participation in market work is also associated with higher levels of childlessness (ABS Cat No 4102.0: 39).

Family separations have also contributed to declining household size. After the spike in divorces following the liberalisation of divorce law in Australia in the early 1970s, the number of divorces has remained at over 50,000 a year. The chances of divorce are rising. For those born in 1999, one in three marriages are likely to end in divorce applying 1997-1999 rates of divorce (ABS Cat No 3310.0 2002: 2).

In February 2003, there were 5,430,200 families in Australia (ABS Cat No 6203.0 2003: 41). Over 80 per cent are couple families, and just under half of these couple families have children (45 per cent). Fifteen per cent of families were headed by a single adult, 82 per cent of them by women. Eighty per cent of Australian children under 15 live in households where there are two parents. However the proportion of children living in lone-parent households has risen steadily over the past decade from 14 per cent of all children in 1991 to 20 per cent in 2001 (ABS Cat No 4102.0, 2002, p. 30).

Putting together the changing story on family structure, and patterns of paid work, we can see the declining role of the traditional breadwinner model of family/work life at any particular point in time. In the 19 years since 1984, the transformation of the work/family pattern in families with children has continued apace. Table 2.2 shows that the proportion of male breadwinning couple households shrank from half to less than a third of couple families with kids, while the number of dual-earner families rose by an equivalent amount to reach 62 per cent of the total. Interestingly, the proportion of couple families with children where men leave the labour market to care for children and depend on female earners remains miniscule.

Table 2.2 Labour Force Participation in Couple Families with Children, 1984, 2003

	1984	2003
Man only in labour force, woman at home	51%	32%
Woman only in labour force, man at home	1%	3%
Both partners in labour force	45%	62%
Neither in labour force	3%	4%
TOTAL	100%	100%

Source: ABS Cat No 6203.0 2003 and ABS Labour Force Survey data on microfiche for 1984. 1984 data include families with children less than 14 years; 2003 data include couple families with children less than 15 years. Note that some families have other types of dependants that are not included in the table.

In 2003, Australian workers are nearly as likely to be female as male, and where they live in couple families with children, they are more than likely to share responsibility for dependants with their partner who is also in the labour market. In one parent families with children, 57 per cent of parents are employed.

Of all couple families with dependants (children under 15 and other dependants), there are now more than *twice as many* where both parents are in the labour market, than those where only the male is in the labour force. The traditional male breadwinner family with dependants has been overtaken by the dual income family. It must be remembered, however, that this cross-sectional analysis obscures the fact that families move into and

Figure 2.5 Labour Force Participation in Couple Families with Children, 1984 and 2003 ('000 families)

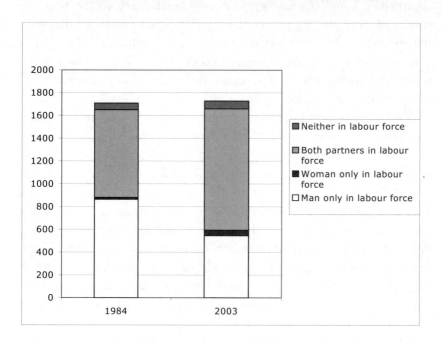

Source: ABS Cat No 6203.0 February 2003 and ABS Labour Force Survey data on microfiche for 1984.

out of types over their life-cycles: today's 'traditional' family is tomorrow's dual earner family, and vice versa.

Of course, the high proportion of part-time workers among women means that many dual earner couple families are, effectively, less than two full-income families: they are modified traditional households with one-and-a-half workers in many cases.

Only a minority of couple families now conform to the traditional male worker/female carer model at any point in time, and the pace of change has been steady over the past two decades. There has been no great compensating rush of men out of paid work into care of dependants. The traditional model has not, however, been totally eclipsed. At this point in time, around 30 per cent of couple families with dependants take the traditional worker/carer shape. More than twice this number, however, now take dual earner/carer shape. This means that Australia's Work/Care regime must be attentive to the require-ments of *both* the 62 per cent majority where both adults with dependants are in the labour market at present, *and* the 32 per cent minority with sole earners and carers at home. The regime must also recognise – and facilitate – the fluid movement of families between various states.

Three other points are important. First, it is vital to recognise the reversal over the last 25 years in terms of which group dominates the work/caring population. While our policies were made in the image of the traditional family, when it was domi-nant, they must now adapt to the new majority form. Second, this analysis is cross-sectional (at a point in time): over a life time, those women currently at home looking after very young children (and the small number of men who join them) will probably spend significant periods of their life in the labour market, while those now in paid jobs will also have periods of care at home. The high incidence of such transitions – concealed as they are in a snapshot – requires a policy focus on *transitions* and how they occur, recognising that today's worker is tomor-row's carer-at-home, and vice-versa. Third, assessing changes in the work/care load and its affects by concentrating only upon men's and women's independent work rates, misses the effect of these *combined* changes in households. It is at the household level, as a result of the combined effects of men's and women's work patterns, that the work/life squeeze and its intensification is sharpest. The combination of more hours in paid work for women, fewer hours for them at home, and longer, more intensive hours for full-timers, creates busy households.

How can we summarise the increasing density of paid work in homes with dependants? One measure is provided by applying average working hours patterns to this changing pattern of family/work structure. Assuming average working hours pat-terns for all women and men, between 1984 and 2002 the rate of paid work being drawn out of households with children under 15 has increased from 47 to 51 hours a week. Applying an alternative method, using time-use diary data, Bittman and Mahmud Rice find that changes in time contributed to paid work out of couple households among prime age couples in the decade to 1997 was even greater: it increased from 50 to 60 hours per week, or 15 per cent (2002: 18).

Dual-worker families with dependants have always been busy households. The major change in Australian in the past 20 years, however, has been the growing *proportion* of Australian families that experience this busyness. While in 1984 more than half of all Australian couple families with dependants lived in male-breadwinner households, now less than a third do. The amount of total hours worked and travelled out of such households has risen, so that both the level of busyness and the proportion experiencing it, have contributed to the growing experience of the personal, family and community work-life collision.

ABS surveys confirm that time pressures are especially strong in couple families with dependants. In 1997 less than ten per cent of those in couple families with dependants never or rarely felt pressed for time, compared to 37 per cent of couples without children. Over half of couples with dependants (53 per cent) felt pressured for time 'always' or 'often', compared to a quarter of those without children. In couples with non-dependent children 15 years or more, 37 felt pressed for time always or often (ABS Cat No 4153.0: 12). Rising work patterns chase increasing spending as households – especially the main carers within them – supplement their own efforts with commodities and services. This intensifies paid work patterns and, in combination with rising material expectations, means that a work-spend cycle is underway in many households.

The life cycle, transition and households

In terms of the model of total labour in Figure 2.1, over the past two decades the boundary of paid labour has expanded while the level of unpaid labour has contracted. We have also seen a change in what is going on *within* paid labour as it has become more intensive, travel time has grown and paid hours have reached more into social time. In gender terms, little unpaid work has been taken up by men, and most continues to be done by women although their participation in the labour market has increased. Women have made greater use of the market and simply done less unpaid work.

Figure 2.1 is, however, a static model of total labour. Real human beings move between paid and unpaid work and care states many times in their lives. The total labour of any individual is dynamic over-time, as Gunther Schmid has highlighted with his notion of 'transitional labour markets', suggesting there are multiple moves into and out of education, for example, and into and out of care (1995). In contrast, Catherine Hakim analyses labour market and care outcomes through personal 'types' and preferences. She has argued that women fall into three 'types': home-centred women who mostly want to be at home with their small children, work-centred women who are inclined to paid work, and 'adaptives' who combine the two (2000). She argues for policy options that meet the three types, and especially women at home who she feels have been ignored too often in the push to accommodate women in paid work. However, *typing* people misses the true dynamic nature of most lives now as people move through a variety of life stages, and not always in a straight line. Total labour is best understood in terms of *a series of labour/care transitions* (as modelled in Figure 2.6) rather than static *personal types.*

Working full-time is a reliable steady state for fewer and fewer Australians. Fifty years ago, men might expect to spend most of their adult lives in a full-time paid job, while women might expect to spend a great deal of theirs in full-time, unpaid work at home rearing a sizeable family. Now, both men and women can expect to spend more years in education and many years in paid jobs, many years combining jobs and caring work at home (with varying gendered rates of intensity), several changes of jobs, and several key transition points where the risks of labour market failure – and loss of income – are high. These

Figure 2.6 Labour/Care Transitions Over the Life Cycle

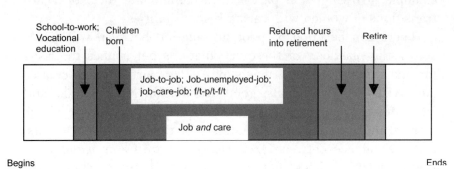

key transition points include from education into paid work, from paid work into care/parenting, from job to job, from part-time into full-time work and vice versa, from unemployment into a job, and from paid work into retirement.

On the basis of European data, Cebrian, Lallement and O'Reilly distinguish three forms of transition: *integrative* (where people become integrated into the labour market through transitional arrangements like apprenticeship); *maintenance* transitions (where people maintain employment through changes in working time); and *exclusionary* transitions (which circulate people into peripheral employment and out into unemployment) (2000). They point out that much part-time work in Europe is of the exclusionary kind, as it is in Australia, with weak integrative and maintenance effects.

The type and number of these transitions is gendered, with women more likely to face exclusionary transitions and men more likely to move between different types of paid work. The institutions that can assist the latter type of integrative transition (like job agencies, employment services, labour hire companies and the like) are more developed than institutions that assist the transition from paid work into care and back again. The latter have weaker formal institutional structure, labour market regulation, and attract less public expenditure or policy analysis. Casualised part-time work is the most obvious example, growing – in part – to accommodate the work/care transitions of women with caring responsibilities.

There can be good or poor articulation between work/care states; the plasticity of these articulations determines the risks for individuals as they manoeuvre. Poor articulation creates large risks for individuals; good articulation reduces risks and facilitates movement. A clear measure of the health of a labour market and care regime is the state of these transition points, and the balance between *exclusionary*, *integrative* or *maintenance* transitionary vehicles. Better articulation between states will assist employees, employers, families and our communities, resulting in a better functioning, fairer labour market, lower personal risks, and higher personal satisfaction.

Explaining Work/Care outcomes: A model of Work/Care regimes

The work and care of Australian's – as modelled in Figure 2.1 and described above – occurs within a complex social, cultural and institutional situation. It is important to unpack and understand its components to consider how they intersect and operate, and to propose workable changes. Bob Connell's theory of 'gender orders' and 'gender regimes' provides a useful conceptual approach on which to draw. He uses the notion of 'gender orders' to understand how men and women and society work (1987), arguing that gender orders are historically constructed patterns of power relations that are 'always imperfect and under construction' but that 'an orderliness' of gender relations exists at any point in time (1987: 116). This order both shapes behaviour and is shaped by changes in behaviour over time and is institutionalised in a 'gender regime' (for example, in schools, the labour market, social practices and so on). In analysing work and care, it is useful to similarly conceptualise a *Work/Care order*, embodied in specific institutions and cultural practices in a *Work/Care regime*. The larger Work/Care order is shaped by the balance of forces between employers and employees, the role and nature of the state, and the gender order. It provides the larger economic and social context of any given set of institutions, established values (or culture) and behaviours. At any point in time or place, work/care outcomes are the consequences of the established Work/Care order and its specific embodiment in a Work/Care regime, as set out in Figure 2.7 (over page).

Such Work/Care regimes are historically specific. While there might be individual variation around the 'orderliness' within any 'Work/Care' regime, and individuals and households can buck dominant practices, there is a 'unity in the field, an orderliness which needs to be understood' which hopefully helps us see patterns more clearly and allows a clearer understanding of the scope of necessary policy changes (Connell 1987: 116).

Work/Care regimes reflect dominant institutional and cultural realities and current behaviours and preferences, and are constantly affected by them: 'imperfect and under construction'. Thus the Work/Care regime is the consequence of the interplay between three main factors: values or *culture*, the *institutions* that prevail, and what people actually *do and want*. The practice of individuals and households in any Work/Care regime is both a product of the dominant values and institutions of Work/Care *and* changes them over time. And the entire regime is gendered: it takes place within a 'gender order' of the kind proposed by Connell, and it is affected by the role of the state and by class forces as employers and employees struggle over elements of the Work/Care regime, like working time, labour law, and leave arrangements.

The three forces that shape the 'Work/Care' regime: values, institutions and preferences/behaviour, are not independent of each other. Over time they shape each other in an interdependent way. Cultures and dominant values are shaped by institutions, which in turn embed cultures and values.

For example, the institution of the market, now extended to the provision of centre-based child care in Australia, has affected behaviour (including patterns of child care provision, work, income allocation and informal care).

Figure 2.7 Work/Care Orders and Work/Care Regimes

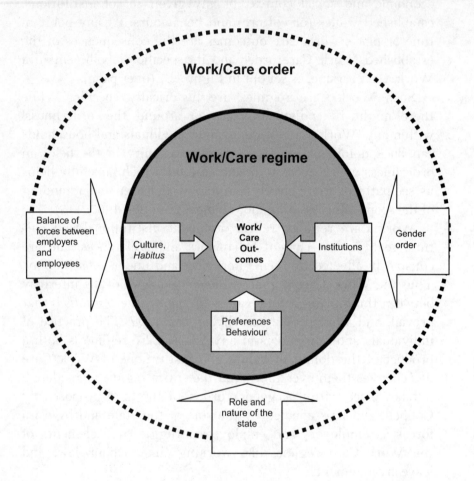

The institutions of industrial regulation intersect with the dominant culture of maternal care of children to give rise to casualised part-time work as the main means of work/care combination for Australian women, while the gender culture has left men's paid work/care relatively undisturbed.

Behaviours like women's entry to paid work or grandparent care of children, change institutions and cultures, which also then affect preferences and future behaviours. Figure 2.8 suggests components of a Work/Care regime.

Figure 2.8 The Components of Work/Care Regimes

Work/Care Regimes	Manifestations
Work/Care Culture *Dominant values and norms:*	What we *think* for example, the 'proper' role of mothers, fathers, and the 'proper worker'
Work/Care Institutions *Specific institutions:*	Shape where and what we do: industrial law labour market child care institutions schools workplaces pre-schools leave arrangements work time government payments family structures
Behaviour, Preferences *What we do and want:*	Behaviour and preferences at a point in time, for example, around participation in paid work, allocation of unpaid work, how we care for dependants

This theoretical model suggests that Work/Care outcomes are the result of culture, institutions and behaviours and preferences (and their components) and that outcomes reflect not only choice but the interplay and contradictions between the factors that make up the regime. Preferences are but one player, in many cases subservient to these other forces, in contrast with Hakim's privileging of preferences as explanators.

Australian Work/Care regimes

In Australia we currently live within an unstable Work/Care regime that is the source of considerable trouble, and gives good signals about where we need to make changes, although many of these are troubles are privately experienced. Institutions, cultures and current behaviour can be better aligned and less discomfort is likely to be the result. At present, work/care outcomes are *sore* because of a dissonance between *behaviour and preferences* (what we do and want), and *institutions,* and *values.* We have seen how much women's labour market behaviour has changed in recent years, and how work itself has changed. However, our institutions (especially labour law and workplaces structures) have channelled much of women's labour market effort into either insecure part-time work or full-time jobs in the image of the care-free male worker, while unpaid labour has not changed much at all. The fit is poor. Against these, in cultural terms, society remains firmly attached to the idea of maternal carers: 'proper mothers'. These mismatches – documented throughout this book – are the source of the Work/Life collision.

It is useful to reflect on the main Work/Care regimes that characterise Australian experience and possibilities: these are set out in Figure 2.9.

The first, the Traditional male breadwinner/female carer household, places the full-time worker at the centre of the workplace, with female spouse a carer at home and the institutions of work, home and government reinforcing that model. It runs deep in Australian culture and epitomised Australia's work regime for much of last century. This social and legal framework – often far from reality in many households – embedded a deep Australian legacy in terms of both wage and social policy and deep-rooted beliefs and practices about the roles of men and women and their treatment in the labour market.

It is far from unique internationally. This practice is replicated in similar terms in many other industrialised countries. In the US, for example, Joan Williams describes a deep-seated domesticity which she argues 'remains the entrenched, almost unquestioned, American norm and practice' with its two features of 'the organisation of market work around the ideal of a worker who works full-time and overtime, and takes little or no time off for childbearing or child rearing' and 'its system of providing for care-giving by marginalising the caregivers, thereby cutting them off from most of the social roles that offer responsibility and authority' (2000: 1). These principles of 'domesticity' structured US work, and William's argues they still structure 'good American jobs' and the roles of men and women in jobs and care.

However, in the last 30 years the growth in part-time work, especially for women, has taken Australia towards a 'Modified Traditional' regime, which gives carers marginalised labour market status as paid part-timers or occasional workers, while carrying main responsibility for care. In recent decades Australian governments have made contributions to supplement women's care of dependants, and women have turned to the market for support. Couple families with children are increasingly characterised by one-and-a-half earners, though the dominant image of the 'worker' is one unencumbered by care and in the main, full-time. Part-time employees in this model are precarious and peripheral. Just over 60 per cent of Australian couple families with children now take the dual-earner shape, with less than a third in the traditional shape, and it seems that most prefer a dual income model: the 1996 Australian Life Course Study showed a strong preference for the dual earner household 'even among women not in the paid workforce' (Charlesworth, Campbell and Probert 2002: 42, Glezer and Wolcott, 2000: 50). These preferences are likely to foster further growth in dual-earner families, as more women enter the labour market over their life course.

The third model is an amended version of one proposed by Appelbaum, Bailey, Berg and Kalleberg (2001): Shared Work/ Valued Care, whereby women and men share access to good jobs and the work of care, assisted by community and public institutions and a 'set of social norms that structure behaviour by workers and firms, that temper employers' demands on employees, and that shape the aspirations of both women and men for the type of employee and the type of parent or family member they can strive to be' (2001: 12). This model holds at its core the promise of genuine choice and the realisation of diverse patterns of work and care, that properly recognise and value the productive work of care, and equally reward various forms of labour and its organisation rather than marginalise the 'non-standard'.

In the half-century to the 1950s, under the Traditional regime the boundaries of market, labour and household were in some ways fixed and in some ways changing. Men of the 1950s no more picked up a tea towel than their fathers, and most income was earned by men in a highly sex-segmented labour market. The domestic/paid work split, and indoor/outdoor roles were constant in the main.

Alongside this, life transitions remained relatively infrequent as people tended to remain either in full-time work or full-time carer roles, to stick with their skills and occupations – even to their employers – and were less likely to move towns and suburbs or to move house frequently. However, other features of work, money and households changed significantly: the exchange of cash for the labour of others embodied in bought produce increased. Homemade products were displaced by market-produced goods. While the indoor/outdoor boundaries were relatively fixed, the commodification of goods used in consumption and production shifted. The exchange of money for the work of others outside the home in shops and distant factories, increased significantly from the early 1900s and continued apace in the latter half of the century.

More recently growing numbers of women have entered part-time work as their income became vital to families and the reach of the market into household consumption grew. By the turn of the century in 2000 the boundaries around 'made' versus 'bought' goods had shifted dramatically: most consumption has crossed the boundary into the market. More households do paid work and pay cash for the food, clothing and care of their children, in a steady cycle.

The marketisation of the care of children is more widespread. While the boundary between kitchen and workplace has broken down for many women, the fence around the kitchen, mop and cleaning chemicals is less often breeched by their men. The wall between kitchen and workplace shows a kind of one way, gendered porosity.

Figure 2.9 Australian Work/Care Regimes

Work/ Care Regimes	Traditional (Ideal worker/carer)	Modified Traditional	Shared Work/Care (Women, Men, state)
Culture *Dominant values and norms:*	Women should be carers, men breadwinners. Proper workers are full-time. Women do unpaid work. 'Good' mothers care for children and are assumed dependent on men	Women should be main carers, work part-time, men main earners. Proper worker is full-time. Women do most unpaid work. 'Good' mothers are main carers but may earn, mostly part-time	Men and women fairly share both paid and unpaid work and care and have genuine choices to share as they choose. Unpaid work is shared fairly. 'Good' mothers are backed by good fathers who share work and care, and various arrangements are supported, not judged
Work/ Care Institutions	Protects full-time worker. Marginalises part-time. Wages system and regulation built around fulltime breadwinner. Wide pay gap between part-time and fulltime. Minimal formal institutional care. Govt spending and action cements worker/spouse carer at home	Primarily protects full-time worker. Growth in marginalised part-time work. Wages system and regulation built around full-time bread-winner with some pro-rata benefits for part-time. Some formal institutional care. Govt spending and action favours full-time earner, with spouse at home	No distinction in conditions of workers based on hours. Institutions give real choice. Equal treatment of part-time and full-time workers. Wages and conditions equal regardless of hours. Both women and men have carer's leave, access to short hours. Narrow pay gap between full-time and part-time. Good institutional support for care. Govt supports work/care arrangements without discrimination
Behaviour, Preferences *What we do and want*	Men's participation in paid work dominant. This preference met, others frustrated. Women do unpaid work	Men mostly full-time, women part time. Preference for male bread-winner met best, others frustrated. Women do most unpaid work, share with market	Diverse preferences can be met. Move to diverse patterns of participation in paid work and care. Women and men share unpaid work fairly and share care with state and market

Draws on models used by Buchanan and Thornthwaite (2001), Williams (2000) and Appelbaum, Bailey, Berg and Kalleberg (2001)

Today, the sale of women's labour, alongside men's, through paid work creates an almost completely naturalised structuring to lives. While it might sometimes be part-time, and 'interrupted' by maternity and parenting, paid work is as deeply natural to many women carer-workers in 2003 as it would have been strange to their grandmothers.

However, not all jobs are the same or treated equally. Time is a matter of rigorous clock watching for the hours of paid work, child care, school, care and rest. And it is *busy* time, as lists and schedules organise the days and dictate a criss-crossing maze of travel between the institutions of care, school, work and home. Travel is a growing part of the day. Women and men now share the task of earning money in order to sustain a highly marketised lifestyle, where muesli bars replace home made biscuits in many lunch boxes, and home mortgages chew through two incomes.

As much as some things have changed – most dramatically, the boundaries between what we buy and what we make and the hours household members spent in travel and more intensive market work – others remain unchanged. The boundaries around domestic and caring roles remain highly gendered, and through them the tasks of rearing children and managing domestic lives. The nature and experience of *time* for women, men and children has changed. The streetscapes in which children grow up, and mothers and fathers nurture, are transformed by traffic and the nine-to-five (or nine-to-three) exodus – into workplaces that are more and more hungry for time and energy, and still carry the legacy of 'ideal-workers' in their structure and assumptions. Expenditure, consumption, over-consumption and debt patterns have changed in ways that earlier thrifty generations would not have understood, and add new impetus to the work-earn-consume cycle that partially drives the increased commitment to market work.

The drive to work more:
The Australian *work-spend* cycle

As we rely more upon the market for our reproduction, production and care, more of our labour is pulled into the market and
the income it generates is exchanged for goods through the
market. A greater demand for market goods, thus drives an expansion in the paid labour market and paid work, and shrinks the
contribution of the unpaid sphere to production and reproduction.

The growth in paid working hours worked out of Australian
households with dependants is explained by two main factors.
The first is changes in Australian workplaces which, responding
to growing international and domestic competitive pressures,
have passed that pressure on to workers in their workplaces and
to workers and carers in their homes. Alongside this, however,
are rising patterns of spending and consumption. These can only
be fed by increased earnings or debt. Australians have been busy
increasing both – but especially the latter.

Juliet Schor has shown how work patterns chase spending
patterns in a US 'squirrel cage' of work-spend (1992: 165). She
advocates action to jump off the 'consumer escalator'. Similarly
in the US, Robert Frank has documented the rising 'luxury fever'
which drives absurd spending and long hours of work among
middle-income households and beyond, and the low levels of real
gain in personal well-being that arise from such spending. Other
American research points to a weak link between personal happiness and rising incomes, beyond a level to meet basic needs
(Lane 2000).

While 'keeping ahead of the Jones' does not appear to result in
commensurate increases in personal welfare and well being – and
indeed may compromise environmental sustainability, widen
income gaps, and reduce welfare through fewer hours for leisure
and community – it has not stopped Australians from replicating
US trends. Indeed the proportion of wealthy Australians earning
more than $70,000 a year who believe they cannot buy all that
they 'really need' is higher (at 46 per cent) than in the US
(Hamilton 2002: vii). While there are many lower-income

Australians who suffer genuine unmet needs for housing, food and clothing, the problems of the 'suffering rich' reflect rising expectations and an Australian strain of consumption fever or 'affluenza'. Rising expectations are reflected in increasing house sizes, with new houses now offering over twice as much space per occupant than they did in the early 1970s (Hamilton 2002, viii). They are also reflected in rising levels of personal debt, especially among middle-income earners. In the eight years to 2002, credit card debt increased eight-fold in Australia, and in the last 15 years borrowing for housing has increased ten-fold (Hamilton 2002: 14). The inclination to spend beyond one's means has risen rapidly, especially among middle-income earners ($31-$60,000 per annum), despite a three-fold increase in real incomes since the 1950s. Hamilton concludes that 'Australian households, and especially middle-income and wealthy households, have an inflated, and perhaps grossly inflated, understanding of how much money they need to maintain a decent standard of living' and, as they become wealthier, their perceived levels of 'necessary consumption' rise (2002: 22).

This is confirmed by data from the Household, Income and Labour Dynamics (HILDA) survey which shows that *extreme* poverty affects only a small proportion of Australians (this survey excludes the homeless). While a larger proportion cannot pay their utility bills on time (almost a fifth), it seems that most Australians think of themselves as comfortable or managing (Melbourne Institute 2002: 16). The mismatch between perceptions of unmet need in the face of rising real levels of average income, and the low incidence of real poverty, suggests that Australians' expectations are outstripping their rising incomes, so that the perceived 'deprivation gap' is widening. Ironically, a remarkably high proportion of Australians also think that we are now too materialistic (83 per cent in 2001 according to Hamilton) and most value relationships with family and friends more than money (Eckersley 1999, HILDA 2001). However, it seems that our spending habits betray our values, at least in many homes.

This has important consequences for market work and care. Those who pursue rising standards of living and perceive a gap between their aspirations and situations, borrow more or seek higher earnings through more paid work. This explains some of the growth in long hours – though far from all of it, given that most overtime is unpaid. Nonetheless, the drive for 'more and better stuff' and the need to 'buy instead of make' especially when time is short, combine to enlarge the reach of the market into household time, and, in turn, the reach of paid work into life. Deeper consideration of consumption patterns is an important part of action to relieve the work/life collision in some middle- and higher-income households.

An international story

It is important to remember that total labour in Australia, the dynamic points of transition, and the current Work/Care regime exist within a complex international picture. An increase in global trade, and financial and human flows, is reshaping households around the world. Corporations and governments are reducing costs and labour forces in the industrialised world, and increasing their presence in low wage, newly-industrialising countries in pursuit of shareholder value – high profits and high returns to shareholders that will allow them to grow. Flows of capital and people mean the dissolving of old communities and families, and the creation of new ones. Production is increasingly globalised.

Nancy Folbre has written of the uncaring nature of global capitalism: 'bad capitalisms drive out good ones. Employers who assume their fair share of social costs by following the rules imposed upon them by democratic governance will operate at a disadvantage. They risk being competed out of existence' (2001a: 186). The corporate charter is – in most cases – strictly economic: bottom lines, growth, profit. Many corporations are irresponsible with respect to caring and to the reproduction of labour – not always because they want to be, but because international market economics require them to be – in the absence of enforced international standards. They are inattentive to community, relationships and quality of life beyond narrow economic measures. They carry no obligation to pay a living wage. Corporations, if they so chose, can be irresponsible with respect to their labour supply compared with times when more immobile, regional corporations faced limited labour supplies, and were forced to increase workers' wages, ensure their reproduction, school their children, develop their skills and – as their limited workforces unionised – raise wages and make greater corporate contributions to the social wage through taxation. The liberation of some corporations from 'place' has freed them from an implicit need to ensure the reproduction of their workforce and its support through national taxation.

The 'business case' for profitably providing family friendly arrangements at work, is unfortunately weak in many places where labour supply is bountiful, legal regulation is weak and corporations can 'free ride' on the privatised costs of reproduction or the contributions of their competitors or government. This strengthens the need for international standards that recognise the cost of work to care and life, especially forms of work that are inattentive to the true costs of reproduction, and care for the sick and the frail.

In the presence of an expanding labour frontier, footloose capital can be – literally – care-free. It can be socially irresponsible: the discourse and practice of globalisation licenses it. A situation like that in Sweden early last century, when a shortage of labour led that country to assist the entry of women into paid work and the reproduction of its labour force through extensive paid maternity and parenting leave arrangements, is now less likely to arise (although it is not impossible in Australia as the total fertility rate falls). Investment decision-makers are keen to avoid countries with high labour and social costs – namely generous wages and leave, shorter hours, and high taxes – those things that permit human and social reproduction on decent terms.

However, declining birth rates in most industrialised countries are forcing consideration of the social, economic and workplace settings that affect birth rates. It is no coincidence that a tighter labour market in England has accompanied improvements in paid maternity leave under the Blair Government. There is a link between birth rates and work-care regimes. Local labour markets still matter, as local capital remains reliant upon a workforce for local services, construction and production. This drives attention to social and human reproduction and refocuses attention upon the role of the state and employers and the condition of our households and relationships.

It is in this larger context that we must make sense of current Australian work and care arrangements, and their implications for our lives. It is important that we understand the interconnected nature of consumption and work; of care and total labour; the dynamic nature of the labour market with all its transition points; and the nature and components of the Australian Work/Care regime, in order to consider the origin of the current collision and what changes might arrest it. The next chapter begins this assessment by considering how changing patterns of total labour are affecting the fabric of Australian community.

CHAPTER 3

How work is reconfiguring the Australian community

What are the implications for our communities of the growing weight, and changing nature of work, being drawn from our changing households? The health and nature of the community within which all forms of work and care occur, shapes outcomes for the individuals who live within any given Work/Care regime. And the nature of work itself, in turn constructs, changes – or destroys – community itself.

'Community' can be defined in many different ways, from a straightforward geographic association, to a shared interest, culture, heritage, or governance. Different definitions of community date back to Tonnies' 1887 distinction between 'community' and 'society', where he linked community 'to the sense of belonging based on kinship, neighborhood and long acquaintance' (Taksa 1994: 23). Robert Putnam's study of social capital in the US focused on community as the 'connections among individuals – social networks and the norms of reciprocity and trustworthiness that arise from them' (2000: 19). When considering the spheres of work and care, there are many forms of community where trust and reciprocity are possible: for example, geographic neighbourhoods, occupations, shared interests, or workplaces. In these spheres, community is perhaps best seen as 'a state of mind, a disposition of *involved neighbourliness*' as O'Farrell has described it (1994: 17, my emphasis). This form of community has geographic location as a primary community – whether at home or at work – but in many cases, other forms of community overlay or intersect with it. The word 'community' is often invoked to rouse feelings of nostalgia, or of real or false common purpose – especially perhaps when 'community' is in decline or under threat. However, a range of studies suggest that social capital and the bonds of community matter to economic, social and personal well-being.

Putnam's US study found that higher social capital and strong community bonds are positively associated with better education and child welfare, better health, safer and more productive communities, economic prosperity, and less inequality. He showed a sharp decline in the bonds of community in the last 30 years in the US which he attributes to many factors, including pressures of time and money especially in two income families (he guesses that this accounts for about 10 per cent of the decline in civic engagement), more commuting through a growing suburban sprawl (10 per cent), more television watching (25 per cent), and the lower participation of new generations in civic engagement (50 per cent) (2000). Putnam argues that 'trust-worthiness lubricates social life'. He distinguishes *bridging* social capital (which is inclusive and builds inclusive links to others beyond the group, for example the US civil rights movement) from *bonding* social capital (which is exclusive and builds bonds within a group, for example an ethnic community) (2000: 22-23).

There are many levels and ways in which 'community' can be measured. Communities of 'involved neighborliness' suggest people with common space and time (Peel 1995). Traditionally, Australian community has had a strong spatial dimension related to neighbourhood and space around the home. Given women's greater association with home, they have been pivotal to the home-centred, neighbourly community. The extended family has also traditionally been important to the making of community: while not always in spatial proximity the extended family has been a place of 'involved neighbourliness' for many. Michael Pusey has analysed community among 'middle' Australians by considering their local affiliations, as well as more formal and remote forms of political citizenship. He makes the point that 'in Australia modern labour markets have long since dissolved the 'associational density' of an older intimate, and sometimes nostalgically remembered world of the extended family, church and local community neighbourhood, each reinforcing the other'

(2003: 113). The high level of mobility of Australians further stretches the threads of extended family, weakening the fabric of geographically-located neighbourhood-community.

With more hours spent away from home by paid workers in Australia, new forms of community are made in new locations, especially the workplace. They are also made at new times, given the weaker integrity of the weekend as social time, and the widening span of 'normal' working hours. Workplaces are places where both bridging and bonding social capital are built: workplaces can be places of solidarity and a sense of group belonging, and they can be places where new entrants find a bridge to new networks. But workplace social capital is different from that of neighbourhood: it is more instrumental, more limited in depth than family or neighbourhood, and conditional on having and keeping a job. And this form of social capital is simply not available to those who do not have a workplace: the unemployed, full-time carers and the retired.

How work is reconfiguring our communities: From street to workplace

Changing patterns of work – whether paid or voluntary – are contributing to a steady reconfiguring of our communities. While traditional forms of community of a generation ago – often neighbourhood based, with the extended family at their core – have not disappeared, those at home with domestic and caring responsibilities talk about their streets as dormitories to a growing number of women and men in paid work. The locus of community has shifted from neighbourhood towards the workplace. Increasing geographic mobility and changing regional labour markets mean that extended families are more geographically dispersed, and the extended family is fractured. This shift is reflected in the comments of those who have been at home for years raising their children outside the paid workforce, as well as those in paid work. Whether working in a traditional factory on shift work, part-time in a shop, or in management positions on high salaries, workers say that increasingly *work* is a place where their community is – at least partially – built. Many describe their streets as deserted in normal working hours: as a male nurse put it 'Well the streets are deserted 9 to 5'.

Community is constructed through both time and place. Part of the pleasure of being in a community is being *known*, and this requires time to create 'long-term witnesses to another person's life' (Sennett 1998: 21). Such witnesses are often lost through geographic mobility, or mobility prevents their establishment. Australians are very mobile, and this has important implications for community and the fabric of extended family. Between the censuses of 1991 and 1996, 43 per cent of Australians moved house, making us one of the most mobile populations in the world (Bell and Hugo, 2000: 22). While mobility has tended to decline in the US, it has continued to rise in Australia in recent years. Most of these moves are not within a local area, but beyond it or interstate. The rate of Australian mobility has tended to rise since the early 1970s, with steep rises particularly during the 1970s and 1990s. The rate of moves Australians can expect to make in their lifetimes has risen by 25 per cent between 1976 and 1996, with the average number of lifetime moves now at about 13 (2000: 31). Australians mostly live in a small number of large cities pinned to the fringe of the continent, and there are large populations that move each year between the labour markets that they sustain. As the job market has restructured away from longer term to much shorter-term employment, geographic mobility has increased. In the US, Sennett argues this has undermined 'those qualities of character which bind human beings to one another and furnishes each with a sense of sustainable self' (1998: 27). Australia's greater mobility and more distant cities suggests that this affect is likely to be much larger.

For many Australians, extended family is not geographically accessible, and those who care for dependants, mainly women, increasingly look to the market to meet their needs for household support. This strategy is widely adopted by a range of women including those in low-income households (in the form of take away food, and occasional domestic support or lawn-mowing) as well as those in higher-income households. However, those with higher incomes make much greater use of a wide range of contracted services – regular cleaning, ironing, gardening, nannies, prepared food, child care, and paid baby-sitting. In terms of general support, people talk about how they can no longer 'lean' on community, but instead pay: 'Now our neighbours work too. It has to be paid! They work too! You can't lean on anybody', as a mother in the city put it. The sense of having people to call on – what Putnam calls 'generalised reciprocity' – is shrinking:

> There is nobody for some of us [to call on]. A friend in an emergency for some, in-laws for others … My mother – I have no hesitation but she's a long way away, but not the mother-in-law – it's too much hassle. She has her own life. (worker in family-owned small business)

Workplace as community, home as dormitory

Many see the workplace as a place where they have laughs, fun and social life: as one put it 'Your work becomes your support network'. This view is confirmed by survey results from the 1996 Australian Life Course Study of parents aged 25 to 50 with children in their households. When asked 'if you had a reasonable income without having to work, would you still prefer to have a paid job?' 64 per cent of mothers (and 72 per cent of fathers) said that the would still prefer to have a paid job (Glezer and Wolcott 2000: 50). A similar result is found in the 2001 HILDA survey.

In general discussion about why they work, women frequently mention the social benefits of work before mentioning any benefits arising from earnings, whether they live in the country or city or on high or low incomes: 'For me, work is like a family' as a mother in a country town put it.

The social community established through paid work is very important. The following comment shows the multiple motivations for doing paid work, with the social side to the fore:

> I initially went back to work for the social side of it because I was stuck at home and I just looked back over my life and the best friendships I had were through people that I'd met at work, so I figured I'd go back. It was the social side of it. Obviously the money. But it was the social side of it as well. (factory worker, city, mother)

A country woman described how her paid work 'made her a better person': 'I actually enjoy working. I'm a better person and a better mother because I work'. Even women in long established community networks describe feeling isolated at home when they have children:

> I really did feel isolated. All the people that I knew, they had different interests and values as me, and so it was very hard. I had always worked, and I needed to go back to work ... My husband was saying 'for God's sake go out and get a job. I want you out of the house', and my mum was recognising the same thing. (pharmacy assistant, country town, mother)

There is wide agreement about the decline in street-based networks, across women in different income levels, occupations, ages, generations, whether at home with children or in paid work, and in the city and country. The entry of more people into paid work, means that those who spend time at home find fewer with whom to make their social connection. As a city mother at home put it 'I can't think of *any* friends who are not in the paid workforce. There is a breakdown in community. It will be women like me who look after our mothers in old age'. Some men in paid work point to the same phenomena. A male nurse describes his family's dormitory street and the effects of his work exhaustion on his capacity to be neighbourly. A co-worker agreed:

> If I think of the street I live in, we built the house and for the first six months none of us had fences and the interaction between the families was amazing. As soon as the fences went up – it was just amazing ... But it's not just about fences. You can hear all the cars go off at 7.30 am and all come back at 7.30 pm

at night. And you're so buggered that who wants to go and talk to Jo Bloggs next door? (male nurse, father)

I was home for four years with my children ... and you just say hello ... People across the street are friendly. They'll look out for your house when you are away. But that's about it. Whereas I remember with my parents they would always go next door, maybe because the wife was home, and they had a bit more time to socialise and the next-door neighbour would look after the kids. (woman, clerical worker, mother)

Women in part-time work in a call centre exchange similar descriptions of their communities, comparing the generations, and explaining why they hunger for the community of their workplaces where they share support about motherhood and other aspects of their lives, as opposed to neighbours they simply never speak to:

If you do stay home, it's not like when we were kids. My mum was home. She stayed home till I was a teenager, but every other mum was home and you were always off next door. There were kids there – you were never home! The mothers did things together, so the mothers got the stimulation. If I stayed home now I could be home all day and not see *anyone* in my street because everyone is away at work. So you are craving by the next day to get back to work because you need that interaction with another adult! That's changed hugely. (mother, part-time call centre worker)

This thinning of street and family community, and the greedy nature of paid work (that leaves paid workers 'buggered' and short of time) has important implications for all kinds of caring. A senior male manager working very long hours in a community service for the aged, with aged parents of his own, put it like this:

We are all still caring ... On and off. But the concept of sacri-ficing our careers for an older person is something that is now foreign ... You have to be very spare in what you can do ... You do what you can. You do it differently. You don't spend the whole day with them. You go there and spend quality time, and you look at sub-contracting out some of the work. (manager, aged service, father)

He uses the language of the market – 'sub-contracting' – to describe care of his parents, and finds reassurance in the 'quality time' argument to explain why he is 'very spare' with his time. As a service provider he also sees how aged care services are changed by this sub-contracting, spare approach of families affected by paid work:

We got a fax from Tokyo this morning from the daughter of one of our residents telling us that she was too busy to take her mother to the optician – could we do it? From a hotel in Japan! They are taking on the part-time carer role from long distance now. (manager, aged service, father)

Clearly, the nature of the caring that can be done by the busy working daughter on an overseas trip, is highly dependent upon paid carers to step into the breech.

Most child care in Australia is done by parents or through informal arrangements. However, increasing use is made of the market and household spending on child care increased more than four-fold between 1984 and 1998/99 (ABS Cat 6535.0). Between 1993 and 1996, the proportion of children under age three who were in formal child care rose by 27 per cent (ABS Cat No 5240.0, 1997). Care of kids, whether babies or school-aged, tends to occur either in the privacy of the home or has moved into institutions and the market sphere – child care centres, out of school hours care programs, family day care. It is less of a street-shared informal reciprocity as the population of mothers at home in any single street has fallen.

'Schmoozing', community and extended working hours

In his US study of social capital, Putnam distinguishes formal community activity from informal activity or 'schmoozing' (2000: 93). While there is evidence that a growing number of Australians are undertaking some form of formal voluntary work, informal socialising and 'schmoozing' is less easily accommodated and it is especially this informal fabric of community that is affected by a changing work regime. People describe having less time for informal talk, their friends, and for unstructured family activity that is spontaneous and flexible.

The growing proportion of Australians who are working very long hours describe a squeeze on *both* formal activity and schmoozing. This sometimes has dramatic effects on the community, for example when new long hours rosters in large workplaces cause country sports clubs to close. Most employees working long hours describe giving up hobbies, sport and voluntary work because of lack of time, because they come home from work exhausted, or because they cannot predict when they will be available. For example, the partner of a doctor working very long hours describes losing touch with his hobbies and interests: 'I have done nothing of my own since 1994'. Long hours have a wide reach, affecting partner's abilities to 'take time for themselves' and maintain fitness and hobbies. As the partner of a teacher working long hours put it: 'I think that if I start doing things we won't see each other [given his hours]'.

Voluntary work in social clubs, charities and organisations like the army reserve is also constrained for those working long hours and their partners, many of whom describe a 'closing in' of their social circle and community: a 'work/eat/sleep' cycle which constrains their days and leaves their personal community impoverished. Those with families find that much of their non-work time is spent together, or trying to be together. When asked about their friendships, several long hours workers asked 'what friends?' and describe how work commitments drain them:

> The only correspondence I have with friends is over the phone, from work and the only time I really ever see them is if it's a birthday, an engagement party. Other than that it's like it's too much of an effort to see them because it's like, let's just sit at home and watch a video. (insurance industry worker, woman, no children)

She sadly points out that her hours have cost her friendships, her relationship with her god-daughter, and that last New Year's Eve she and her partner – who also works long hours – realised they had no network of friends to call on. They spent it at home alone. A strapper in the racing industry who works long days points to the cost to her own hobbies and larger community:

> You don't have time. You are too tired, When you are home you sleep. I gave up all my [other horse] work, I don't judge now, I don't compete. As far as going out for dinner, even to my mother-in law's-for tea you make sure you are out of there and home by 8.30 pm otherwise you don't get up the next morning. (strapper, racing industry, long hours worker, mother)

Long hours create serious social disabilities for employees. Their social communities shrink, their physical activities are cut back, while basic activities – like keeping a dog – are restricted. A postal worker describes his social life as a 'downward spiral'. He often broke social engagements because of work, which eventually led him to no longer attempt them. As his hours lengthened he gave up playing weekly squash and his golf club membership. He would like a dog, but his hours prohibit it: 'If I had time to walk the dog, I'd buy one', describing his loss of social interaction as the greatest cost: 'That social interaction is the greatest [loss] … for me, and from what I see from my peers, [it] is the thing that suffers the most'.

The growth in street traffic and increased commuting time for workers also contributes to the shrinkage of local community, and the retreat to the private sphere of the home. Many parents are very aware of its affects – and their contribution to it: as one full-time worker and mother said 'The level of traffic is so different. The roads are so different. And then you add to it by driving your kids everywhere!' Putnam's analysis of the effects of longer commutes on US social capital leads him to conclude that 'In round numbers the evidence suggests that *each additional ten minutes in daily commuting time cuts involvement in community affairs by 10 per cent* … And time diary studies suggest that there is a similarly strong negative effect of commuting time on informal social interaction' (2001: 213, his emphasis). By this calculation the average increase in commuting time of 30 minutes week for Australian workers between 1992 and 1997 would have reduced community involvement by 30 per cent. On top of this, more street traffic makes neighbourhood life less safe for children and their parents.

Community through leisure, sport and live performance

Overall, the shift into the labour market for women over the past 20 years, and the slow decline for men, suggest contrasting paid work effects on social attachment. For women, paid work increasingly constitutes a source of social interaction with less time for social attachment around the space of home, and through non-work social activities like leisure, sport and volunteer work. There is clear evidence of a decline in time available for leisure and recreational activity, despite much talk of the leisure revolution. Time series studies for 1992 and 1997 show that the average amount of time people spent on recreational pursuits decreased significantly between 1992 to 1997 (ABS Cat No 4153.0, 1998: 9). Over this period, there was a 'marked decline' in involvement in formal and informal sport, especially in the 15-24 age group (ABS Cat No 4153.0: 8). Attendances at live theatrical performances also fell in the 1990s.

Formal voluntary work in organisations

Survey data about participation in voluntary work in formal organisations or groups in Australia is imperfect. It appears, however, that participation in voluntary work of this type has increased, bearing in mind that the available measures do not capture a wide range of less formal activities like talking to friends, caring for neighbouring children and others, and informal socialising: Putnam's 'schmoozing'.

International Social Science Survey data suggest an increase in formal volunteering from 27 per cent of the population in

1995 to 33 per cent in 1999 (ABS Cat No 4441.0: 38). ABS data suggest that the increase was even larger but the 1995 data understate real participation and 'should be used with caution' (ibid: 39). Thirty-two per cent of those over 18 years 'gave unpaid help, in the form of time, service or skills' to an organisation or group in the twelve months of 2000 (excluding volunteering in the 2000 Olympics and those who performed voluntary work to qualify for government benefits) (ABS Cat No 4441.0: 3). Time-use data shows that in 1997, Australians on average spent 22 minutes a day on voluntary work, with women contributing six more minutes than men, and a one minute increase since 1992. The participation rate for this measure fell slightly between 1992 and 1997.

Table 3.1 Annual Hours of Voluntary Work, 2000, (million)

	Men	*Women*	*Persons*
Community/welfare	81	101	181
Sport/Recreation	92	56	148
Education/training/youth development	31	69	100
Religious	45	73	118
Emergency services	18	4	23
Other	51	77	128
Total	**318**	**380**	**698**

Source: ABS, Cat No 4441.0, 2000: 27 Data includes hours worked for up to three organisations.

The incidence of formal voluntary work is highest among the 35-44 age group when work and its combination with care is often most intensive. Women with dependants have the highest rates of voluntary work (45 per cent, compared to 38 per cent of similar men). Around half of 35-44 year olds who do voluntary work, do so out of personal or family involvement, mostly connected to the sport and schooling of their children. Social contact motivates less than one in five in this age group (ABS Cat No 4102.0, 2002: 150). Interestingly, voluntary work is higher among those in the labour force than those outside it: only 27 per cent of women not in the labour force did voluntary work, compared to 31 per cent of women working full-time and 44 per cent of women working part-time. The reverse is true for men, with more full-time males doing voluntary work than part-timers and volunteering among unemployed men lower still (ABS Cat No 4102.0).

This suggests that a load of formal voluntary work accompanies the tasks of parenting, but that not all parents take it up in the same way. While the incidence of voluntary work is lower among those not in the labour force, they tend to work longer hours when they are involved. Parents in the 30–55 age range tend to have shorter periods of voluntary work.

Two types of voluntary effort claim over half of all volunteer hours and the highest participation: community/welfare (working in organisations like Rotary, Meals on Wheels and the Smith Family) and sport/recreation (especially among men). The most common activity of volunteers is fundraising which accounts for 56 per cent of activity, followed by management (45 per cent), teaching (44 per cent) and administration (41 per cent). Two-thirds of the voluntary activities of those in the 35–44 year age group relate to fund-raising, and more than half to management of organisations like sporting clubs. This suggests that much of the effort of working parents is related to the instrumental tasks related to keeping organisations going: raising money, running committees, administering activities and coaching.

The volunteer participation rate is much higher in country settings than cities (38 per cent compared to 28 per cent), especially in community/welfare and sporting/recreational organisations. It is very low in Sydney, where the volunteering rate was only 15 per cent compared to 26 per cent in Melbourne. Men and women tend to volunteer in different sectors, with women more involved in community/welfare and in education/

training/youth development work, and men in sport/recreation and emergency services.

Many voluntary workers speak very positively about what they get out of voluntary work – and these rewards closely mirror those that arise out of paid work: to escape the house, to meet people, to join a community and to be social. As one put it 'I only stay if I can build friendships and relationships'. Others feel rewarded in their religious beliefs or reminded of their own luck: 'It makes me feel good. Sometimes I feel sorry for myself, and it makes me realise there are people worse off'. One volunteer who 'graduated' to chairing a busy child care centre committee and taking on a paid management role in it for a short period, describes the process – and its rewards:

> I was dragged into it and for me it was probably the best thing that could have happened because I was at home, starting to feeling like I was never going to get back into the workforce, that I wasn't worth much, my confidence was just going down the drain. I got called onto a sub-committee here and the next minute they asked me if I wanted to be on the management committee and then next thing I was the chair and I knew nothing about being chair. And then I became director for a while. And it was the best thing that could have happened because I could actually see what I have to offer. I regained my confidence and that just perpetuates more giving. (student, mother, volunteer)

Volunteers saw their involvement as generating friendships, community and intimacy:

> We get a sense of community and intimacy from being on the committee … In becoming a mother your life is changed in other ways so it makes up for possibly other friendships that have changed because you've become a parent and so you have more in common with these people than you have with other people in some ways. Some of my primary relationships – it sounds crazy, and the others on the committee are probably unaware of it – but my *primary* relationships are here, and with my other voluntary group that I'm very committed to. They are my

family. We've done a lot together over six or seven years. (mother, volunteer, part-time worker)

Women doing voluntary work sometimes face the kinds of conflicting demands that are mentioned by those with jobs – that is, doing their voluntary work as well as meeting the needs of family, especially – in the case of grandmothers – those of the extended family and working daughters.

The effect of paid work on community participation

The participation rates in formal voluntary work suggest that many parents with jobs participate in fundraising and management of organisations associated with their family and children. The higher rate of such participation among those of prime parenting age who are in the labour market, than those outside it, suggests that paid workers may be determined not to shirk their involvement in formal organisations. However, qualitative data suggests that entry to paid work affects informal community involvement, and that those working long hours find it very hard to participate in either formal or informal activity. The increasing entry of women into the labour market and the growing average hours of work of full-timers have especially affected informal community involvement. First and most obviously, they have reduced people's availability for these contributions, like collecting children from school and taking them to sport. This is true in many different types of jobs – whether in factories or office work. Second, it seems that many people combining paid work with care manage to undertake formal voluntary work in organisations, especially fund-raising and management committee participation. They have found it harder, however, to keep up their informal social and community participation. Third, people feel regret at these losses – at not being at the school for their children, or giving up organised sport or hobbies – and they report pressure from their children to be there for them:

I used to be a guide leader but I actually gave it up to look for work. And then when I got afternoon shift, which was more relevant for the family, then I had to give it up. (factory worker, mother)

I used to work at the primary school when the kids first started but that went out the window as soon as I started full-time work. (factory worker, mother)

I used to do reading. My daughter has been begging me to work as a volunteer in the canteen. But doing morning/afternoon shifts, it is too hard. I tried to explain to her that I can't. She said, even if you do it once a year, please do it. So I am going to ask if I can do it once a year. (factory worker, mother)

Similar regrets are common among employees working long hours. Those picking up the informal work in the neighbourhood or school are not always happy with the reallocation.

Women at home: 'I'm doing yours!'

Some women who work in the home feel that they are 'picking up more' for those in the workforce, and this causes resentment:

I'm annoyed with people in full-time work sometimes. I'm coordinating sports teams after school. There are very few women who do anything. It's left to women who are at home. There is an assumption that you will look after their children. There are not enough people. (mother at home)

I felt put upon. I get asked 'My girls don't want to go to before school care – can they come to you?' (mother at home)

Women in the country also speak of resentment when voluntary work falls to the shrinking population of people available to do it:

Years ago we were all expected to do it, and if you weren't there you were really noticed. Now, a lot of the mums are working and you get those few who will come and do the volunteer stuff. (country woman, worker, mother and grandmother)

Grandmothers and grandfathers and the extended family community

Grandparents have always been important to many communities in Australia, sharing the care of children and assisting parents. They remain vitally important to working mothers when emergencies and sickness hit households. Around a quarter of care of informal care for children is provided by grandparents. Grandmothers primarily provide this care, although some grandfathers set aside their tasks to 'baby sit' children:

> We are sharing it more with them. Grandpa is supposed to be paving but he's been baby sitting for the last three months. (grandmother and full-time worker, city).

This role has many positive sides. Many mothers talk about how wonderful extended family has been for their children, as do grandmothers. On the down side, however, is the risk that grandparents, having raised their families, now do more care than they would freely choose. They do it to help their daughters and sons, who they see trying to juggle demands. Some grandmothers talk of being torn, and feeling guilty for not doing more, just as their daughters do. A number of women observed the growing demands on grandmothers:

> My mother looked after my brother's kids. Because that allowed by sister-in-law to work. She thought it was something that she should do. I think you see more grandparents taking on the role and I think there is more of an expectation that they should, especially for those who can't afford child care or who work casually. (woman, no children, casual worker)

> With my friends, they seem to have a regular day where they look after their grandchildren and then they may go to child care on another day. Sometimes I think they like it as they have a permanent relationship with their grandchildren. But several I know also feel restricted and feel they will let their kids down if they stop. (grandmother of two, casual worker)

Some grandmothers were very conscious of the pressure to do more, and women in their communities supported their right to 'choose' as this exchange suggests:

> I'm pretty busy and sometimes I feel as though I am in Coventry with my daughter. There is definitely pressure to be there. But for the first time in my life, this is my time and I'm not going to give up my fitness class (which she teaches). (retired mother and grandmother, country town, volunteer)

> It's different to years ago. Grandparents are expected to look after the kids now. Parents need someone to look after them. Grandparents have a bigger role to play nowadays. (grandparent, country town)

Others elected not to involve their mothers because of differences in values or ideas, or because the expectations of reciprocity were burdensome. As one woman put it 'I hate relying on my mum. I don't like it. Because she acts as if you owe her a favour. Being beholden. And I don't feel good about it'. Concerns about emotional reciprocity were expressed by city women, as well as those in the country: 'I'd rather pay for it than feel the guilt' as one put it.

Clearly grandparents are often an important element of the extended working family's community. This role is not without its complications, however, in terms of 'limit setting' for the voluntary grandparents, reciprocity of exchange, and predictability for working parents. Some grandparents find a clash between their roles as part of this extended web, and their volunteering interests or own preferences, and others are at work or pursuing their own interests, thinning their capacity to offer more to their family's extended community.

Women from non-English speaking backgrounds are more likely to talk about their reliance upon, and access to, extended family support. This includes women in management positions or running their own business, along with women in lower paid jobs. In both cases, family support is crucial to women's jobs.

Though the sample is small, Aboriginal women interviewed are also less inclined to make use of market solutions for care and support, relying more upon the extended family and community. Indeed, some are perplexed by the problems of non-Aboriginal women in relation to finding after school care and so on. This may reflect the constraints of lower incomes, but the community fabric appears more resilient in the urban lives of these women than those of many non-Indigenous women.

Making community through the market?

Some clearly prefer the purchase of market care over the emotional exchanges that are implicit in inter-family transfers of labour – whether in the form of grandparent care, food or cleaning. They would rather *buy* than *owe* their parent or friend. The greater role for the market in lives and households makes non-monetary reciprocities less common. What are the rules for 'owing' each other when one cares for another's children within a set of often emotionally complex, familial ties? Some choose the market because it conveniently sets a rate, free of unspoken reciprocities. These shifts and preferences for market solutions have important implications for communities. Mutual, non-monetary exchanges have embedded within them – indeed *create* – personal and community relationships. These obligations are the stuff of community and generalised reciprocity. They create trust and long-term witnesses to one's life. A shift to the market has significant implications for the web of local and family relationships. Sometimes new communities are built through new connections made through the market – with the Family Day Care Worker, for example, or the child care centre that is a community hub. Certainly, commercial connections are places where some form of community can also be made. But the growth in such connections has, as its cost, the reciprocities that make families and neighbourhood communities through non-monetary exchange. While the market hungrily offers its commodified supports (food and all kinds of services delivered to the door) where the prospect of profit exists, the engine for non-monetary community creation – not driven by profit – is a weaker machine, one that is starved in the face of time pressures in streets where work sucks both time and place.

Conclusion

The decline of local street community sometimes makes the business of being at home, an unexpectedly lonely and disconcerting experience. Interestingly, this shift of the locus of community, while clearest in the city, extends to the reshaping of country towns and women living on farms and working off them. The greater mobility of workers, families and households has also fuelled this shift, with extended families increasingly scattered geographically and inter-family support often intermittent, infrequent, or 'virtual' by means of the telephone or the Internet. The Internet and greater use of mobile phones has strengthened the role of telecommunications in creating new forms of community, including for those at home, and Australians have enthusiastically – if expensively – adopted it. Between 1996 and 2000, the number of households connected to the Internet grew from under 4 per cent to 37 per cent, though access is highly skewed by income. Similarly, our use of fixed and mobile phones has increased rapidly (ABS Cat No 1370.0, 2002: 130). While these technologies create new ways in which community bonds are formed and sustained, they do not replace the social and spatial basics for most: community is made through actual meeting, and more of this is occurring in workplaces, and less of it in neighbourhoods.

Traditional reliance on intergenerational support is thinning. As one country woman put it 'Many grandparents are now too busy, or now too far away'. Those with extended family nearby face the pressure points of work/family life with greater resources. Grandparents provide the 'give' in crisis, picking up sick kids or doing the spring cleaning that mothers in paid work cannot get done. For those that have it, such support is a precious resource. However, the extended family is not always an uncomplicated support – it is sometimes a source of complex, tense reciprocities.

As women's participation in paid work increases, many report a shift in community and social life from neighbourhood to workplaces. The rising level of participation in paid work among older women has also reduced the role of grandmothers in support of some families, while the growing proportion of Australian workers locked into the work/eat/sleep cycle of long hours impoverishes their neighbourhoods and limits their time for both formal and informal social and community life. While some long hours workers are firmly attached to the community of their workplaces – and clearly see them as a positive complement or even substitute for neighbourhood or home communities – many do not.

The workplace has become a kind of family for some. But it is a different kind of family or community. It is centred outside the home and on identities created as workers in workplaces. For many it does not extend beyond paid working hours, or to deeper forms of support for individuals or their families. For those outside this community – carers at home, the unemployed and the retired – it creates exclusion and loneliness. For those whose work is precarious it is an unreliable or inaccessible form of community. In the US, Putnam finds various forms of evidence about work satisfaction 'hard to square with the hypothesis that the workplace has become the new locus of Americans' social solidarity and sense of community' (2000: 91). He points out that employers have significant controls over work time, including over work communication, and that paid work serves 'material, not social, ends'. (2000: 91).

In the US, Richard Sennett is also deeply sceptical about the character of the workplace, arguing that the diminished sense of place through home-based community arouses a longing for community elsewhere, but that it is not found through paid work because 'the uncertainties of flexibility; the absence of deeply rooted trust and commitment; the superficiality of teamwork; most of all, the spectre of failing to make something of oneself in the world, to "get a life" through one's work ... impel people to look for some other scene of attachment and depth' (Sennett 1998: 138).

In Australia relationships at work are shaped by workplace hierarchy, competition for position, work organisation and changes in employment. They can be suddenly terminated. They are mediated by workplace, position and money. The fabric of workplace community today is different from the workplace community of 50 years ago. It is less sustained by steady occupational relationships or formal organisational links (like the associational density of trade unionism), and work is increasing in intensity. Working harder for any given period of time, means people run harder, concentrate more, take fewer or shorter breaks, and socialise less. The workplace has also changed with the gender and caring responsibilities of those within it. Carers do not hang around after work chatting when there are children to collect from school and get to sport, or there is a child care centre that heavily fines late parents.

Building a community of relationships – of involved neighbourliness – relies upon becoming known at work in order to develop 'long-term witnesses' to one's life. With over a quarter of Australian employees now working on a casual basis and increases in short-term and limited contracts, opportunities for community at work are undermined. Precarious work arrangements are inimical to community-through-work and they remove the first requirement for any form of community: stability over time.

For some women, especially those at home with children, the street remains an important positive focus for their family and children. For others, the street comes alive at the weekend and provides a lively social community. But many talk about a decline in their local community, depopulated by the growth of paid and unpaid work, or drained by its effects. This means that those who spend time at home with young children, or in retirement or unemployment, often face a quiet street or town or unit block where they know few people well and where there are far fewer other people in their situation than has been the case in recent memory. This affects trust and safety. Maintaining the street as a place where neighbours know the local children takes time and effort: as one mother at home put it 'You have to work at it'. Many women raise issues of safety and feel that their children are less safe on the street than during their own child-hoods, particularly with the nine-fold increase in city travel since the 1950s. This constrains an easy street, suburban or town social life for children.

What are the long-term implications for Australian society of the shift of community from home to work, and from non-monetary reciprocal exchanges to the market? New forms of community, and a thinner community around home, reshape the environment of Australia's Work/Care regime. When carers at home find themselves without social connection in a thinned community neighbourhood, they look to workplaces for com-munity; they might return to paid work more quickly and turn to the market for care; or they may simply feel isolated at home. These shifts in the locus of community raise important practical problems. For example, in 1998 over half of those 65 years old or more who were receiving informal care, did so from their adult children (ABS 4201.0 2002: 40). With a reduced capacity to offer such informal care as a result of the shift in paid work patterns and the thinning of local community, the costs of this care will either shift to the state, be paid by families through the market, or the standard of care will decline. People will 'subcontract' it or be 'spare' in what they offer. While the proportion of people undertaking formal voluntary work has grown, much of this effort is focused on the instrumental work of keeping groups functioning: upon raising funds and managing organisations.

For those who value community for its value *beyond* its capacity to substitute for market goods – through social life and a richer human exchange – the shift in community to workplaces carries other potential costs. The decline in leisure, informal sporting and hobby activities, and less time for simple talk and 'schmoozing', all affect the quality of our communities and potentially our physical and mental health along with broader social, economic and political institutions and outcomes (Putnam 2000).

In the short-term at least, the shift from streetscape to work community creates the need for new forms of community for those who are not in the paid workforce, whether through volunteer activity, or facilities for those at home with young children or caring for the aged. Specific challenges exist for urban planners and governments, as their actions can either leave the shrinking proportion of home-occupiers in private isolation, or make better use of shopping centres and community facilities like online access centres, libraries and child care facilities as stronger hubs of strengthened communities.

Paid and voluntary work create new forms of rewarding community. And these rewards and new sources of identity – along with financial necessity – mean that there is no prospect of a return to an old and romanticised community streetscape. Women and men have left the street community for many reasons – some of them very positive. Any impulse to call for women's return to the home by day, is absurd. However, it seems that some of the longer term implications of this shift for those who still spend their days there – or who may come to rely upon it more in the future when retired, unemployed, less mobile or caring for others – are uncertain and less positive. The shift of community from street to workplace has important implications for those who do not have a workplace in which to 'build community', and for those who have periods away from it. For some, it makes being at home with young children or other dependants, unexpectedly isolating as we see in the next chapter's discussion of motherhood.

CHAPTER 4

Mother wars: The market meets sacred motherhood

The Work/Life collision is nowhere better illustrated than in relation to mothers. Increasingly Australian mothers are workers with care responsibilities. Fewer women now leave the workforce in the peak childbearing years. Over the past 20 years, the participation rate among women in this age group has risen by 12 percentage points to reach 71 per cent in mid-2002 (ABS Cat No 6291.0.40.001). Two thirds of women in the peak childbearing age group of 25-34 years are in full-time work while the remainder work part-time. The highest share of full-time work is among women in this age group, so most Australians now come to motherhood with an identity partly rooted in paid jobs.

A growing proportion of mothers are in paid work when their children are young, and that rate of employment rises with the age of the youngest child. There is a steady increase from lower rates of participation when children are less than one year old (when 35 per cent of women are in paid work), to much higher rates as youngest children reach pre-school age (59 per cent), and to 75 per cent when these children are in upper high school. While two thirds of women are not in paid work when their youngest children are very young, a third are quickly back to paid work. Among sole female parents, less are in paid work, but a similar pattern of rising participation occurs as children grow up, with two thirds in paid work when their youngest children are in upper high school.

Two thirds of mothers work less than 25 hours a week when their youngest children are very young, but this reverses as children age, so that three quarters of women in couples are working more than 25 hours a week when their youngest children are in upper high school.

Table 4.1 Women's Participation in Work By Age of Youngest Child, 2001

Age of youngest Child	Employed <25 hours	Employed 25-34 hours	Employed 35+ hours	In work
Couple				
0	24%	4%	8%	35%
1	28%	7%	14%	48%
2	28%	8%	16%	52%
3	28%	9%	19%	55%
4-5	28%	10%	21%	59%
6-13	27%	14%	29%	70%
14-18	22%	14%	38%	75%
Total	26%	11%	24%	61%
Lone Parent				
0	9%	2%	4%	14%
1	14%	3%	6%	23%
2	16%	4%	9%	30%
3	19%	5%	11%	35%
4-5	20%	6%	13%	40%
6-13	23%	9%	21%	52%
14-18	18%	11%	37%	66%
Total	19%	8%	20%	47%

Source: Unpublished ABS Data

The proportion of mothers in couples with jobs has increased very significantly over the past 25 years, doubling among those whose youngest child is less than one year old. It has increased regardless of the age of the youngest child (Figure 4.1). The majority of women with children under one spend time at home, and a large proportion make use of part-time work as a means of combining paid work and care of their young children. Since 1976, workforce attachment of mothers has increased very significantly, even among those with very young children.

Australians have steadily adapted the traditional worker/ carer archetype with a small fall in men's participation in jobs, while most women have added a half time paid job to their workload with little redistribution of their domestic work. Mothers and fathers follow very different paths of transition around children. Men's patterns of participation barely waver, while women's shifts very significantly, with two thirds of women at home with new babies, and a steady increase in their participation in jobs as youngest children reach pre-school age, mostly through part-time work. A three-staged transition is

Figure 4.1 Proportion of Women and Men in Couple Households who are in Paid Jobs by Age of Youngest Child, 1976 and 2001

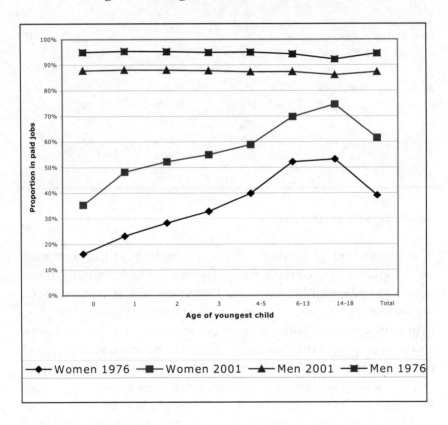

Source: Unpublished ABS data.

common for women: in paid work prior to birth of baby, out of it while children are very young, a gradual return to work – especially part-time – while children are at school, then a shift to full-time jobs. This, however, is the *average* pattern of the majority. There are many variations around the mean. Many women spend extended periods at home especially with multiple children. On the other hand, a third return to paid work relatively quickly after having their last baby. Clearly, a comprehensive suite of policies to meet the needs of mothers – for whom the work/care collision is sharpest – requires policy that assists those at home, those who combine paid work and care, and especially the overwhelming majority who do both and must make transitions between – most commonly – full-time work, full-time care, and work/care combinations that involve part-time and full-time jobs.

'Proper mothers', 'sticky' culture

While we might expect these changes to have unpicked some of the traditional stereotypes of 'mother', instead we find much continuity, giving rise to guilt and over-compensating behaviours. The Australian *habitus* of mothering is *sticky* when it comes to change, like thick mud in which mothers must live and push through, despite very rapid change in the circumstances of mothering and households. While women question the idea of a 'proper mother', they agree that a mythology of 'proper mothering' runs deep in society – including in their own homes. Clearly, women mother in diverse ways and not all carry the same version of 'proper mothering' in their minds. However, there are entrenched and powerful expectations about 'proper mothers' that shape children's expectations as well as those of the extended community and family, and encourage guilt when they cannot be achieved.

These expectations and cultures, revealed in interviews, are also validated through larger surveys. A survey of Australian attitudes about what mothers *should* do, for example, suggests that attitudes run behind what women *actually* do (Evans and Kelley 2001). While this survey is not unproblematic (for example, it forces a judgment between three closed options about what mothers of small children *should* do – work 'full-time, work part-time or not at all'), it suggests that Australian women may be more conservative than those in similar countries. Sixty-nine per cent of Australian women surveyed in 2001 indicated that women should stay home when there is child under school age (n=392), and attitudes moved against mothers in paid work between 1994 and 2001(International Social Survey/ Australia Program (IsssA) surveys; Evans and Kelley 2001: 30). In reality, the paid work participation of women with very young children has doubled in the past 25 years and increases rapidly, as we have seen, as the young child proceeds through school. The IsssA survey reveals a dissonance between what more mothers are choosing to do, and what is still seen as 'proper mothering' by the larger group of women, many of whom do not have responsibility for dependants and are outside the prime childbearing age. Qualitative evidence supports this picture of dissonance:

Marie: My daughter sees all the other mothers [around the school]. Yesterday she said to me 'Why can't you be like other normal mums?' I said 'Well I don't know, love, there's nothing abnormal about me'... (factory worker, mother)

Interviewer: What do the kids think is a 'normal' mum, a proper mum?

Anna: A lot of them, I think, it's the one who is at their beck and call. (factory worker, mother)

Marie: When I was on nightshift I was there when they woke up, and I would take them to school and pick them, and go to work at night. But on morning shift, things [are different]. And she doesn't like that ...'Normal' to her is somebody that brings her to school in the morning and picks her up in the afternoon. Like I used to do.

Interviewer: And why did you change [from that shift]?

Marie: Because I had to. The company wanted me to do that. There was no negotiation ...

In this exchange a 'proper mother' is one with a lot of time and flexibility to be available to her children, whose job is not pitted against children's needs, or non-negotiable workplace demands. This caricature is alive in women's minds and society despite the fact that many cannot 'live up' to it:

Denise: I know a mother who virtually spends every minute with her kids. She is a really great mother. (full-time worker in the country with two children).

Denise can never be 'a really great mother' by this standard and many mothers in paid work would have difficulty achieving the status of such 'proper mothers'. The ever-nurturing mothering standard remains strong, especially in country towns:

Heidi: We are perceived as not such good mothers. I think it's a country town thing. (mother in paid work, country)

Denise: Because you are not there morning, noon and night, you are perceived as not a proper mum (mother in paid work, country)

Of course the conflict between family and work is not new: older women with grown children talk about the guilt that they felt when rearing their children. The difference today is that so many more women are attempting what Denise describes, reporting similar feelings of being 'always torn' and guilty, and facing the surveillance of their communities. Some talk of an ongoing critique from their work colleagues, with fellow-mothers active participants, 'running the guilts over you':

Claire: I get most of the [other] nurses saying, 'Don't you think you ought to be at home?' When one of them is sick they say 'Shouldn't you be at home?' I say 'What's wrong with Malcolm? He's at home. He was there for the three minutes unskilled labour [at conception], why can't he be there when the child's sick?' I mean, the pressure! I mean Malcolm's very good. But the pressure has been enormous from my working colleagues both senior and junior. (nurse, mother)

Interviewer: Both men and women?

Claire: Actually the men probably sort of say we don't know how you do it …

Interviewer: Is it mostly people without children?

Claire: No it's mostly women with children. Women without children don't even acknowledge that I'm a mother! Those that know, who are really paternalistic, like to run the guilts over you.

Some were emphatic that they were better mothers for being working mothers; nonetheless 'mother blame' is still strong:

Meredith: We are the majority now. But mothers are still copping it. Mother-blame is alive and well. It is still there.

The cross-criticism of mothers

Interestingly, women with jobs feel criticised for being working mothers (called selfish and 'money hungry'), while on the other hand, women at home feel criticised for being lazy, incompetent, or unable to 'get a job'. As one country woman and mother of three put it:

There is a real false representation. If you are home with your kids, you should be out working. If you are out working you should be at home with your kids. And you can't win either way. That's the feeling I get.

While working mothers felt criticism of them was unfair, they were sometimes critical of women at home for socialising and 'not keeping up with the ironing':

Mary: When they have something on at the school I know that I take time off of work to go there, and most of the mums [at

home] don't. And its three other mums who are there supporting our kids' class, and we all work, and we have to take
time off of work to get there and the other mums don't worry
about it. They are probably at home having cups of tea together
building their own friendships! I don't know ... (mother with
job, country town)

Joan: I had a friend who had kids at the school a few years ago.
Monday morning was a religious coffee morning for all the
mothers but she never ever went to any of the school things and
yes she was sitting at home doing nothing and it used to drive
me nuts. Just to sit all day – how do you do that? All the friends
that I have that don't work, don't get their ironing up to date
and don't seem to do anything, because they have tomorrow to
do it. I had one friend whose mother would come out and do her
curtains and that kind of stuff for her a couple of times a year,
and I'd think, you're kidding me! (mother with job, country
town)

Ironically, in this discussion, women who enjoy social contacts
through paid work are critical of women at home for their 'coffee
mornings'. On the other hand, mothers at home speak of feeling
shame, anxiety and guilt for *not* working, for not 'being professional', or being 'looked down upon as a low life':

People think that it is not that we choose, but that we can't get a
job. Sometimes its jealousy. (mother of four, at home)

I feel shame about being a mother at home, personally. For that
six hours when the children are at school, I don't sit down. I feel
anxious, I have to be productive. The message is that you have
to be superwoman – so I feel guilty. It's complicated. I feel like
I'm sponging. I feel anxiety as middle age approaches. How do
you break into the workforce? I didn't decide consciously to stay
at home with the kids. (mother of two with postgraduate
qualifications).

Some mothers at home criticise working mothers for treating
their children 'as an accessory' and 'farming out responsibility'.

Mothers with jobs, however, contrast this with the compliments that their male partners receive for 'helping' at home and the absence of any critique of working fathers. As one mother of three, who worked part-time while also supporting her builder husband, put it:

> Everyone says to him: 'What a wonderful father!' But I don't get 'What a wonderful mother!' (call centre worker, part-time, mother)

There is not a parallel debate about 'good' fathers alongside the discussion of 'good' mothering. Some fathers are aware of the over-scrutiny that applies to their partners – and resent the assumptions that they are not contributing:

> My husband is resentful that people ask how I cope with four children – and says 'Because I put a lot of work into the children too'. He resents not being seen as an equal partner. (call centre worker, part-time, mother)

Many mothers are very aware of the contradictory messages that abound about motherhood and the clash between the economic self-interest that dominates society and the under-valuation of the care they provide. The longstanding under-valuation of mothering and its 'sentimental valorisation' (Hays 1996) was described by many women:

> You get mixed messages about being a mum. It's said that it's held in high regard but the fact is that it isn't because everything in society values what you produce. Not being a mother. (mother at home, city)

Those at home debate the nature of rewards that they sought, weighing 'money' versus 'respect'. Some want motherhood to be pulled into the paid sphere through a wage, for example, seeing this as the only means by which real recognition will flow, while others wanted 'respect rather than cash'.

Super-mothers and 'intensive' mothering

Women recognise the pressure to be 'super-mums' and the increasing rate and standard of mothering around them. Sharon Hays characterises contemporary mothering as 'intensive' with its consolidation through child-rearing manuals, experts, the media and the market (1996). This apparatus of ideologies and cultures of motherhood, along with the physical facts of maternity, conspire to load up the 'sacred logic' of motherhood with an increasingly large model of 'intensive mothering', as mothers are expected and 'trained' to provide, a limitless 'willingness to nurture the child, to listen to the child, to decipher the child's needs, to respond to the child's desires, to respect the child, to consult the experts for suggestions on what the child may require, to search long and hard for the appropriate alternative caregivers to watch the child should the parent be unavailable – in short, the willingness to expend a great deal of physical, emotional, cognitive and financial resources on the child' (Hays 1996: 128). Many Australian women strive to provide intensive, super-mothering, while others recognise the 'gold-standard' even as they fail to achieve it:

> I try and do everything perfectly, but you can't. You need to admit you are not super-mum. There are real emotional ties with kids below school age and when they are at school, and when there is something special on and you can't be there you feel terrible ... I always seem to have to prove myself because I am a working mother. I never buy a bought cake for my children's dos. I always cook them myself. You are constantly proving yourself (all nod in agreement). I don't see Lisa Kenny as a super-mum. She has a trainer and a housekeeper and so on. *We* are the super-mums! (country woman, full-time worker, mother)

Denise is aware that she is striving too hard, that her self-surveillance is too vigorous. She sees the home-made cake, alongside her full-time work, as the marker of her proper, intensive mothering which she must constantly 'prove herself' through *because* she is in paid work. Others in the group encourage Denise to make greater use of support or to lower her standards: 'Kids don't notice the difference if you didn't bake the cake. We put so much pressure on ourselves'. But Denise is not alone:

> I work full-time and about 20 hours in our business. I do [all the housework] at home. My girls do callisthenics and I would stay up till the small hours of the morning sewing on sequins to get things done so they didn't miss out. (country woman, full-time worker, mother)

Others describe growing pressure to be super-mums and to more intensively mother. As one put it: 'The pace moves a lot faster now. There is more pressure to be a super-mum.' A retired woman who now does voluntary work argued that women 'brought this upon themselves' and that they need to build clearer boundaries around mothering, so that its demands are less intensive, more shared, and less debilitating for women – including her own professional daughters:

> Women are too committed to both family and work. They don't set boundaries. We seem to have more to prove. We get anxious about trying to prove ourselves. I'd like to know why women think they have to do more? Do we need to prove our worth and add the extra stress? (volunteer, country woman, mother, now retired)

The pressure to 'prove' themselves as mothers, especially among those with the most choice to work or not, is powerful. It is bolstered by the strength and pervasiveness of the dominant cultural model of intensive mothering, which has proved so sticky in the face of significant change elsewhere. The discussion about motherhood and the controversy it creates reveals the deep roots of 'proper mothering' and its *intensification* with the onset of paid work. These affect women, and they provoke criticism of women who are mothers – whether at home or in paid work. Women look for more support to assist them to mother well, regardless of their 'work' choices, whether through a variety of child care arrangements, paid leave, or better appreciation and support for those with young children who are at home.

It is not surprising to find that Australian mothers undertake 'socially necessary "ideological work"' by adopting rationales for their decisions, to make sense of the contradiction they experience between 'what they believe and what they actually do' as Hays describes this 'work' (1996: 133). Such ideological work to bridge the gap between the dominant vision of the good mother and its lived realities, is 'simply a means of maintaining their sanity' (1996: 133). Some of that work is undertaken through critique of those who have made other decisions so that the 'rationality' and 'goodness' of their own choices remains plausible. This is partly at the root of the cross-mother critique of mothers-at-home of mothers-in-paid work and vice versa. Its other sign is an epidemic of guilt – that most gendered of emotions, to use Michael Pusey's phrase (2003) – as many mothers fall short of the intensive 'proper mothering' that the cultural stereotype leaves unrenovated at the centre of the family and their own selves. Where is the father in this model?

Being at home

Some mothers enjoy their time at home with young children without reservation. One who had raised her four children on a single wage that she described as 'basic', loved 'all of it ... I never had a day when I felt bad'. She felt free of guilt about being at home and had no qualms about 'putting my feet up and having a coffee'. She had reluctantly taken on some paid work, because 'My husband likes me to work because he feels it is fulfilling for me'. Others talk of the delight of being there for the first steps, the importance of being there when the kids were sick and of their discomfort with, as one put it 'the idea of handing over care. I wanted to be their mother! Once they go to school they belong to someone else'. Women working full-time in a factory who had come back to work with small children expressed regret at losing early times with their children: 'Just being with them in that time when they are at home – and the bonding. A lot of people take it for granted but if you don't have it, you miss it … We've missed out'. An older country woman recollected with real pleasure her years at home amidst a supportive community, pointing out that this community had now shrunk with farm restructuring and more women going into paid work. Thirty years ago women on nearby farms and organisations like Mothers and Babies provided 'any excuse' to go out.

However, for many mothers today ambivalence about being at home with young children is common. The thinning of the community in which it is located, intensifies mothering for many individuals and creates isolation:

> When I had my children, I had always worked full-time. I did not like being at home. Now I look back and I wish I had been better, I wish I'd liked it more. Because it was probably my chance. I didn't have to work, but I found I had demands, the kids were demanding, they were close together and I found the days were so long and the nights so short! And I didn't enjoy it, and now I'd love to stay home a bit more because no one's there and I just love it! (mother, part-time worker, city)

The decision to do paid work or to stay home is, for many, not easy. On the one hand, women at home feel the isolation; on the other, women with jobs feel sadness at their loss, and that of their children. And many women have experience of both, having spent years at home and then taking up a job. Unfortunately, the need to defend 'your' situation often crowds out exploration of this ambivalence and fuels an over-estimation of the divide between mothers at home or in jobs. The isolation of mothering is often mentioned, and sometimes drives an unanticipated quick return to jobs. A new mother in the country, with a wide social network and a well-established country town community around her, who might be expected to comfortably enjoy early mothering nested in her community, describes unexpected isolation:

> I was itching [to get back] when he was two months old, I said 'I'll come in voluntary' – even though I was on maternity leave! I feel I need that – the people. I'm not used to being home on my own. I felt isolated. I had a caesarean, and I didn't drive. Mum

said 'How can you feel isolated? You're in the town and everything!' but I said I'm here but I feel I can't get out. The baby needed me at home. I felt I had no one until Frank got home at night and then I'd say 'Here you are, you have him'. And I didn't cope as well as I thought I'd cope. (new mother, country)

Others simply hated being at home. Several women referred to 'the four walls': 'I had to escape those walls!'. As a professional woman in a country town put it:

I hated it. Well I was in a small business of my own, I employed a locum to help and I was breast-feeding for the first 12 months. I chose to go back to work. My mother-in-law said I'll look after the baby, but as soon as I said I was going back to work, all services were withdrawn! Everything, except from my mum who was a long way away. Because I chose to keep my business, and not change my name and return to work. So I employed a nanny and wherever I went Nanny went, and I fed the both of the children for 12 months. So I had to make it work. In private business you can do that, if there's an avenue to do it financially. But here [at the hospital] I can't. It's very different. My children have grown up in my workplace, but now they can't … The work is totally different.

This woman's choice to work with her children nearby, was clearly shaped by the nature of family support available (and her mother-in-law's judgments about her choices) and by the nature of her workplace: in her own private practice, she could choose to work with her children nearby; in a larger workplace on a salary, this choice was not available. Income, family and workplace arrangements condition her choices, along with the fact that she 'hated' being at home.

Women with extensive work experience before becoming mothers are more likely to want to return to work after having children. They speak of feeling isolated. The growing proportion of women of child-bearing age who now have up to a decade in paid work before having their first child, increase the probability of such feelings.

Why mothers work outside the home

The motivations for paid work include social contact, money, a sense of accomplishment, independence and utilisation of skills. We have seen how many experience paid work as a source of community and social life; these motivations for paid work are often named ahead of economic reward. The drive to avoid isolation is strong:

> If I had to stay at home all the time – like on the school holidays – I'd kill the poor kids! (country town mother of two)

Many mothers feel that they would 'go barmy' if they didn't work, that they were 'more sane' because of time away from their kids. Some talk of being housebound. As a doctor put it: 'I had that terrible feeling of being scared of going outside. I realised that I needed to get out'. For many, work remains a financial necessity. They feel no real degree of choice about their 'decision' to take a job. As one woman working in a factory put it, with the general agreement of the group: 'I work for money! It's a necessity nowadays. One income is just not enough'. Casually employed workers shared the same motivations – often mentioning a combination of both financial and personal issues:

> It pays the bills. It goes a long way to making life a bit more comfortable. It give satisfaction. You feel like you are worth something.

> Yes it's a self-esteem thing …

> It's money and the social things …

> I don't know what I would do if I was at home. I'd go mad. I'm not a person who can be happy in a context only at home with four children. It's that balance – fulfilment of yourself of what you have achieved as a professional and as a wife and mother.

For many it is now too hard to live on one wage and enjoy some quality of life: 'One income is for necessities – food, mortgage. The other income is for the extras, which you won't be able to afford without the second income'. Economic necessity was especially the motivation for sole-parents to work, and some found it very difficult. It was very far from their preferences:

> Before my partner and I separated we were surviving on one wage, but now being separated, I have to work. (she cries) (full-time worker, city)

Mothers were also motivated to work to 'make a contribution', to consolidate their 'skilled identity', and to gain a return for the years that they had spent in education. Given the rise in qualifications for women of child-bearing age, and the link they see between their skills, occupation or qualifications and their identities, this impulse is likely to become stronger:

> It's not so much a need to work as also a *want* to work. If you've been in the workforce, if you've been educated, and then get married ... you still have that desire to make a contribution to your family unit, being just a mother is not wholly and solely your identity. (mother, country town)

A variety of obstacles and life circumstances stand between women and their personal work/care preferences, not least the cultural expectations of their husbands, and a struggle – sometimes long term – for who has 'the say':

> I always liked to work between each child until I had my fourth child and my husband didn't like me to work. He enjoyed the money but he put these extra pressures on me to do everything but now I've had four and a half years at home before I've gone back to work, he's actually done the full circle and realised that it's okay, he's encouraged me to go and work. (mother in paid work, living on farm)
>
> Do you think that's because his mum didn't work?
>
> Absolutely! His view was you don't go and do anything physical because that's the man's job: 'You stay this side of the ramp [farm gate] and make sure that toilet's clean'. Of course I'm *really* good at that! (laughs ironically) ... I think he thought I

should go out and play bridge and play golf. I mean, this would be his ideal – to make me the traditional farmer's wife – where it's a lucrative income and you could afford to go out and do good things.

And then they can have all the say!

Interviewer: So what shifted?

He actually realised I really wasn't very good at cleaning toilets! He actually said 'You're not going to change are you?' I said 'No. This is me. This is how I am.' He hoped deep underneath, right under there, that maybe I'd change. He's accepted that I won't now. Now we have a cleaner!

'Mothers' or 'workers': Identity and the value of mothering

A loss of identity – being 'only a mother' – is significant especially for mothers with qualifications, professionals, and those with pre-motherhood work experience (especially many years of it). It is less of an issue for casual, part-time or less skilled, lower paid workers – though not irrelevant. Women in middle and senior management talk about how work contributes to their identity, to 'who I am':

> I strive for the best I can. I am to an extent *who* I am at work. It defines me. My work is worthwhile, especially when you have responsibilities. It is all tied up with my self-worth and who I want to be. (manager, call centre)

> Yes. Just because I have a child doesn't mean that I have to give up who I am. (manager, call centre)

The low market valuation of motherhood also constructs identity. Many women are keenly aware of the low valuation of 'mere mothers', and reject the inadequacy of identity through being 'just someone's wife. Just some appendage'. Their sense of identity was weakened by motherhood – 'you get treated differently once you have kids' – and they sought to build it through paid work. For a significant proportion of women, 'being someone' means having some occupational identity:

> Jenny: When I was on maternity leave I used to be embarrassed when I would be introduced to someone and they would say what do you do?' And I'd say 'Oh, er ...' and I'd think 'I'm just at home with my kids and there's absolutely no value put on that'. And then I'd be embarrassed. And then I'd say 'I'm currently on maternity leave', and suddenly, well, that was okay! (laughter) It was okay to say that! It made you equal with them. (country woman, full-time worker, mother)

Describing herself as 'on maternity leave' rather than disappeared into the non-identity of 'mother-at-home', retrieved for Jenny a sense of worth and identity that was significant to her community and perhaps to herself as well. The need to be 'on maternity leave' – and still a worker with a workplace attachment – while a mother at home, is symptomatic of the increasing 'non-person' status that our community confers upon carers – despite sentimental valorisation of motherhood. Those who respect full-time mothering and those who do it, work against the grain of society where so much of personal worth, value and self is shaped by a worker identity established through the market. The greater emphasis on work attachment in the making of identity, effectively lowers the status of mothering even further – in the minds of mothers and their friends and community. This leads women like Jenny to rename themselves as 'temporarily away from work' rather than fully occupied in the productive work of raising children. Effectively, the increasing reach and power of market work into life – its measurement and creation of 'value' – further devalues motherhood in the minds of mothers and others.

Women in paid work adopt other shielding and renaming behaviours: some hide their breast-feeding or child care commitments, and their maternal status, recognising the liability that a carer label creates for them at work. The pressure to maintain the appearance of a non-maternal worker contributes to decisions to reduce family size. It is part of the 'emotion work' that is necessary from women as they 'cover' for their situations and attempt to resolve the gaps between who they are, and who or what they 'should be': to make everything "fine"'. This is the complex internal 'emotion work' undertaken to bridge the gap between what mothers can personally deliver and what the ideal demands, to find some emotional resolution by rationalising their 'choices'. Arlie Hochschild defines this as the work of '*trying* to feel the "right" feeling, the feeling [you] want to feel – to make and keep everything "fine"' (1989: 46). Part of that work involves critique of those who have not made the same choices. The failure to completely bridge the gap between ideal and reality is revealed in the widespread incidence of mother guilt.

Guilt

Australian motherhood is suffering an epidemic of guilt. Guilt was raised by women in every discussion and infects women at home with children, women in paid work, and rural and urban women. It is no respecter of income, age or occupational divides. Feelings of guilt sit heavily on women caught between the roles their mothers played and traditional expectations of motherhood, and the expectations and financial demands of society now. Many women are affected by it. Most women spoke of the remorse they felt at not being able to *do it all* – be there for their kids, and meet their family's financial needs, the expectations of motherhood, and their own ambitions or experience.

Even when their children are grown up, women felt guilt about how their decisions to do paid work might have contributed to problems years later:

> My guilt says I am responsible for what is happening in their lives, which are drug-related problems at the moment. Was it because I wasn't there? That I didn't make the right decisions? I am beating myself up really well. I can't give to work or my team at the moment. I don't have any more to give. (team leader, office, mother)

This woman's self-criticism in relation to her sons' current difficulties was very painful to her and she looked only to herself for its sources and solutions without mention of their father. Another woman, whose children were also older, spoke of her guilt, always wondering when things went wrong for her children, whether it was her fault for working and 'not being there':

> Both of my sons are schizophrenics and although I know it is genetic I still think 'did I pull the trigger by not being there?' I feel so guilty. (call centre employee, mother, city)

Other possible explanations for her sons' mental illness were no protection from guilt for not doing enough and not being there with unlimited time to nurture. This contributes to exhaustion:

> Legitimising time for yourself is really hard. If I am not doing anything I get guilty and think of what needs to be done. I see empty time as wasted time. I always feel guilty, even my time off is guilty time. (call centre worker, mother, city)

Professional women in small business shared these feelings. A successful consultant and private business-woman, for example, questioned her earlier choices to work, as her children grew and wanted to have less time with her:

> I am finding I want to be with them more, like they have missed out on something. Feelings of guilt are starting to appear. I think that society puts that frame of mind (guilt) on mothers. Even the kids take it from society. (mother, full-time worker, city)

While this mother feels a 'frame of mind' is created to 'put' guilt onto mothers, she is in its grip nonetheless. Professional women with small babies talked of the guilt they feel on leaving the house or child care centre:

> She [the baby] is getting easier, not so upset, she sometimes waves and smiles when I leave. That makes me feel better. There are times when I am in tears – it makes me feel so upset, but I can't do it – can't stay at home without being in huge trouble at work. (journalist and mother of toddler).

Only a handful of women said they felt no guilt. A couple of these were single mothers who had, as they put it, 'no choice' but to work for money. The absence of choice demobilised powerful motherhood ideologies (though not all single mothers were immune):

> I regret missing out on their early years but I had no choice, my husband died early and I had to work. (call centre employee, widow, mother and grandmother)

> I told my children, 'I have two lives, one for you and one for me'. I had to have one night a week when I socialised with my friends. Community was important. I didn't feel guilty, I felt saddened. I was doing the best I could. No I didn't feel guilty because I knew what I was doing was for the kids anyway. (health worker, single mother)

This single mother rationalises her time for herself on the basis that it improves her mothering: it was 'for the kids anyway'. Both mothers at home and those in paid work rationalise their situations in terms that serve their children and reinforce their sense of being a good mother (as Gilligan and Williams also observe among US mothers (1982, 2000)). At one extreme, paid work saves one mother from 'killing' her children. At the other end, women at home give up the prospect of a higher income in order to serve their children better. Both mothers at home and in paid work 'remain attentive to the central tenets of the ideology of intensive child rearing' and – as in the US – there are signs that middle class mothers 'go about the task of child rearing with the greatest intensity' (Hays 1996: 151). It was a rare Australian mother who felt so impervious to mothering norms, that she was both guilt-free and felt no need to rationalise her choices in terms that made them 'good for the children'. One example was a young mother in a full-time clerical job with two young children who said she felt no guilt: 'I've never felt guilty'. People would criticise her choices 'no matter what', and she had decided to just get on with it. She reallocated the discomfort, arising from the gap between her reality and social expectations, to her critics, robustly *refusing* to feel guilty:

> There is always someone who is going to criticise the way that you live your life … [There are those who say] all mothers should stay at home with their kids and you get other people who say all those single mothers [who stay at home] are bludgers. That's *their* problem. You do what you have to do. (clerical worker, mother)

Another mother of two, who had suffered post-natal depression felt that her 'huge think' when she was hospitalised and under psychiatric care had helped her 'resolve' the gap between 'the good mother' and what she could realistically manage:

> I had to do a huge think a few years ago because when my two and a half year old was two weeks old, I was diagnosed with post-natal depression, and I ended up in hospital for a bit … and then it was a year to climb back, with support. We did a lot of this stuff: what is motherhood? What is a good mother? And as a result I've come out stronger and more resolved so I don't need external measures to feed me, I know what is right for us, and I haven't had to do it based on my mother's role model which was wrong for me. I've had to create my own parenting and our family life. It might not relate to anyone else's, but it's right for us. (student, mother, city)

Maggie rejected the dominant paradigm of motherhood and had decided to be the kind of mother that was right for 'us/me'. The period of depression after the birth of her second baby had also helped her partner adopt an active domestic role – he was thrust into taking a newborn home on his own. She felt relatively free of guilt in relation to her choices, and regularly took time to 'selfishly' look after herself and do what she wanted to do: 'My kids have to compromise for me, it's a balance'. Maggie has deliberately – and with professional help – unpacked the ideological and familial models of motherhood available to her, set them aside and refused to recognise a gap between ideology and practice. As a result she does not feel guilt.

A number of less guilt-afflicted women had been raised in working class or immigrant households. For example, Leonie felt relatively guilt-free and wondered if the fact that she was raised working class, and her partner was the son of European migrants, led to less guilt. She pointed out that her immigrant mother-in-law, who had always had a job, never questioned her decision to work, while her Australian-born mother did. There are class and ethnic differences at work here, replicated through the vehicle of their own working/'non-working' mothers. Some level of guilt was, however, very widespread among *most* women – whether working in a factory on nightshift or in management positions. Young women without children did not anticipate feeling guilt: as one put it, 'I don't think I'll feel guilty because I'll know I'm doing it for them', readily adopting a frame that aligned her own wish with the projected positive effects for her children, but other older women in the focus group warned her to expect it nonetheless.

Guilt emerges as the outstanding emotional consequence of the gap between 'realistic mothering' and 'intensive mothering', between mothers with jobs and the cultural distortion of 'proper motherhood', and between women's mothers and their own reality. Women worked hard to align what they see in society's mirror with their sense of themselves and their situation. Their self is destabilised by the incongruence between being a hard working mother-at-home with the 'non-worker/nobody' signal that others take from being 'just a mother'. Guilt is part of the penalty of the gap and the measure of its imperfect resolution and it affects mothers with jobs or at home.

Motherhood and materialism: Buying love, spoiling kids?

Australian motherhood is increasingly overlaid with a market dimension. This marketisation is reflected in many behaviours ranging from loading up children's extra-curricula activities to commercialised recreation and celebrations. *The Australian Magazine* recently highlighted the changing nature of childhood, pointing out that in 1997 Melbourne's Yellow Pages telephone directory did not even list children's parties, but by 2002 included 688 listings for performers that can be hired for children's birthdays – clowns, magicians and theatre groups – with a 43 per cent jump in the most recent year. They also note increasing spending on toys: 'total spending on toys and games has jumped by 151 per cent in the past decade compared with a 68 per cent rise in total retail spending' (Stewart 2003: 1). However, this spending does not necessarily mean healthier or happier children, with increasing obesity and diagnosis of depression among young children. It does mean more shopping, management and coordination, especially for mothers.

Children are described as very alert to the guilt that parents feel and they mobilise it to their material advantage: 'kids pick up on the ambivalence'. Mothers are open about their complicity in commercially compensating for their absence or 'inferior', time-poor mothering:

> A few weeks ago I worked nightshift and next day I took my kids to the supermarket and spent it all, because I felt bad for not being there.(factory worker, mother, city)

Women salving their guilt with material objects for children, who are alert to the advantages of their mothers' pay packets, as factory workers discuss:

> My neighbour says I spoil my kids by giving them things to allay my guilt. You supplement money for love and over-compensate.

> We do spoil our kids and that is part of why we work, so that we can spoil them.

> When I said I'd give up work, she (child) said 'No. If you stay we get more'.

Some feel that the material pursuit game is unending and unsatisfying – and perhaps unnecessary: 'People could survive on a lot less ... A lot of kids are brought up to want more. The pressure is put on by society'. The role of the cultural frame in creating pressure to 'want more' is recognised and some mothers talk of the absurdity of trying to 'keep up with the Jones' and the endless demands of kids for labelled clothing and expensive toys.

Women report a wide range of opinions among their children about their paid work. There is no sign of a parallel controversy in relation to the paid work of fathers. Women actively engaged in discussion about the costs and benefits of their paid work, encouraging their children to see the financial benefits ('the stuff') it brought. Women working in a factory discuss their kids views:

> My youngest one actually said thank you! She gets a lot more now. She said you can't leave [work] mum, because we get more.

> My youngest has said, she basically wants it all. She wants me there in the evenings, but she wants the stuff as well. I said we can only have one or the other. When I started this shift it was very hard for her and she said I want you to stay at home. I listed all the things that I'd bought for her or done for her in the last three or four months since I'd started working and its like 'Oh, okay'. I had to make her understand that it's a means to an end, that you can't have it all.

> I have to explain to my daughter that if I don't go to work then I don't get paid, and if I don't get paid then I can't buy her the things she wants.

Many women talked of the material things that their children now had because of their jobs, and how they believed that their children would not have been happy without them:

> I think if you say to your kids would you rather I stayed at home all the time or would you rather do this because we can afford to, I think the kids are smart enough to make the decision that they would rather you go off to work so that they can afford what they want as well. Mine do that at six and seven [years old]. No question. (country woman)

Others felt that it was *time* that children wanted, not things. In sum, mothers' guilt results in compensating spending patterns in both low and higher income households. Time-poor mothers substitute material goods for their presence and to salve their sense of guilt. The mirror of expansive 'intensive mothering', held up to their practically constrained time, energy and capacity to nurture, creates an uncomfortable dissonance. As more women enter more paid work, the dissonance grows. It is further intensified by the growth in hours in paid work among those who work very long hours. And it is sensitive to comparison – especially to mothers who do things differently. The thinning of the community within which women must mother – with fewer people in the street and less extended family nearby to comple-ment their efforts – also takes effect. The market offers one means of feeling better, through the hope that spending eases pain, loss or blame from the child. It also offers an important means of replacing direct caring labour, through bought meals and services. These links between mothering, guilt and con-sumption are fine friends for the market and capitalism. The habit of replacing mother-time with goods also encourages young people into consumerism, creating a new generation of diligent consumers who associate emotional comfort with consumption, making the connection between 'feeling better' or 'being loved', and 'having stuff'.

Powerful ideologies are at work here. The unconscious, internalised *habitus* of contemporary Australian motherhood is influential. It is surprisingly intact in its traditional terms, despite the changes in women's paid work. Some recognise 'society's pressures': that society 'puts that frame of mind (guilt) on mothers'. Nonetheless, most women experience guilt and they do not mention a parallel guilt among their male partners. This is not to say that men are not actively involved in the care/ expen-diture economy of their families, but their role has not been our focus here. Women attributed behaviours in their adult children – like drug use and schizophrenia – to their work/ mothering choices, when a great variety of things might have caused these things, including absent fathers, structurally inflexible work-places, frayed social structures or weak state supports.

Mothers are much more likely to see the fault in themselves, attempting to meet their 'deficiencies' through super-mothering, than they are to look to their partners or to critically examine the rigidities imposed by their workplaces that leave, for ex-ample, factory workers, lawyers and doctors locked into 'greedy' work patterns, and shift-working factory employees without the option of part-time work or maternity leave. The link between fixed and inflexible work arrangements and mothers' 'inade-quacies' is obscured.

A critique of cultural standards of motherhood is weak except among a few who mobilise it against guilt. Women live within the established *habitus* of motherhood (motherhood's 'unthought orientations' (Lash, 1994: 154)). They may refer to society's 'frame of mind' and talk about its influence – and they attempt to create their own frames to rationalise their behaviours as good for their children (whether they elect to stay home, or enter paid work). But it seems that this *habitus* of motherhood is sluggish to catch up with the fact that women's capacity to mother 'inten-sively' is increasingly compromised by their participation in paid work, by the thinner community base out of which mothering is done and by the intensification of paid work and long hours of some parents. There are few signs of an active critical decon-struction of traditional motherhood among middle class women, the traditional vanguard of social change, and surprising silences about the role of men, the state or the workplace.

The growing reach of the market around motherhood has two important effects. First, the dominance of its schema of valuation (what is exchanged for money, is valued) drives a devaluation of care-work, so that the only means suggested to increase its value is by paying it – pulling it into the market.

Second, while mothers in our study show little attachment to 'the calculating logic of the market' (Hays 1996: 173) and it cannot explain reproduction or most caring, the market never-theless increasingly encroaches upon the terrain of motherhood through the substitution of market goods for love and care. Market economics makes very little sense of the economies of care (and it seems probable that only non-carers could have invented the assumptions of neoclassical economics). Mothering is built upon emotional, cultural and biological realities. While they occur in the context of one economic system or another – more or less marketised – they cannot be analysed with the tools of economic rationality. Being a mother is simply 'uneconomic'. In this sense, the market denies motherhood and love. It might exploit it, work with it, try to mould it (often successfully), but it cannot explain the non-economic decision to mother and to nurture. Indeed the market runs counter to this care. It creates competing motivations. Most mothers can make more money out of paid work than mothering (calculating its gains in terms of the child's potential long-term reciprocal earning and caring capacity). So the pull to the labour market drains the direct caring part of motherhood. Thus the only way that mothers in the labour market can persist with the loving care they want to give, is by super-exploitation of themselves or even lower paid women workers, or a greater contribution from their partners or other social contributors like the extended family, or the state.

Ghosts

Overshadowing this discussion are four ghosts. One is the absent father. While men are now more involved in their families and caring work (as we discuss in the next chapter), the shift is hardly seismic. As they have entered paid work, mothers have had to devise their work, labour and emotional strategies without a compensating shift in men's fathering and caring patterns. *Hope* that they will do so has proved a weak impulse for change. The mud of gendered care is sticky and thick.

The second ghost is the weak extended family and community support that continues to leave mothers in nuclear families carrying the central load in a paradigm of increasingly intensive mothering.

The third ghost is the workplace. All too few mothers find themselves in workplaces that assertively recognise their caring life and motherhood. Many working women veil their maternity, and squeeze it around the established professional and workplace norms which face them.

The fourth ghost is the largely untouched discourse of boundless motherhood and its shadow, guilt. Its hold is powerful among most mothers except where no element of choice existed, or a determined effort has been made to uproot it. It is weaker – but far from dead – in some working class, single parent and non-English speaking households where the 'choice' is narrower or nil in the face of economic necessity, and where women have experience of their own working mothers. Familial patterns matter.

While some women are confident and sure of their mothering, in other cases we can see a confusion of guilt and money. Earnings are used to compensate for guilt, and we see a range of levels of comfort and discomfort with these compensations and consumption. These confusions spill over into a discussion about the meaning of motherhood, and its 'proper' shapes today. As more mothers enter paid work, without liberation from the vision of the boundless proper mother, the incidence of guilt will rise especially with increases in intensive mothering and the thinning of community. It is already an epidemic. Some hope that young women will be free of it and assert that 'young women will demand more flexibility from their partners, their employers ... and themselves' (Mackay 2001). Unfortunately, the 'demand' does not make the change. If this hope has not been realised amidst a generation of women – and men – many of whom were affected by second wave feminism, it is no more likely amidst younger women who lack as yet better equipment to unpack and reconstruct the large, deeply rooted, social constructions of 'proper' motherhood. While some women are optimistic about their chances of doing things differently, they are not yet accompanied by male partners who have taken up in equal measure the load of parenting or housework, or supported by a state that will be more active, or by reformed workplaces. Very few Australian men elect to take time off paid work for extended periods to care for their children, and the tenacity of male resistance to domestic work is remarkable. Hochschild's double shift – extensively documented in the US in the early 1980s – remains powerful 20 years on. As long as these burdens remain unequally shared, intensive motherhood remains an impossible vision for women who can deliver its promise only rarely. It over-shadows motherhood – increasingly expensive, complex and 'professional' – where the incursion of the market and contraction of other forms of community, loads up expectations of them.

Mother wars

The collision between work and care takes many forms in relation to mothers. Several outright wars around motherhood are frequently fostered in public discussion, with skirmishes between mothers and non-mothers, and between mothers-at-home and mothers-with-jobs. These wars are useful to those who benefit from women's preoccupation – or assumed preoccupation – with squabbles among themselves and from women's self-critical introspection, focused on personal limitations and failures to 'live up to' the ideal.

Over-reaching both of these wrestles is a third larger contest between the market – and its underpinning logic of competitive individualism and personal gain – and the nurturing non-economic logic of 'sacred' motherhood. The market is hungry for the benefit that can flow to it from the practices of contemporary mothering, and women's attempts to assuage guilt through its devices, earnings and materialism. Motherhood is one of the modern market's most powerful contradictions, but elements of mothering are increasingly within its thrall.

There are major losers and several beneficiaries from these three motherhood contests. The major losers are women in general and mothers in particular. These wars both divide women and blunt their capacity to cohere into political voice that influences change. Instead women's voices are fractured, individualised or silenced, as men in governments or business discuss –

or ignore – their situations. Differences in the needs of women are both consciously and unconsciously magnified in order to immobilise. A stalling 'in the gender equality agenda' in Australia can be traced to conflict around motherhood, given that the fastest gender advances have usually occurred 'around a clearly articulated and widely shared common purpose' (Probert 2001: 9).

Most obvious beneficiaries from mother wars are, first, those men who abscond from active parenting and leave housework and care to women and, secondly, the state and governments that would rather spend public resources on many things other than care. The third beneficiary is the market which gorges itself upon the consumer substitutes that mothers (and sometimes fathers) offer children out of time-pressures or their guilt, and children enthusiastically claim as the material fruit of 'intensive mothering', which is increasingly measured through market expenditure on children – whether their private schooling, labelled clothes, fast foods or commercialised leisure. The market increasingly mediates motherhood and other forms of dependent care, and the price is high, with the returns vague and unsatisfying. Women's guilt does not seem to abate no matter how many toys and shoes are fed into its maw, but a handy new crop of enthusiastic consumers is reared and delivered to the market as its side-product.

The contradiction between what people *value* and what material goods *can deliver*, is starkly revealed in surveys by The Australia Institute (and HILDA 2001) which show that large majorities – over three quarters – of Australians rate family and friends above other things as very important to their quality of life. At the same time, more than 80 per cent feel that society is too materialistic. However, most continue to look for more goods and feel that they lack enough money to satisfy their households needs despite 'the fact that Australians are richer than ever, and around three times better off than their parents in the 1950s' (Hamilton and Mail, 2003: vii; HILDA 2001).

Consequences

How should the Work/Care regime change to liberate mothers and all women from the worst effects of the collision between work and care? On an individual level, women are looking for liberation from judgement of their choices – whether by other women, their children, community or extended families. Some of this liberation will only happen in the short term if women can individually understand and then refuse the impossible model of 'intensive mothering' and instead opt for reasonable personal standards. Personal refusal of stereotypes is hard work – especially if one's husband and children are actively on their side. Women in our study managed it with psychiatric help or a robust refusal of others' opinions, sometimes through the mobilisation of the tools of feminist analysis or the support of their partners and friends.

Decisions around consumption and the substitution of 'things' for time and love are also made at the individual level. Fed by advertising and competitive desires to 'keep up' – these are individual decisions that parents must make carefully and perhaps more consciously. The dissonance between what people value (friends and family) and what many strive for (more stuff), and the weak association between more stuff and happiness (beyond a decent standard of living), must partly be resolved at the individual and household level. Current patterns of materially-compensating-mothering (and parenting) are hardly in this direction.

At the level of the community, women value neighbourhood communities when they can find social support and positive exchange. At home, however, with the decline in neighbourhood community, isolation is not uncommon and, for many, work-based relationships do not always extend into the home. Communities around playgroups, child care centres and schools are very important to mothers when they are at home. Many women make use of shopping centres for their outings, but most offer little non-commercial interaction. Much better use could be made of public spaces that facilitate social exchange. The integration of online access centres, public libraries and other social infrastructure into shopping space provide one example. Better urban planning has considerable potential to better meet the needs of those who care.

At the level of public policy, the provocation of mother wars between mothers and non-mothers and between mothers-at-home and mothers-at-work, must be seen for what it is: a useful cover story for policy paralysis. As long as women 'fight' over who should benefit from public spending, then progress is held back. Of course, mother-wars are a war within a single gender. Men are absent from the battlefield. They make no sacrifice, take no injury. In the same way, governments and states are absent from this 'private/public' war among women, while markets benefit from the intensification of motherhood and its emotional/material substitutions. Many love to see women fight: they find the mud wrestle salacious. But it does more than sell newspapers and entertain the public: it protects the beneficiaries of the present arrangements. It is therefore important that the larger goal of improvement in the terms for *all mothers* (and fathers and carers) be the dominant goal. Most women will spend many years of their lives in paid work and the majority will have dependants for significant parts of this time. Most mothers want to spend part of the very early years of their children's life with the option to be with them more than full-time or even part-time work allows. Facilitating these states, and mobility between them, with minimal penalty should be the goal of policy.

CHAPTER 5

The hidden costs of work:
Love and intimacy

How is work – in all its forms – affecting our most intimate relationships? In this chapter we consider three significant connections. First, the effect of long working hours on intimate relationships; second, the effect of women's paid and unpaid work on intimacy and personal life; third, given the important con-nection between housework and the quality of relationships, we look more closely at the nature and effects of domestic work on the quality of personal life.

Often the most poignant stories collected in the qualitative studies around which this discussion is based, are about intimate relationships and finding the time or inclination to be with a partner. This arose early in discussions about being a paid wor-ker. The struggle for intimacy is an important consequence of changes in the nature of work and in working hours, and of the combination of paid and unpaid jobs. While many are shy about talking intimately, they see a connection between work and love. They tell stories that reveal a close connection between work and intimacy, with large gaps between societal expectations about relationships, and their realities. Those in more senior or higher paid positions are less likely to openly discuss this aspect of their lives, and are more protective of themselves. Those in lower level office or factory jobs, however, are often jocular and open about these issues. Most Australians rate their family and friends – relationships – as very important to happiness (Eckersley 1999). Three quarters rate more time with family and friends as very important to their happiness (Hamilton 2002). However, pressures of time increasingly place a spontaneous, easy intimate life out of reach and people talk of 'working at' their intimate connection or scheduling it. For those who work long hours and their spouses and families it is not just *time* but its quality that are obstacles to easy intimacy, with grumpiness a common state for tired workers.

Modern discourses of love, intimacy and romance are complicated. They are embedded in social and historical myths and realities. While our public life has a large focus on sex and sexuality, the focus on intimacy is much weaker. Giddens has argued for the transformative power of the 'pure relationship': that is, a modern intimate relationship between equals (1992: 2).

There is all too little evidence of the ideal, pure relationships of the type that Giddens refers to in many households. This is not to say that many people are not in happy and satisfactory relationships. But tensions arising from work, relationships and inequalities are not uncommon. Larger survey data results substantiate a widespread clash between 'equality' discourse and real household practice: for example, the 2001 HILDA survey shows that most men and women believe couples should share housework if both work. However, the practice is very different. And this inequity *matters* to the majority of women who see it as unfair. The feelings of unfairness that surface in the qualitative material discussed below are widespread. In this chapter we explore the two work-related spokes in the wheel of intimacy that are most obvious: first, the struggle for time and energy to be intimate and to communicate and, second, inequality in the allocation of unpaid work and its effects on relationships.

Changing work patterns drain households of common couple-time. Many see communication as an important component of successful relationships (even where they do not have much of it), and they are supported in this in a wide range of popular literature about building and maintaining healthy relationships (Biddulph and Biddulph 1999; Jansen and Newman 1998). A first requirement for communication is time. The second is energy. The collision between time and easy intimacy is especially sharp where long or unreasonable hours are worked by at least one partner, but it is not uncommon more generally in the rising number of households where both partners work, jobs are more intense, and where one or both are 'drained' by their paid work.

The second powerful spoke in the wheel of intimacy is the inequality that persists in the allocation of unpaid work – especially the work of care and housework. The double day of household work and paid jobs contributes to physical exhaustion among women in particular, and it carries a high emotional cost as well. Household expenditure on convenience meals, gardening, child care and cleaning has risen much faster than total household spending over the last decade as women have turned to the market – not their partners – for help.

Many Australians say that intimacy, sexual activity and physicality are at a low ebb in their relationships. For some this is a source of loss, regret and pessimism. While some women talk about a need for closeness that does not include sexual intimacy, for many there is a general lack of interest in sex because of tiredness and lack of both personal and relationship 'space' because of the demands of children, other dependants and work. Some women take purposeful steps regularly to enable intimate communication and connection. Others see it as a past preoccupation that has little place or time in busy, stressed lives. Many are philosophical or humorous.

It is here more than anywhere else that the 'super woman' image comes unstuck: the seductress, the lover, the sexually liberated woman is often too tired, too stressed or totally disinterested. This loss of communication, intimacy and time has many effects. Among couples it is implicated in the breakdown of relationships and divorce. While this study does not include the voices of children, other studies show that children particularly value time with their parents – especially *unstressed* time (Galinsky 1999 in the US, and Lewis 2001 in Australia). So children are also relationship casualties of the time-poverty and low energy in many households where paid work patterns have grown. This time-poverty has wider reverberations in terms of the self-care of individuals and the fabric beyond their household among friends and extended family. We look first at the connection between longer hours and intimacy before turning to the effects of work more generally on relationships, and in particular the connection between the unequal distribution of housework and intimacy.

What long and unreasonable hours do to intimate relationships

Interviews with long-hour workers and their partners about the impact of their hours reveal very few positive comments about the effects of long hours on relationships. Sometimes more money helps the family generally, but over half of all overtime in Australia is unpaid so families do not necessarily feel a financial benefit. While some long hours workers love their jobs, their partners do not share the passion. Almost all couples feel that long hours negatively affect their intimate relationships, and partners of long hours workers describe themselves as *defacto* single parents. Tiredness emerges as the enemy of intimacy, so that couples struggle for time and energy to talk and to spend enjoyable time together.

Many describe their partners who work long hours as 'grumpy'. They approach them carefully, choosing their time to talk. Irritability, short tempers, and simple unavailability all contribute to a dearth of intimacy in many long hours relationships. In some cases the hours simply *spoil* relationships and put marriages at risk. The choice is between the marriage and their pattern of hours:

> Well, working in the construction industry, the hours can vary from anything from ten hours a day to 16 hours a day. Having spent 38 years in construction I didn't know what a 40 hour week was. You could work seven days a week, year in year out. It was a large contributor to the break up of my first marriage (man, partner to public service worker)

> I said to him, 'It's not worth our marriage, it's not worth what it's doing to us, just go and speak to someone,' because I said, 'you can't keep this up'. So he did … We decided that wasn't the way we wanted it to go, 'cause my father and Larry's father both

worked two jobs or three jobs and we never saw our dads and we said, 'no we don't want that for our kids'. Money's not that important if you haven't got a relationship or a marriage that is workable. (woman, supervisor's partner)

Many couples report arguments 'over who was going to do what' or describe 'living in survival mode'. These arguments occur around domestic work and activities, especially when one is tired. The time poverty of these households makes communication problematic. A technician describes how his long work hours strain his relationship with his wife:

She resents a lot of it, there's no two ways about that and rightly so too. I'm not there to help out with all the domestic chores and duties and all of that sort of thing a lot of the time ... By the time I get home, I basically have something to eat and go to bed and then I'm up again in the morning before everyone else and gone to work. Yeah that gets tiresome on the relationship.

He believes his relationships would be different if he worked less hours although he is worried that the family budget has expanded to depend on his overtime earnings. The choice is between earning extra money that his family needs or spending time with them instead. A number of those working long hours bring work home, and frequently think about it while with their family, then dream about it. So being *home* for these workers often does not mean being *available*: work contaminates home. This contamination is widespread: 29 per cent of a 2001 TMP Worldwide survey of 6,000 Australians said they took work home on weekends, 11 per cent of them for more than eight hours a weekend (*The Advertiser*, 22 September 2001: 6).

Unpredictable hours – when workers are unexpectedly called in for extra hours or are phoned at home – compromises intimacy. Many find their social lives as a family sharply constricted. Long hours undermine the vision of a 'Brady Bunch happy family' and turn workers into 'visitors in their own home', 'out of sync' with the rest of household and intermittent partners. As the partner of a flight attendant put it, with sadness and anger:

I miss him. I miss him very much and I get very angry about that. To the point that I don't want him home any more ... sometimes I don't know what's worse: to have him leave or having him come back. Yep I think it has definitely affected our relationship in a negative way ... He has a vision of coming home to a Brady Bunch family because he misses us so much and we can never match that. And because he's tired, he's intolerant and that leads to a lot of conflict and resentment on my part, I think 'I waited all effing week for you to get back and this is what you ... you know and he thinks 'Why am I here? I'm just a visitor in my own home'. It has had a lot of negative impacts and I think it's more the hours he works, than anything else ... It's the time. He needs more *time*. If Jason was home more often, I think we would be a stronger family unit. We would do more things as a family. We would go out to dinner as a family. We never do that. (woman, partner of flight attendant)

In a manufacturing workplace, a long hours worker describes how he physically collapsed leading his wife to demand that he take a serious look at how his hours were affecting their relationship:

I know I was the guilty party. It just got that any minor thing that my wife or kids had, you'd take it out on them by maybe not talking to them or isolating yourself ... Maybe I'm one of the lucky ones that woke up to the reality of what the important ingredient is and it's not work, it's the people that you're home with ... When I was in hospital, she come in that particular night [after I had collapsed] and she said to me, 'look you either get something that doesn't take the hours, or you leave the job you're doing' and like she said, 'it has affected the marriage, it has affected the children, and you're obligated not only to yourself, but to us, to look after you're health'. I think it was mainly the collapse I had and the hospitalisation that brought it to a head. (man, supervisor)

Intimacy: 'Your sex life doesn't exist'

Not surprisingly, tiredness, lack of time, moodiness and tension around hours in many households affects sexual intimacy. Some grab their chances, with 'sex on the run', as one describes her strategies with a laugh. Some feel exhausted: 'we're so tired…we just go to sleep'. A male supervisor commented 'It got to the point where physically I wasn't interested – to the point where I used to come to bed and go to sleep more or less'. Others describe the difficulties of finding time to be together and create intimacy. The dearth of intimacy crosses occupations and industries:

> I was doing a lot of nights in obstetric anesthesia – we hadn't actually seen each other for 26 nights out of the month. And that's when we start finding things becoming disruptive, because we can't organise social functions, there are a whole lot of things we can't manage to do because of the schedules not matching up. (woman, doctor)

> Yeah it affects your relationship. Like your sex life doesn't exist. (woman, strapper in racing industry)

> Well I don't see a lot of my husband. I don't see a lot of my mum. My mum lives like two blocks away from me, from where we are at the moment. I don't get to see a lot of friends. Because I'm stressed and I don't see a lot of my husband, we do fight a lot more. Yeah and it's over little things like the rubbish hasn't been put out, you know, meaningless things. So I know that's happening and basically your sex life goes. Yeah because you're just so tired, you just don't feel like it (woman, finance sector)

The work/eat/sleep cycle, which many long hours workers name, creates a drought of intimacy. Electricians and miners describes similar experiences while working long hours:

> You didn't have any leisure time. You were basically going home, eating, having a shower and going to sleep. That was your leisure time. Have a bit of a chat and you're too tired to do anything else. (man, electrician)

I come home, I'll have a drink, have a shower and then go straight to bed. (man, miner)

The 'second shift' for long hours workers and their partners

Many women say that running the household falls to them when their partners worked long hours: 'he doesn't do anything'. However, even when the woman is working long hours, sometimes with a partner who works them too, the burden of household management and work still falls more often to women, and this contributes to relationship tension:

> When I'm at school I'm fine because you're involved and it's fine. But then I come home I sort of think 'Oh, no!'. 'Cause there's so much [to do] at home and I find I expect the boys to do more and more to help and they're getting to the age where they want to do less and less ... I get enormous satisfaction out of it when I'm [at work]. It's just when I get home and look at the mess and there's no dinner cooked and there's clothes that need washing and people need to be taken to basketball, soccer or whatever, and you sort of feel you're being pulled in many directions ... (woman, teacher)

Those who are doing both long hours in paid work and a second shift caring for dependants, find their lives very demanding. An outline of an average day for the manager of a post office explains why:

> I've had fairly heavy health problems in the last two years and I think it is ... because if you take a typical day for me ... I'm getting up at 5.30 - 6 am, getting lunches ready, getting the kids ready, I've got a bed wetter at home ... I do that all before I get here ... I've got 20 staff here, I'm looking after them all day ... I pick the kids up say around 6-6.30 pm and then it starts again, got to get the tea ready, empty the lunch boxes, sit down with them with their homework ... the first time I sit down at night at dinner at 7 which is quick ... I don't actually sit down to relax until nine. A lot of friends of mine they just shake their heads,

they don't know how I do it … If you can get a happy balance between work and personal life, you're pretty lucky I think – it doesn't happen in the real world … I suppose if you had a supportive partner and someone who would take the pressure off at home it would be so different. That's probably the worst thing you can do – is learn to live with it … Mine's just a chaotic life. (woman, postal manager, with partner and young children)

Not surprisingly there are over 30 people at postal manager level in this employee's region and only a very few manage the job and have small children.

Who does what work at home: Sex, divorce and housework

There is a close connection between unpaid domestic work and intimacy in many Australian households, according to women. Its unequal distribution is a source of unhappiness and anger. It exhausts many who now do paid work with little change in their load of work at home. As discussed in chapter two, unpaid work in Australia has been extensively analysed, with women doing, on average twice as much as men. We have seen how changing overall patterns of paid working hours and the spread of the two-income household has been accompanied by little change in the gender distribution of unpaid work. This squeeze has intensified the heat around domestic work. This heat is also turned up by the hold of 'equality' discourse in households and society. The dissonance between 'equality talk' and work distribution at home is a source of pain for many.

Many women are torn between providing the necessities of a clean, nurturing and efficient home and the time they want to spend with their children, spouses and on their own. There is considerable guilt and frustration at not being able to fulfil, to a satisfactory degree, the functions of paid worker, partner, mother, and domestic worker on an ongoing basis. This leads to resentment about male partners' failure to help while also failing to appreciate what women are doing on a day-to-day basis to maintain both the emotional and physical health of the family.

This directly affects intimacy – across occupations and among both rural and urban women. As doctors and lawyers discuss it:

> I think you build up a resentment but you bury it. Instead of going over well-travelled ground you put it away and I think this impacts on our intimate relationship: 'if you are not there for me, I am not there for you!' It's not enough to leave for, but it's there. (doctor, mother)

> I agree, there are very, very deep feelings of injustice. He can't see things, he'll say he's done the lounge and I can't see a thing has been done. I used to get angry that he can't 'see'. We have had huge arguments and now I have dropped my standards but the resentment is there. (lawyer, mother)

> I feel the same way and yet sometimes when my partner *does* say he does appreciate what I do, I wipe the slate clean of resentment – it has that much effect on me. (doctor, mother)

> My partner does do things I don't have to think about and it makes a huge place for the relationship to be better, it feels like a partnership. (doctor, mother)

A now divorced community worker talks with her co-workers about the devaluation she clearly had felt in relation to domestic work:

> When I was married I did the bulk of housework and – it was like my husband didn't value what I was doing, didn't know what I was doing all day, and took it completely for granted. So I felt devalued by that and I think if you work as a partnership and you share stuff, and you share a bit about each others lives and about the problems – that makes a better bond.

> I agree totally. I think it's a measure of respect. (manager, father)

If you focus and help each other then you have time as a family. It's important to keep the quality between you and your partner. (clerical worker, mother)

My wife is appalled that at our school, out of our female friends, a 100 per cent of their husbands do nothing! (man, nurse)

The linkages between housework and divorce were remarked by women in many locations and circumstances. They took several forms. Some women had divorced their husbands over issues that centred around housework. The failure to share it, or to recognise the double load, makes many women angry, and the failure to be 'heard' on this issue makes them feel disrespected. They hate nagging, but they hate not being heard more:

I was cleaner and tidier than him, it was a real issue in the relationship – now he has to do it for himself. (divorced, part-time clerical worker, clerical)

My partner got retrenched. He stayed at home and became a real disciplinarian and he didn't do anything other than cook. I used to have to nag to get anything done. He wasn't willing to give and take. He didn't do anything at home and then used to complain on the weekends when I was doing the housework instead of spending time with him. (divorced call centre employee)

Some see at least one positive out of such divorces: men learn from them. Several have partners who had been married before, and they believe that this contributes to their partner's domestication. Women point to a direct link between sex and housework: anger and tiredness affect intimacy and in one focus group women laughingly discussed the withdrawal of sex as punishment for the failure to 'help'. Housework, its allocation, and communication about it, are far from trivial issues in terms of domestic harmony. One woman, a mother two, from a non-English speaking background, doing factory shift-work describes with sadness how her husband's expectations were entirely out of kilter with her self – and led to a small rebellion:

> I was in bed and my husband came in and said 'Get up, my friend is coming over and I want you to look beautiful'. I got up and looked in the mirror and thought 'It would take $200 for me to make myself look beautiful!' I got dressed, left the house and caught the bus into the city. I had breakfast at McDonald's and read the paper. I had a really nice time. Then I rang my husband and asked him if he wanted to come in for lunch but he said no, so I asked if his friend had gone and he said yes, so then I went home. He was very nice to me after that and offered to take me to work the next day. It was the first time in 18 years of marriage that I have done such a thing!

Women at home shared feelings of guilt and concern about not 'being there' for their partners as a result of the effort they put into their paid work or study and care for children. A full-time student and mother described it:

> That's what I feel guilty about, not giving my partner enough. I wouldn't blame him if he had an affair, in a way I would understand it. I take time for myself before I give time to him.

Women in private business agreed:

> I regret not being with my husband in that way but I really don't want to. Your focus shifts, our relationship has changed. You don't have the physical intimacy so then you don't have sex. I want the physical stuff, warmth, reassurance, but I don't always want the sex. I want to go to sleep! (woman, family business, company director, full-time worker)

As the mother of a young child she went on to laugh about the need for more 'fuel' for love:

> You subjugate your sexuality, I consider myself an attractive person and if someone came into my life I could be attracted, not that I would probably follow it through, but it is there. It's just not there between my partner and I. I could appreciate other men, but it [intimacy] doesn't seem to have an outlet in our

relationship. I heard Margaret Throsby talking about this philosopher who believed that there was this sort of temporary love dust that gets sprinkled on you to get you to fall in love, procreate, have children and after that you just have to get on with the arduous task of bringing them up. Just enough to fuel you into the thing and then leave you. I need more love dust!

The sources of the lack of intimacy were not hard to discern: tiredness, lack of time, multiple demands, as several comments show:

We are too tired to be intimate.

Lack of intimacy is the result of being both a worker and a mother, there is just no personal space.

There is no time for me as a woman. So many other people's needs come above mine. It affects us negatively. I find that a lot of the time I am emotionally exhausted, I run out.

Male partners were sometimes disinterested also:

When you are so tied up in the day to day child rearing it is hard to find the time. Sometimes I want a little romp and he is not there for me either.

The absence of communication was seen as a serious difficulty for some:

My husband is an understanding man and understands that my work affects the time and energy I have for him .... but I know of a lot of people who don't (understand). I know a lot of people whose lives are falling apart. There is jealousy if the wife is earning more than the husband, loss of understanding and communication between partners, different shifts to accommodate the children. There is no time to communicate.

For factory-based shift workers the stresses were even greater as being in the same place at the same time was very difficult. Three of them describe their situations:

We are like ships in the night.

We sleep in different rooms because we work different shifts.

We have a phone relationship.

Each of these women was working shifts as a means of child care (that is, they worked opposite hours to their partners to be available to care for their children). Others made formal arrangements to keep intimacy alive:

> We make appointments to see one another and on Thursdays we talk to each other for an hour ... Then on Friday afternoons no-one is allowed to visit us! That's our time.

Unequal housework: 'My work, your work'

There has been much more *talk* about change in who does what around the house, than real redistribution between spouses (Bittman and Pixley 1997, Baxter 2002). This is confirmed by the 2001 HILDA household survey which shows that this dissonance is widespread: over 90 per cent of women and 80 per cent of men agree that household work and care of children should be shared equally when both partners work, but 63 per cent of women think that they do more than their fair share (Fisher 2002). More than twice as many women as men over 18 years and living in couples do more than 41 hours per week on all family related work. Sixty per cent of women living in couples with children and working full-time do 11 hours or more of housework each week, compared to only 12 per cent of the men they live with. Forty-one per cent of mothers in couples 'never have spare time that they do not know what to do with' compared to 27 per cent of the men they live with (Fisher 2002: 27).

Women's know that they are still doing the majority of domestic work. Many find it boring and repetitive, contrasting it with other things they find more rewarding:

> I moan and I get sick of it. I feel I am forever cleaning. We have all been trained to clean. I get so bored with it. I have all these things I have to do or want to do but instead I clean and next thing I have to do it again. (woman, part-time worker)

As women take on more paid work, many drop their standards of domestic maintenance, as the ABS time-use surveys confirm, with the slight narrowing of the gender gap in domestic work between 1992 and 1997 explained more by women doing less than men doing more. Lower standards often lead to feelings of frustration and inadequacy:

> I have lowered my standards, and we eat out more at Hungry Jacks and so on – things I thought I would never do but I am so tired and I just want to feed the kid and feed myself. Every now and then we have a mass clean up which takes all day. (woman, full-time worker)

Many women struggle with the reality of falling standards: 'why should I have to put up with things badly done, or the fact that he just doesn't *see* dust?' Incorporating the family into lifting these standards is often unsuccessful or takes too much nagging or training – so women turn to the market and/or lower their standards. There is more resignation than expectation that the rest of the family will pick up the housework load voluntarily. Some men are frank about their tactics to minimise domestic work:

> Like most males I do housework that's noisy so it's noticed. Like mowing the lawns, vacuuming, things like that. (male, nurse, father)

A male nurse in his late 40s, with two small children and wife in full-time work, he went on to point out that he never cleaned the toilet. A second man in his workplace focus group concurred, and they continue:

> Michael: I don't clean toilets and showers. But I do everything else.

Abe: I think women think that cleaning the toilets is 70 per cent of the housework! (laughter) Men never clean toilets. Men cleaning toilets!! No!

Jenny: I live in a male household and it's the same thing. Obviously cleaning the toilets is such a pain in the arse job. The vacuuming and mowing the lawn are always more fun.

Susan: I love mowing the lawn!

Although Abe and Michael do traditionally feminised jobs – nursing – in their paid working lives, their home tasks remain sharply segmented by sex, with a clear line drawn around the toilet, which they argue women over-dramatise as a housework task, but refuse to do themselves. On the other hand, Susan loves mowing the lawn and insisted that she be allowed to do it when she married, although her father had refused to teach her. Clearly, the choice between mowing the lawn and cleaning the toilet is simply unavailable to many women, including some who might be married to men who might be described as Sensitive New Age Guys (SNAGs). Abe describes himself as 'semi-housetrained' – a condition that he traces to his years as a single man.

However, his training does not extend to the toilet. Several women referred to their partners as an extra child 'to look after'. Many men relied upon women for their most basic self-care and maintenance: 'He would wake me up to make his sandwich!' according to a divorced, rural woman and mother of two. Many women are resentful about the inequitable load. They see a connection between housework and intimacy. Clearly, the issue of domestic work and how it gets done is no small matter. It affects the quality of family life, and in many cases is a source of friction. It is an issue that many women care deeply about.

Strategies: 'Equal sharing', 'part sharing' and 'not sharing'

Three forms of arrangement exist with respect to getting housework done: 'equal sharing', 'part-sharing' and 'not sharing'. These parallel Hochschild's models of 'egalitarian', 'transitionary' and 'traditional' gender ideologies of marital roles (1989: 15). In some households women say that their partners 'share equally'. In these households, women are likely to be working full-time hours – at least equivalent to their partners, and many have shifted large slices of housework to the market. They then share the rest. These 'sharing' couples are relatively rare, and HILDA data confirm that they are in the minority, given that so many more women in full-time work do much more domestic work than their partners (Fisher 2002). With contractors to provide meals, clean, garden, iron and care for kids, these households have less to apportion. Women in these households clearly use their greater income to buy solutions rather than argue about them. In the face of men's unwillingness to share this work, women have turned to the market, or lowered standards. Many have also turned to their children or mothers.

Much more common is the situation where working women carry the main burden of housework, despite their part-time or full-time hours jobs. In these 'part-sharing' households women frequently use praise or threats to convince their partners to do more. Many women find the continuing argument over who does what debilitating.

One woman manager who worked night shift in a data processing centre describes her situation – and its costs:

> Rita: He stopped doing anything after my daughter was born. He thought that if he minded my daughter when I worked that that was all he had to do. I asked him over and over to talk but he wouldn't and then I got to the end of my tether and I threatened to walk out. This went on for weeks and then he asked me did I think our marriage was on the rocks? I thought 'Am I going through this on my own? Doesn't he get it?' Then one night we started talking. He thought I was angry because I was

working nights or still had that thing, you know, post natal depression …

Kerin: He would have had an axe through his head if you'd had that! (laughter)

Rita: But it wasn't that! It was the amount I had to *do*. He now understands that if he wants a relationship he has to put as much effort in to it as me.

A year after these comments, Rita had left her husband and found a new partner.

In the third kind of arrangement, 'not sharing', women simply did most or all of the work, and many were angry about it, including women at home with their children:

Domestic work? I think you mean slavery! (mother at home with children)

Women living in the country also faced the 'not sharing' situation:

Sarah: My husband doesn't do anything. (hospital worker, rural)

Amanda: Hang on! *I'm* married to him! (farmer, rural)

Some women living on farms were more accepting of their greater domestic load: as one pointed out, her husband worked long hours out of doors and she didn't expect him to help inside as well. This acceptance of delineated roles (with the woman working in the home, and the man outside on the farm) is associated with less resentment and anger. Not all farm-women were so reconciled, however:

Over the past ten years I have learned to operate most of the machinery on this farm. I can do most things. But he hasn't changed his role at all really.

Women who had increased their hours of paid work while not seeing a compensating shift in unpaid work were much less sanguine.

The most widely recognised form of 'housework' is physical: the straightforward hours of cleaning, washing, ironing, putting away clothes, gardening, cooking, and caring for kids. However, women point to a range of other forms of housework that also fall to them, and are ignored by many partners: the work of *management* of the household, and the *emotional* work of family maintenance. Women in professional, rural, factory and home situations manage the household, seeing what needs to be done and organising it. Men are 'helpers' who pitch in (or not) but leave the identification and organisation of tasks to women.

> I live my life according to priorities, feeding the kids, bathing the kids, getting tea on etc, but my partner will come in and sit down and read the mail or the paper. He'll do the lowest priority! (doctor, mother)

Professional women in particular refer to the emotional labour they do in their households – the work of listening to kids, thinking about their social and friendship needs, helping them sort out their problems, and being alert to individuals' non-physical needs through to more basic tasks like dentist and eye appointments. These tasks take time, just like cleaning the toilet. While men are more likely to take time to play with children, generally the primary organising roles are assumed to lie with women:

> I always check with my partner as to his whereabouts but it is assumed that I will always be there. I feel guilty if I go out for say three nights, whereas he will go away for a week without giving it a thought. I am the primary minder, the child minder, the organiser, the pick up, orchestrating everything. (office worker)

While the ABS time-use diary data includes the physical tasks of housework in its calculations of unpaid work it is harder to count the management and emotional labour that many women identify as significant, and largely falling to them. Many women have to ask for 'help' and report the expectation that they should be grateful when they get it:

He'll help out if I blow my top – and then suggest that I should be so grateful. (factory worker)

My husband does the cooking, cleaning and washing but he always says 'I've done *your* cooking, cleaning and washing'. I say 'It's not *my* work. It's *our* work'. (call centre employee)

I do it. I always have. We were always renovating. The words were 'helping'. The men 'helped'. Never the language of sharing. Not 'pull your weight'! Women say 'I'm lucky that so and so helps me'! (call centre employee)

While the distribution of housework has changed a little for some, it tends to revert when women are 'there'. Some women responded to this phenomena by making sure that they regularly are 'not there', so that their partners have to do it:

Things have changed but there is still a long way to go. My husband is excellent when I am not there, but as soon as I walk in the door I have to do the meals, cleaning, shopping. He does sometimes throw things in the washing machine but then all the colours get mixed up. He does sometimes hang out the washing and he irons his own shirts. He can manage when I am not there and he is good with the kids. (nurse)

Men are more reluctant to do some tasks that others – many women mentioned folding and putting away clean clothes as a particular point of contention, as this exchange between professional women shows:

My partner takes the clothes off the line and puts them on the bed.

My partner puts [the washing] on my side of the bed and then gets into his side. If I move it to his side of the bed he gets into my side!

'Cover stories': Housework and intimacy

The mismatch of discourses of 'equality talk' and the reality of unequal sharing of domestic work is not new: it has been discussed in the US by Hochschild in her study of the 'double shift' in the early 1980s (1989), and by Bittman and Pixley in Australia (1997). 2001 HILDA data confirm its ongoing reality in many households (Fisher 2002). These studies point to the painful gap between the egalitarian ideologies of gender equity, and the practices of daily housework and care. Bittman and Pixley use the concept of 'pseudo-mutuality', defined as the 'ideological embracing of mutuality without any adoption of mutual practices', to explain the contradiction between ideology and practice (Bittman 1998a: 31, Bittman and Pixley 1997). Under pseudo-mutuality, men discursively minimise what women do (like Abe when he says 'women think that cleaning the toilets is 70 per cent of the housework') or inflate their own contributions, while some women collude in these practices (like the finance worker who describes fights over 'meaningless things' like housework) or attempt to resist them unsuccessfully. Arlie Hochschild refers to the same phenomena as a 'cultural cover up' which for many women results in intensive 'emotion work' as women deal with 'all the feelings that naturally arise from the clash between a treasured ideal and an incompatible reality. In an age of a stalled revolution, it is a problem a great many women face' (1989: 45). Both writers mention divorce as a part of the solution, or overshadowing its 'non-resolution', and many writers have puzzled over the tenacity of inequality in housework (Probert 2001).

Interestingly, it seems that the general issue of the inequitable distribution of home tasks crosses the class divide affecting women in well paid employment and private business, as well as factory and office women on much lower incomes, but it seems that professional women – with a stronger ideological commitment to gender equality – resent it more. While more likely to be married to men who are closer to egalitarian or at least sharing partners, professional women speak with bitter feeling:

The SNAGS are worse. They know they are doing better than average so they don't allow you to push it! (doctor)

They have better tactics at protecting their privilege. (lawyer)

This comment is suggestive of Hochschild's notion of the 'going rate' of domestic contribution from men: 'a subconscious sense of the going rates for a desirable attitude or behaviour' relative to other comparable men (1989: 51). While men may have a sense of the common going rate in middle class households and stay just ahead of it, their partners know it is well short of equality.

Working class women are not immune to anger over domestic work. However, professional women are more likely to be using market supports to bridge the equality gap. Nonetheless, when the toilet cleaning remained 'in house', they do more of it.

Turning to the market: Buying help

Women use a range of tactics to meet the demands of the home. Most commonly they contract out housework, lower standards, take shortcuts, train their children or use labour saving technology. Predictably, contracting out of tasks is much more frequent in higher income households. Clearly, the contracting out of tasks like meal preparation through the use of prepared and convenience food, and care of elders and children (in aged care and child care centres) have achieved a high level of community acceptance. Table 5.1 shows the growth in household expenditure on a range of domestic services over the decade to 1998/99.

Women are increasingly making use of market goods to get food on the table quickly, maintain the house and garden, and care for children. The greatest growth in household expenditure on goods and services that substitute for domestic labour is in packaged and prepared meals which increased more than four-fold in the decade – almost three times faster than the increase in total household expenditure. The use of gardening services also increased at more than double the rate of general expenditure.

Table 5.1: Expenditure on Selected Household Items 1988/89 to 1998/99

Item	Change 1988/89– 1998/99	Per cent change greater than change in total expenditure
Total Expenditure on Good and Services	139%	0%
Packaged prepared meals	414%	275%
Gardening services	249%	110%
Pasta	231%	92%
Childcare services	214%	75%
Frozen prepared meals	205%	66%
Housekeeping and cleaning services (including ironing)	190%	51%
Household services and operation	171%	32%
Cakes tarts and puddings	154%	15%
Biscuits	147%	8%

Source: ABS Cat No 6535.0

Expenditure on marketised child care, cleaning and house-keeping also rose much faster than total spending.

Most women feel comfortable about contracting out domestic work and do not have concerns about paying other women to do 'their' housework. Many say they would do so if they could afford it. Some raise the issue of fair remuneration for domestic work, or talk of the importance of 'sharing the money' around. There is little concern about the creation of a pyramid of wo-men's work – with working women on higher pay, relying on women receiving lower, intermittent or 'cash-in-hand' pay – which is often mentioned as a feminist scruple (Meagher, 2000).

Interestingly, a common task mentioned for contracting out (after the use of prepared meals and forms of care) is lawn mowing – traditionally a job done by men. With spending on gardening services up by 249 per cent in the decade to 1998/99 (compared to the increase rise of 139 in total household expen-diture), many households are spending more on an activity that men do more of, than some other kinds of housework done by women. Women are not unaware of the irony: when a factory woman described her decision to hire a lawn mowing service; her co-workers argued that it was a fatal mistake to mow the lawn: '*never* mow the lawn – you end up with it for good!'. Many women find it easier to organise a service to do it, than to depend upon their partners.

Immigrant and Aboriginal households

For migrant households, especially older generations, issues around domestic work appear to entail strong resistance. Some women in these communities describe how domestic work is 'culturally linked' to being female – just as it is across most cultures. Men suffer loss of status and credibility if they are seen to be either doing 'women's work' or submitting to women's will. There is social stigma and embarrassment if they try to accommodate the changes in their wives' lives – 'They think they have less importance if they do women's work. If they do women's work they lose status' as one immigrant woman describes the impact on her husband.

> Sometimes in the Chinese or Vietnamese community a man is not employed and the woman is, but he is still the boss and he can't do the housework. The woman must do both the housework and the paid work. Sharing domestic work is a problem. (Chinese immigrant woman, mother)

Others agreed, and looked to the help of extended family to make it work:

> He thought he was marrying a typical Polish wife and was a bit disappointed when I didn't do all the cooking and socialising. I still try to do the cooking and parties and so on, but it's an added extra to my life. That's where mum helps me out … In my community the cultural upbringing still means that family roles are divided and it is the woman's role to do the domestic work. This means that a woman is always tired and this impacts on all her relationships, she is too tired for a proper relationship with her husband. Families maintain cultural roles. Also as mother she

often feels guilty for working and does extra things for her children which makes them do less to help her. (Polish immigrant woman, mother, divorced)

However, generalisations need to be made with care:

Domestic tasks are sometimes shared in the Cambodian community but there are still very strong cultural divides. There are some changes. You can't stereotype all families as they are all different. It is changing, yes, but not much. Women still do most of the housework and get too tired and don't have any energy.

Like most others, urban Aboriginal women are also affected by the dominant pattern and recognised their own attachment to established habits:

I took over where his mother left off. I felt that my role was in the home and even though a man goes out to work and I'm working too, his dinner has to be on the table at 5 pm. I did everything. I was brought up that way. It has been hard for me to change from the old ways. (Indigenous community health worker)

Conclusion

Of the many Work/Life issues covered in focus groups and interviews, none drew more laughter, anger and sadness than the issues of domestic life and intimacy. While so much has changed, the unyielding resistance of men, in the main, to doing more domestic work is remarkable. It imposes very significant costs of adaptation and over-work on women:

I think the pressures of the world are so great that women can't do it all. I think they (men) have come a distance, but not as far as we would like. Those days of the dad coming home to his TV are over. (manager, government agency, permanent casual)

Not everyone is pessimistic. And some women recognise that they must also change, lowering their standards and giving up control:

> Men are responding. They are being made more responsible, they share the role which is good. It's good. Women are realising that it takes two people to make a relationship work. (Indigenous community health worker)

Women question the assumption that a working woman can still be all things to all people without some personal toll on health and well being both to the individual, the family and the community. These are the hidden costs of our work arrangements now. They are the consequences of the weight of domestic work and reproduction, the growth in paid work among women, and the growing pressures in many workplaces.

Are we prepared to pay the price of diminished personal relationships, sex and intimacy as a result of these changes? This question is barely on our community's agenda – mainly because the effects of work on intimacy and relationships are privately experienced. Guilt, tiredness, lack of personal space and strained relationships are affecting many. They are partly the price of an idealised vision of motherhood, around which work arrangements – whether domestic or workplace – have inadequately adapted. The necessary accompaniments are absent in many locations – affordable, quality child care; paid maternity and carers leave; shared housework; equitable workplaces. Many unconsciously turn their frustrations, perceived shortcomings and inability to be the idealised image, into private concern and guilt with significant consequences for intimacy and relationship stability. The higher domestic burden still falling to women regardless of their paid work loads, is an important part of the wall of unchanging institutions into which fast moving changes at work, crash. A redistribution of domestic work – and not only to the market – is essential if the destructive power of that collision is to be mitigated.

CHAPTER 6

Long hours: Family unfriendliness at work

How have changes in working hours affected Australians and contributed to the collision of work and life? In this chapter we examine the growth in long hours of work and their implications for individuals, their households and our community. Some of these effects are felt directly in intimate relationships as we have discussed in the previous chapter. But their effects reach well beyond the individuals who work them – to their spouses, households and they reverberate through the community.

The hours spent in paid work are increasing in Australia. We are not the only country where this is true. Juliet Schor has written of the increase in the post-war working week of Americans, despite massive rises in productivity which would have permitted halving of work time in the post-war period. Instead, the length of the American working week has continued to increase. In the US, the annual hours of paid employment increased by 163 hours on average in the 20 years to 1987 (and much more for women than men), so that Schor estimates that Americans contributed an extra month of labour each year by 1987 compared to 1969 (1992: 29). The US remains at the long and growing hours end of the international industrialised spectrum, where it is joined by the UK and Australia (Campbell 2001).

As discussed in Chapter 2, the average working hours of full-timers grew by 3.1 hours a week between 1982 and 2001 (Campbell 2002a) and they are contributing an extra months work each year compared to 1982, most of it unpaid. Disaggregating the effects of part-time work, full-time Australian employees work hours similar to Koreans and Americans (Campbell 2001).

Australia has a large and growing proportion of employees who work long hours, especially *very* long hours (ACIRRT 2001). At least 31 per cent of all Australian workers are working more than 40 hours a week (up 23 per cent from 15 years earlier) and a quarter work more than 45 hours a week (Campbell 2001, ABS Cat No 6359.0). The 2001 HILDA survey shows that many want to work less: a third of full-time workers want to work less, and 58 per cent of those working more than 49 hours a week would like to. The proportion of long hours workers who want to reduce their hours has grown by 20 percentage points in the six years between the AWIRS and HILDA surveys, from 37 to 58 per cent (Wooden 2002, *Workplace Express*, 16 August 2002). Much of the growth in extended hours is unpaid overtime. Almost half of full-time Australian workers are now working regular unpaid overtime of an average of eight hours a week, according to a 2002 Job Futures/Saulwick Survey. Not surprisingly, 40 per cent of those in this survey said their stress levels at work were high (*Workplace Express*, 23 September 2002).

In this chapter we rely on the views of more than 50 long hours workers (37 men and 17 women) in 12 industry sectors, and 35 of their partners (15 women and nine men) (Pocock, van Wanrooy, Strazzari and Bridge 2001c). We weigh their perceptions of the impact of long hours on those who do them, the partners they live with, and their families and communities. Much of this evidence reinforces the results of studies in other countries (Schor 1992, Hewitt 1993, Galinsky 1999, Pocock 2001b).

Long hours take many forms: they include simply *long* or *very long* hours, hours that are worked on continuous rotation around the clock, hours with inadequate breaks, very pressured working conditions, or working hours that are unpredictable or provide poor rest between shifts. Those who work long and/or unreasonable hours have a variety of motivations. Some are motivated by money. But this does not explain the majority of overtime in Australia, most of which is unpaid. Up to two thirds of all overtime hours worked in Australia are *unpaid* according to Campbell's estimates (2002b). Some of this might be motivated by the hope for financial gain in the longer term, through promotion or bonus.

Unpaid overtime is concentrated among certain occupational groups – especially managers, administrators, professionals, associate professionals and intermediate and advanced clerical and service workers, and among public sector workers. But a proportion of the overtime worked by most groups of workers includes some unpaid hours. So direct monetary reward does not explain a very significant slice of extra hours.

Understaffing, a commitment to the job, supervisory pressure, or a combination of these forces explains many long hours. Some workers feel that they have little control over their hours and little chance to refuse them. Strappers in the horse racing industry, for example, feel that they cannot refuse their regular unpaid long hours or their animals suffer, while those on building sites often feel pressure to work long hours under threat of losing their job. Doctors fear losing training opportunities if they refuse long hours. Very powerful, skilled employees are concerned about the impact on their jobs, promotion or training if they refuse to work long hours. Many employees do not have the individual power to resist the pressure to work long hours, whether that 'requirement' is a direct request, or arises – very commonly – in an indirect way as a result of staffing levels and/or client, student, supervisor, animal or patient expectations and needs.

Some have tried to take control of their hours by changing jobs, going part-time, taking demotions or changing employers. A recent Newspoll survey of 981 Australians showed that in the past ten years, 23 per cent had 'downshifted' – that is, made voluntary changes to their lifestyle that resulted in lower earnings (excluding retirees and those who returned to study). The most common downshifting action was to reduce working hours: 29 per cent of downshifters had taken this step in the past decade. Twenty-three per cent had shifted to a lower-paid job. More than a third of those who decided to reduce their earnings were motivated by a desire to have more time with their family –

by far the most common motivation for reducing earnings, and most were happy with the change (though some missed the money) (Hamilton and Mail 2003). Strategies to reduce hours can work if households can adapt to lower earnings. Long hours are increasingly entrenched in a culture of long working days across a range of Australian workplaces. These hours have created, *de facto*, a kind of new hours standard for many workers in workplaces that are hungry for their contribution. They raise the 'hours bar' for all in some occupational groups or workplaces or industries that have been permeated by a long hours culture.

This effect is compounded by the powerful perception that the pace and rate of work is now harder and more intensive.

Many employees agree to work long hours because they love their jobs. 'I absolutely love it' said a paramedic whose children are in child care from 7.30 am–4.30 pm on her work days. Love of horses drives strappers' long hours: 'the industry runs on passion' as one put it. Commitment to students, patients and the public, drive the long hours of teachers, doctors, paramedics, postal workers and public servants.

Long hours are worked within a set of complex relations at work. In many cases, the mechanics of this power relation are veiled from view. They are created by the demands of some industrial agreements, job deadlines, staff formulas, complex teaching demands, or deeply ingrained workplace cultures. The decline in union density (given that unions often ensure that regulations and health and safety are enforced), the fracturing of industrial regulation, and weak industrial inspectorates have also contributed to the growth of hours. In many workplaces, employees work long hours *not* because someone asks them to do them, but because 'it is just expected' – with the clear implication that those who do not, will suffer disadvantage. In some cases, this means no chance to specialise or be promoted, or being side-lined to undesirable jobs. In other cases, it carries very serious consequences: the sack, failure to be re-employed on future jobs, or placing the safety of co-workers at risk. Long hours occur within a set of workplace relations where even highly paid, highly skilled workers like doctors, engineers, electricians, teachers, technicians and middle managers – many with long-term employment records – are not able to control their hours. It is startling that employees with such high skills and experience cannot contain their hours of work. As a doctor put it:

> To say – before you get on the training program – that 'I think 96 rostered hours and then an extra 30 or 40 hours a fortnight is unreasonable', well, that would be career suicide, probably … If you want to get into a training program you need to keep your nose clean and your mouth shut! (man, doctor, in specialist training)

These hours burn out employees and burn up their commitment, as employees shift from loving their jobs to hating them. Rates of pay for working such hours are often seen as inadequate compensation for the effort, and of course those who work unpaid overtime – the majority of those working overtime – are not paid for their extra efforts. Their benefits are almost entirely anticipatory: 'Maybe I'll get a promotion' or 'Maybe this means I will hang onto my job'. For some, unpaid overtime has become an entrenched and non-voluntary part of the work contract: it is, in fact, labour theft.

'Pushed to the limit': one story

One case illustrates many of the effects of long hours. Frank lives with his wife Bronwyn and they have two young children. Frank's employer, a manufacturer of large equipment, faces deadlines that are very tight, and are met through long hours. This means that employees are often closely supervised, in a tense environment where bullying is not unusual. This intensifies the effect of long hours on individuals, their families and their communities. Frank's case also illustrates the pressures that can be repetitively applied to highly skilled workers in the context of work deadlines.

Frank has worked 50-60 hours a week for a long time. He is on a contract that annualises salary, building in his overtime.

Once he has reached a certain hours threshold, he receives an annual bonus, but thereafter his extra hours are not paid so there is an incentive for his employer to push for long hours. A supervisor and job planner, Frank buckled under the pressure of working around 60 hours a week for extended periods:

> I used to spend an eight hour day with the men, and then an hour before work and an hour after work of paper work, so that was making it a nine, ten hour day five days a week, and a half a day Saturday, or all day Saturday … We were working extremely long hours, sometimes from six o'clock in the morning through to eight o'clock at night. Often I wouldn't have my lunch break because if you did it would be a cup of coffee and a sandwich at your desk while you were doing more paperwork. And it just got progressively more and more and more, just keeping on adding to our jobs … and then one morning … bang! … I actually went to work, and it was a really, really hot day and we had a seminar on health and safety for some reason. And I got home at about three o'clock in the afternoon, got away early, and I came in and I was really hot, really stinky, and my wife was on the phone with a friend. I came in − and the kids were just playing − well one was just born and the little bloke was just three and was playing, and I did my block. And I told my wife off, had a go at my kid and then realised I was just tearing the hair out of my head. And it was all because I'd just had enough of it … I'd started to bring work home − mentally − for months before that. Like on the weekend I'd come home from work on Saturday or whatever it might be and just lie in front of the TV and didn't want to talk to nobody, just wanted to be left alone. At night I'd be dreaming. Like you'd be in bed and all you'd be doing is dreaming about work … I ended up, once I had got to the point where I brought my work home and realised that there was just too much, I was virtually suffering from severe panic attacks, during work, at home. Every little thing was upsetting me. If I saw something which I thought wasn't right, it'd create this panic attack where I'd feel hot and sweaty, very, very nervous, or agitated and it might last for anything from 20 minutes to an hour or two hours. And it got to the point I saw a doctor about it and he wanted me to go on medication,

antidepressants or whatever. I wasn't interested in it. But then that day when I came home and blasted my wife, and had a go at my kid – my wife, she rang the doctor and made an appointment and sent me down. And I remember breaking down and crying and going into the doctor's surgery and telling him what was going on and he gave me time off work immediately and I ended up having six weeks off. That turned into burnout – I went into depression, and I ended up having the full-scale mental breakdown.

Frank had 'a very, very bad eight to 12 months and had suicidal thoughts before being put onto anti-depressant medication'. Despite this severe experience, his employer shortly afterwards asked Frank to extend his hours once more, and once again he broke down:

But over the last say six months I've been seeing a psychiatrist and my GP, and taking my medication, I've been feeling better. Up to possibly a week or two ago [when] they put me under [pressure again]. So it got to the point where I virtually did a breakdown at work in the manager's office. I went in there to tell him, 'Look, it's just too much for me.' And I actually broke down and he's since – I've got a track record I guess – so he's cut down. I think he now realises that a man can only do so much.

I actually said to this manager, I said, 'Every person's got a bucket of water they've got to carry it around' and I said, 'I had too much water in that bucket – it overflows' and I actually asked that certain manager, a while ago to get someone to give me a hand because work was starting to increase and they wouldn't give me no one to help me, they just said, 'no, no, you just keep on going the way you're going and we'll see what happens, we'll see what happens'… Until I virtually broke down again. It's only been the last two or three weeks where I thought 'Bugger them, I'm not going to go through that again'.

Frank's first breakdown had resulted in a successful worker's compensation claim where it had been recognised that his long hours and the pressures placed on him at work had directly contributed to his breakdown. Despite this 'track record' as

Frank calls it, he returns to work and faces a renewed set of pressures that result in long hours and a repeat cycle of panic attacks and mental collapse: 'but they are still pushing me to do extra hours. And I feel strongly about not doing them … I don't think they know they are actually playing with people's lives'.

Frank's commitment to producing quality work, and his employer's reliance on his skills and experience are clear. However, his managers are resistant to recognising the problem – despite having received medical reports from their own sources that establish that Frank's problem lies, at least partly, in his long hours of work. His doctor and psychiatrist offer to mediate between Frank and his employer to try to keep his hours under control:

> I spoke to my GP several weeks ago, and I told him, 'look, they've been pushing me to work six days a week again and I don't want to. I feel I'm doing 45 hours which is ample'. And he said to me straight off, 'look, if they push you, give them my number, get them to contact me'. I also spoke with my psychiatrist. I told him the same thing and he also said, 'the company wants you to work more than 40 hours a week, let me know and I'll deal with it'. So last Friday week it was when I went into the manager, I was pretty emotional, pretty tired. I tried to explain to him, but I couldn't, I was pretty, I broke down, upset. So I organised a meeting later on that week, the following week, and I said to him on that day, I said, 'look, if you think I'm mucking around, either the [Human Resources] division or yourself can ring up my GP and you talk to them. Because this isn't a Mickey Mouse issue. It's fair dinkum. You're playing with my life insisting I do these hours'. Some people can work ten, 12 hours a day six days a week and just do a hobby on Sunday and just come back to work on Monday. But other people can't.

Frank believes that employers like his 'use' people – that they find people who will do the long hours and get them to work long hours until they are 'scrapped': 'And then the next person will just come along and fill your place … They've got no life. They only live to work. They expect you to be like them … I look at it: I work so I can live. I work so I can enjoy myself, not live so that I can just continually go to work'.

How long hours affect individuals

Frank – like many long hours workers – describes his life when he worked long hours as a repetitive work/eat/sleep cycle. His hobbies fell away:

> It was a very long day. And most nights you'd come home, have your dinner, have a shower and go to bed. And if you weren't sleeping, you were travelling to or from work, or having your tea ... Most Sundays were off, but if you were required to come in you'd have to come in ... To an extent if the guys wanted to work and the work was there, we had no choice but to come in.
> ... My social life, put it this way ... before [changing jobs and increasing hours] I used to play tennis once or twice a week. I'm interested in fishing. I go fishing as a sport and keep a boat. The day I stood down from being a supervisor I went to see my doctor, he said ... 'okay, I want you to go home. Stop all your activities that you're doing, everything that you do and just do nothing.' His exact words were, 'be dumb for a week. Do nothing.' I got home and I recall lying on the floor and I'm thinking, 'what should I stop?' and I had nothing left to stop because I no longer played tennis. I no longer went fishing. I no longer ran my boat. I had no interest to do the gardening, 'cause I had no time for it.
> So all I was doing was virtually living and working...A lot of the interests I had were gone.

Having made the decision to cut back on his work hours, despite the constant pressures of his employers, he has started to regain his interest in, and his ability to engage in, outside interests and play with his children.

Unfortunately Frank's experience – while extreme – is not isolated. He recalls three co-workers with similar health effects of stressful work and long hours, including for example, a co-worker who stood down at the same time as him for the same issues 'because he found it too difficult to continue doing what they were asking of us'. Some workers accept long hours in Frank's workplace. In his view this puts pressure on every one else:

> The company uses those people as a benchmark. So, 'so-and-so's doing x amount of work. Why can't you?'. They use that scenario on me. When I first hit my manager with the hours and needing a hand several months ago, he said 'it's a bit difficult when Andrew who is working beside you is working half a day Saturday. Why can't you come in? How are you going to explain it to him?' So they try and put the guilt factor onto you. I said to him, 'Well if he can carry two buckets of water good luck to him. But I can't'.

Frank's story is at the extreme end of the long hours spectrum. He faces a very pressured workplace and his story shows the direct 'spill-over' effects of his working life on his physical and mental health and his wife and children. His paid work contaminates his home. His relationships suffer. He pulls back from the brink – just. However, many of the effects he describes are experienced by those who work long hours. Fatigue is a consequence of long hours, and its costs are high as many studies show. Fatigue has been shown to be four times more likely to be a cause of workplace impairment than alcohol or drugs (Dawson, McCulloch and Baker 2001: 21). For many workers and their partners the health effects of long, pressured hours are a serious and primary concern:

> You get absolutely exhausted … You get to the point where you are really struggling to get out of bed in the morning to get there on time. And in the racing game, you are running the whole day – it's *run*, its not just walking at normal pace – you are in a hurry to do everything. There is nothing called slow. You get extremely tired, very ratty, very irritable, you obviously don't eat properly because of the funny hours you work. Sometimes you come home and you are so tired you can't eat. It affects your moods, really ratty, really bad tempered and short tempered and you really run on a short wick. (woman, strapper)

Physical affects include high blood pressure, long-term fatigue, constant tiredness, and poor sleeping patterns. Depression is not uncommon, along with moodiness, 'being grumpy' and being short tempered. Stress is also a common consequence of long hours – and not only for the worker:

> My primary concern is about the long-term effects on his health. He eats really late. We rarely sit down to a family meal. [That] is really missing. I eat with the children so he doesn't eat til 8 or 9 pm. He rarely eats breakfast, and he has lost his relaxation skills ... He is constantly stressed. He has physically aged, he has put on weight. If he doesn't take lunch with him, he doesn't normally have lunch, and even then he doesn't break – he eats at the desk. I mean, we have spoken about all these things and I guess I am pretty hard on him in that I hammer him and say you know nobody else can change this but you ... you should take lunch, it is part of your award. (woman, partner of public service worker, mother of two)

Fatigue results in accidents, death and significant public health expenditure, along with the consequences of major national and international disasters including oil spills, industrial accidents and plane and train crashes which have been traced to fatigue. Doctors, paramedics, electricians and mining truck drivers talk about being 'zombies' at work – falling asleep at the wheel, horse riding falls, dangerous electrical 'shortcuts', being pierced by needles and near misses on building and mining sites. Long hours place lives in jeopardy – both the lives of those who are 'worker-zombies', those who work with them and those who share the road with them. Many partners are very concerned about their partner's drive home from work when they are very tired. Given the accounts of 'nodding off at the wheel', they are right to be.

The effect on families: Time poverty

What are the effects of long hours on home and families? First and most obviously, long hours mean less time for home. This affects single people but especially those with families. Workers, partners and children – by their parent's reports – feel that they are missing out. However, the effects of long hours reach well beyond a simple time-drought at home. Many feel that the *quality* of time at home and with family is contaminated by bad moods, tiredness, short tempers and the effects of general exhaustion that directly result from long hours. 'Moodiness' and 'grumpiness' are repetitive complaints of long hours workers and their partners. As a doctor described her home: 'The whole environment within the house is very tense'. A medical specialist describes how doctors in specialist training have no real choice: they must 'abdicate' their families to do their training. Many in high pressure, long hours jobs are entirely dependent upon their partners to rear their children and run the household. Predictably, it is women who take on the traditional role at home.

The gendered work/home patterns that evolve around long hours workers forcefully exaggerate the traditional worker/carer model. The long hours worker – more often male – earns the majority of household income, and the partner at home – most often female – builds her more peripheral paid work hours around the long hours worker and does all the unpaid and caring work at home. This means the parent at home is dependent on the worker for money – both day-to-day and over the life cycle, while long hours workers are dependent upon their partners at home for care, not only of themselves, but also their offspring. This might be seen as a balanced reciprocation of money for care in the 'breadwinner/carer' tradition. But it is a precarious imbalance: many long hours workers have very limited relationships with their children:

> I know this one particular person who works every [overtime] amount there is and he's the first there, last to go sort of thing. He's a carpenter. And there's another carpenter I know and he leaves 3.30 pm – goes home. And they were talking about their kids. And the guy who leaves early was saying when he gets home, his kid can't wait to see him, you know. And the other guy who's never at home said, he was amazed, because when he gets home, the kid runs away. But he's, I guess, so far with the work

he doesn't realise – doesn't twig – his kid doesn't *want* to see him. He probably says to his mum, 'Who's that guy who comes here every night?'(male, electrician)

A number of carers describe their worker-partners' remote relationships with their sons and daughters: they have 'visiting rights' to the family. This money/care imbalance, introduces particular vulnerabilities into relationships that exact high costs when they become unstable: the divorced worker is at risk of losing any relationship with his children and the divorced carer risks poverty. Given the probability of divorce – perhaps especially among those working long hours – this is not a low risk.

A number of women married to long hours workers describe themselves as single parents. They do all the cooking, cleaning, care of children, chauffeuring, bill paying and financial and emotional work of parenting on her own: 'I'm the mother and the father' said a miner's wife. She is not alone:

I have no social life, virtually none. I can't make plans for the future. It's very difficult ... I do get very stressed because I have to deal with so much on my own. I'm raising three children as a single parent who gets support occasionally. (woman, teacher and partner of flight attendant)

Another mother describes herself as 'a 1950s wife'. Prior to giving up paid work she had the higher paid and more senior job. She is the one now at home with three children, while her partner works very long hours and regularly travels for his job:

What it reminds me of is a nice neat 1950s family. Sometimes I think all I need to do is go and buy a pinny. Because when I look at *my* peer group that is what things seem to have returned to. Mum at home. Dad going away and Dad walking in the door of the perfect house with three scrubbed kids on the lounge and the car parked in the drive way ... but Dad actually doesn't have time to kick a football. And it's almost unreal. But it *is* a reality and it seems to be a reality everywhere. And the women make the adjustment. (woman, partner of public service worker)

Long hours mean long days for carers at home. Many full-time parents at home talk about the loneliness they feel, and their need for adult company. Partners are often sympathetic. An electrician, describes how his wife nearly 'cracked' doing it all on her own:

> I think a lot of the pressure went on her cooped up in the house with two kids … Sometimes all she needed was a half an hour to leave the kids with me, just to get out and not have them in her ear, 'cause as little kids, they're, 'mum, mum, mum, mum', and that's non-stop from when they wake up, til when they go to bed. I found that she was going around the bend when I was doing all those hours. I could see she was close to breaking point. (male, electrician)

A consistent pattern of 'residualness' is noticeable among the partners of long hours workers. Their lives are frequently built around their partner's, in terms of paid work in particular but also in patterns of household activity, parenting and family activities. The hours of the worker assume a kind of automatic priority in households and 'drive' them. Partners and children fit around these hours – in terms of meals, leisure, family time, sleep and work-recovery. This affects whether partners take a paid job at all, their hours, the type of job they take, and whether that job is casual or permanent. It also sharply constrains their careers: some had given up their jobs while others had foregone promotion, or other opportunities in order to take over the domestic sphere and support the 'main' worker. Many long hours workers rely upon the full-time support of a worker at home, especially where dependants are present. Others rely on a part-time support person at home, or one who works their own jobs around the long hours worker, by running a small business or holding a very flexible job. In some cases, households support two long hours workers, and these strain under the burden. The careers of carers – mainly women – along with their lifetime earnings, are particularly affected by this accommodation.

How long hours affect children and parents

The general impact of long working hours on children is seen as negative for the great majority of parents. This sometimes reaches extremes with one father saying 'It got to the point where I could not handle my own kids' because he spent so little time with them.

Interestingly, a number of parents of very young children do not think that their long hours are 'a huge deal' for their young children. They feel – or hope – that their infant children are unaware of their absence. Others feel that their young children are affected by these long absences. Almost universally, however, parents felt that *they* were missing out on their young children, and this was a source of great regret:

> Thank heavens for the video camera or he would have missed everything! (woman, flight attendant's partner)

> [My son]'s off to bed at 7.30 pm and you might not see him at all. You're gone before he gets up in the morning and see him for about 20 minutes when you get home ... I don't like it much it at all. I'd rather spend more time with him. (man, engineer)

Most parents who work long hours are concerned about the number of significant events they miss out on: performances, school events, reading at school and sporting events. The great majority report complaints from their children or resignation and sadness about parental absence. Many feel a general time shortage that creates stress for children:

> We spend most of the day saying 'Hurry up! Hurry up!' And that's what we spend a little bit of the night-time saying. We're basically saying 'Hurry up, tie your shoes. Hurry up, brush your teeth' and so it's – pretty much – stress right through. Which again is something that you become so habituated to, you actually don't notice after a while. (man, public service worker, partner)

Oh yeah, definitely [it affects them]. Even at this young age (four and two). They get disappointed a hell of a lot because they want to bounce all over you, and … my fuses are a lot shorter in those circumstances because I'm that tired and I just physically can't do what they want me to do so they notice it directly. (man, flight attendant, long hours worker)

Electricians who had cut back their hours felt that their relationships with their children had improved in ways that no overtime pay could compensate for:

The little girl, she's just a happy chappie, but the little boy, I found he wasn't as close to me … now when I come home he just drops everything and runs straight for me, where before – I'd come in at 8, 7, 6 pm whatever time – there just wasn't that closeness. Now when I do grab him, when I do come home from work, and go to the park or go to the shops, I mean they can't wait to come up to me and that's worth any money or any amount of overtime, or anything. (man, electrician, previously a long hours worker)

You are 'family' or you are 'worker': mummy and daddy tracks

The tendency for women to take 'the mummy track' when they try to combine work and family has been widely noted (Schwartz 1989, Hochschild 1997, Wajcman 1998). A 'mummy track' exists for many women who put their caring responsibilities squarely alongside or in front of their paid work. This track is a second-class career track, in that women drop back in status, pay or career to secure conditions that accommodate motherhood.

A much larger proportion of women than men working long hours would like to reduce them: over half of women working between 41-48 hours a week would prefer less hours, compared to a third of men (*Workplace Express*, 16 August 2002, reporting HILDA data). Many step back from their careers or current jobs when they become carers, and the widespread pattern of long hours enforces this choice vigorously. 'Ordinary careers' are hard enough for many mothers. Jobs that demand long hours are much harder and many simply give them up, while others take a 'mummy track' and drop back to part-time work, change fields, swap jobs or take a demotion.

Flight attendants, postal managers, public service workers, teachers, strappers, paramedics and doctors all struggled with this 'choice'. While some managed to work long hours and maintain careers as well as be active parents, most did it at considerable cost. This cost was to health, relationships and time with children. Each had a partner. While this partner's contribution varied widely – from equal sharing through to little help – no women in our study managed to combine long hours with family, without a partner's presence.

The greater the proportion of long hours jobs in any labour market, the more carers are forced into 'mummy tracks' that lock them into second class paid jobs. Further, when their male *partners* hold long hours jobs, carers at home are more strongly pushed into accommodation strategies in the labour market – taking casual, short term and lower status jobs that give them flexibility to work around their partners, remembering that many of the latter's hours are unpredictable. There are, therefore, multiple factors arising from long hours that foster and embed the secondary labour status of carers, and push them towards a 'mummy track'.

There is evidence of a parallel 'daddy track' for men who refuse to work long hours in workplaces that are imbued with a long hours culture. Men who refuse extra hours, try to restrict their working week, ask to work part-time or refuse promotion to avoid long hours, find themselves viewed with suspicion. One described his request to work part-time as 'dangerous' to his career. He need not have worried: it was simply ignored. Some feel they are viewed as not serious about their work, and thus in danger of disappearing down a 'daddy track'. A limited time commitment or a desire to work part-time are read as 'bad signs'. This creates a barrier for couples where either or both would like to work less hours, but neither feels they can do responsible, senior, rewarding jobs *and* be active carers. Their case also illustrates the practical contradiction that exists between 'family friendly' policies and entrenched long hours cultures. The presence of family friendly policies is no antidote to the real hold of long hours culture and the archetype of the 'proper, long hours' worker who fits them best, as Probert et al's research in the 'family friendly' finance and education sectors reveals. As they say: 'despite significant and welcome formal provisions for flexible working, and industry claims to family friendliness, employees in both these major sectors appear to be experiencing a deterioration in their ability to balance work and life on a daily basis' (2000: 42). They trace this deterioration to the patchy reach of such conditions, the context of over-work that limits real access, and the fact that existing formal provisions are 'unequal' to the problems of overwork and intensification.

Long hours: Embedding systemic disadvantage for carers

Women's larger responsibility for the domestic sphere shapes their paid labour market status. If that responsibility grows through taking on a larger caring role in response to the long hours of male partners, women's disadvantage in the labour market is reinforced by two mechanisms.

First, long hours increase carers' responsibilities at home: the time that they must spend on child care, care for other dependants, domestic work and household administration, compensating for the absence of their partner, increases in ways that weaken their foothold in the labour market. While there are examples of men who take up the greater role at home, women do so much more commonly. As their domestic burden grows in support of their long hours partners, their labour market situation weakens.

Second, an increase in hours standards means that those with more responsibility for care – traditionally mothers and daughters – are increasingly unable to meet the standard of the 'long hours' workplace: it is remade in a yet *more* carer-unfriendly image. Many drop back to part-time work, change jobs, or leave the labour market. While some men take these choices as well – or at least try to – it is much more common among women. This means that in the presence of gendered patterns of caring and paid and unpaid work, long hours forcefully embed a workforce pattern that further disadvantages women who make up the majority of carers. While not all women will elect to make such decisions, for example to work part-time or take a demotion, most women are tainted by the *expectation* that they will. This means that a gendered long hours-of-work/caring regime is contributing to increased indirect discrimination against women. Further, the alignment of 'long hours' with 'serious worker' makes the penalty higher for men who want to refuse them in order to actively take their place as carers and parents. A 'daddy track' may await them and further stigmatise, penalise and inhibit men from care.

The effect on extended families, communities and volunteers

The time famine in long hours households has significant effects on the fabric of the extended family. Some workers feel that they do not see grandparents or grandchildren enough, and that they often miss family events. Further, many feel that their contact is built around 'asking for help' – for child care or other support – rather than an unfettered social exchange. Some feel guilty that their hours, or those of their partner, preclude *offering* help to their extended families.

Many regret the loss of time with their extended family, and some feel that it is a very important part of life, which a reduction in their hours allows them to reclaim. Pat, a busy public service worker and grandmother explains the effects she notices for her grandchildren of her regular overtime:

> If I worked 38 hours I would have more time for the grandchildren [she has six]. My grandson is at the age – he is four – he'll pick me up from the train sometimes with granddad and he will say 'I waited to see you cos I haven't seen you for

such a long time because you've been at work again!'. I'd definitely like to see a lot more of them. I'd like to have a day just for the grandchildren. My kids say we need to see more of you ... Grandparents are an essential part of the child's growing up because they can have a relationship with the child that it can't have with you parents and you lose out a lot by not having grandparents. I took my children away from their grandparents when they were [young] and it did impact on them drama- tically. My eight year old admitted later that she hated me for the first two years after we moved because I took her away from her nanny and granddad. And from the reactions I am getting from my grandchildren, they need their grandparents just as much as the grandparents need them.

It is striking that so many working long hours give up hobbies, exercise and sport. Most Australians value their health: the most common reason for giving up income among 'downshifters' without children in the 2002 Newspoll was a healthier lifestyle (Hamilton and Mail 2003). Many workers without dependants find that the first casualty of their working lives where hours are long, is their personal health and well-being. In the opening story in this chapter, Frank describes the loss of his hobbies and larger life as his long hours took over and 'work became life'. Like Frank, long hours workers let their hobbies, sport and social lives decline and this affects their health. Once again, the time poverty arising from long hours is not visited on the worker alone but transmitted to partners:

> I have done nothing of my own since 1994, and I've now got a car to rebuild as of two weeks ago. But that's going to take a long time because I can't ... guarantee to get myself time, like four hours at a stretch, I can never guarantee that. I always do whatever I can by sneaking in an hour or two usually. (man, doctor's partner)

Workers in a variety of occupations describe giving up forms of sport, and/or hobbies because of lack of time, its unpredictability, or exhaustion. This has significant effects on whole communities. Miners describe the decline of their local football club and golf club as a result of 12-hour shifts in their town. The implications for community fabric, for friendships and for community are obvious. Voluntary work like social clubs, charity work and participation in the army reserve is also constrained. Many families affected by long hours describe a 'closing in' of their social circle. Those with families find that much of their non-work time is spent together, or trying to be together. Others work hard to maintain their community of friendships which they see as invaluable support for their jobs: being able to easily call on neighbours when called to work, for example, relies on a good community of neighbours and friends.

The growing grip of a 'long hours' culture which corrodes community in privatised ways

The pictures that arise from the lives of long hours workers reveal a long hours culture that has taken a strong workplace hold. This is not a marginal phenomenon. One in four Australian workers work more than 45 hours a week, and one in two full-time employees work around eight hours overtime a week, more often unpaid than paid. It reaches into many households, where the symptoms of grumpiness, exhaustion, poorer health and time poverty are common, along with loss of intimacy and risk of divorce. Yet the linkage between work patterns and divorce is rarely made. Moralistic exhortations to 'stay together', or proposals to stiffen divorce laws, make no sense if the source of family breakdown lies in increasing hours of work – as it does in some cases.

There are many forces that combine to establish the hold of a long hours workplace culture. Some workers want higher incomes through paid overtime, and there are examples where this income is firmly built into household budgets. For others, their overtime, whether paid or not, is not voluntary: in under-staffed workplaces there is extensive evidence of workers under strong pressure to work overtime. Many workers are pulled into long hours because they want to get the job done or because their supervisors and employers demand it: money is not their motivation. This commitment provides fertile ground on which to structure staff shortages and run lean budgets. The dollars that are saved, however, do not come without costs – to the individuals who work them, their families, friends, and the larger community.

Many workers describe their workplaces, one way or another, as places where long hours are entrenched, where refusing them means being tainted as a 'bad' worker, destined for negative treatment, redundancy, undesirable tasks, or the sack. New technologies like the mobile phone extend the reach of that culture, and take it into the hidden workplace of the home and car.

The corrosive effects of long hours are frequently experienced privately. They are the externality costs of long hours of work. While some corrosive effects reach the public sphere of the health, workers' compensation and social welfare systems, many are privately experienced through the loss of amenity in private time, relationships, family life and a diminution of community. And they reach out to affect many beyond the worker – to their partners, children, parents, friends, social group, and community. They entrench a new standard of work and raise the 'hours bar' in ways that affect not just those who work long hours. They have implications for all those who populate the workplace because they create a new standard.

With long hours growing in many workplaces, many employees find themselves either trying to meet the new standard, or failing in comparison to it – carers especially fall into this category. There are strong arguments for the re-creation of model worker standards in a new image that allows family life to occur without strain, and without taking on 'exceptionalism' status in the labour force. Workers with families are not exceptions in labour markets. Most workers will have dependants for significant portions of their working lives, creating a strong argument for reigning in long hours and practices.

Long hours place extra stress on women with families who must work double shifts in paid work and domestic labour. They exacerbate inequities in the division of household labour where a parent – usually the woman – must step into the 'mother and the father' roles and become a *de facto* single parent. They cause some divorces. And they embed second-class mummy and daddy tracks for those workers who want to actively parent.

Extended hours in paid work undermine human and social capital formation with significant negative implications for health, economic growth, democracy and citizenship (Putnam 2000). Social capital building activities, which include the socialisation of children, volunteer activities and civic engagement are significantly affected by increasing pressures arising from patterns of long hours, with implications for social cohesion.

Long hours exist in workplaces where employees know them to be unsafe – especially in combination with shifts (Heiler 2001). And they exist in highly unionised workplaces among highly skilled workers who exercise considerable labour market power. These factors do not prevent the acquiescence to long hours, testament to the powerful effect of long hours cultures. What is more, these hours persist in the face of employers' knowledge of the 'suicidal thoughts' of some workers, and obvious signs of stress in many more. The pressure to get the job done is a powerful force in Australian workplaces and appears to have taken a firm hold. It exists despite statute, agreement and award provisions that regulate 'reasonable overtime', impose a duty of care on employers to provide a safe and healthy workplace, and specify meal, shift and rest breaks. These have not been enough to stem long hours in many workplaces, and they create a strong argument for new circuit breakers to stem the systemic hold of long hours in Australian workplaces.

Control over time is a critical ingredient for happiness and having a good life. For many, more time at work is not associated with *either* more money or more happiness: more time at work *might* increase job security or promotion prospects, but it is *highly likely* to compromise home life, relationships, health, and relationships with children and within communities. Grumpy people do not made great lovers, fathers, mothers, drivers, neighbours or golfers.

Conclusion

The impact of long hours on the one in four Australian workers who now work them, are profound. They extend, also, to many self-employed and small business people and farmers, whose lives are structured around long and demanding days. It is time to weigh their costs, especially the hidden, private costs, and take action to curb them. The collision between work and life is being given added momentum by increases in hours of work that see more Australians working long hours, and an increasing proportion of these who do not want to. The changing long hours regime in Australia frustrates both men's and women's preferences to work reasonable hours.

For most of the last century, formal hours of work in Australia have been determined by employers and unions, mediated by industrial relations tribunals at State and federal level. These standards have been enforced by industrial inspectorates and active unionists and workers. The weakness of our industrial regulatory regime and its enforcement contribute to the increase in long hours. Since the late 1980s the system of workplace regulation in Australia has changed significantly with fewer employees covered by awards (now less than a quarter), more by locally bargained collective enterprise agreements and up to 40 per cent by individual contracts (ABS, Cat No 4102.0: 154). An environment of intensified international competitive pressures and pursuit of shareholder value, alongside shrinking real expenditures on human services, has contributed to intensified work and longer hours. Bad contracts now exist (of the kind that Frank works under in a highly unionised workplace, for example), a diverse range of contracts and standards now exist (rather than industry standards), and many contracts and awards are not enforced. Each of these issues must be addressed if the growth in long hours is to be stopped, and – more ambitiously – reduced.

Regulatory options

Long hours of work can be reduced by several means. These include reducing standard weekly hours (to less than 38), preventing unpaid overtime, capping paid overtime to specific limits, extending annual leave or public holidays, and expanding other forms of leave like parental leave or rostered days off. Each of these, as Iain Campbell has argued, presents an option in Australia, and there are overseas examples where each has been applied (2002a). The first possibility is a cap on total hours worked, as has been adopted in the UK (Campbell 2001). While exemption from this limit is possible, the requirement for most to stay beneath a minimum is an important advance. Given the high public and private costs of extended hours in Australia, is it vital to place a cap on total hours. It is also, however, vital to simultaneously reduce unpaid and unregulated overtime. This will require legislation and/or award changes.

In 2001, the ACTU attempted to convince the Australian Industrial Relations Commission (AIRC) to introduce into industrial awards a definition of unreasonable hours, a right to refuse to work them, and a new leave provision if they were worked. While vehemently opposed by employers, and not won in its entirety, the AIRC granted a new right to refuse 'to work overtime where the working of such overtime would result in the employee working unreasonable hours' (AIRC 23 July 2002, para 277). However, the AIRC refused the approach of compensating long hours with special leave saying 'the appropriate course is to fix the problem, not to provide *"a beneficial recuperative effect"* (AIRC, 23 July para 268, italics in original). The 'appropriate course' is to cap long hours – whether paid or unpaid – so that employees can neither choose to work them, nor employers require them. The medium-term objective must be to reduce average working hours overall, through a reduction in the length of the working week. Work contracts represent a wage/effort bargain, where wage rewards, along with hours of work and employee responsibilities, are specified. Work arrangements with – effectively – unspecified and unpaid hours of work beyond those paid for, is theft. Preventing this theft requires industrial regulation of unpaid overtime, clear wage/effort/hours contracts, and enforcement of new rights that clarify rights and prevent exploitation.

This requires two important supporting initiatives. First, as we have seen, long hours are the result in many cases of understaffing. Agreements about staffing levels and ratios relatively to workloads are essential in many workplaces if hours are to fall. They have been negotiated in some workplaces, especially where people die if employees do not work long hours (for example among paramedics and nurses). In less lethal situations, staffing agreements are essential to underwrite the end of long hours. There is no sensible reason – beyond the realisation of profits through exploitation and theft – that banks, the racing industry, manufacturers and public services – should run their predictable day-to-day operations around increasing levels of unpaid overtime. Ending this theft will require strong measures to name, prevent, and redress workplace bullying and victimisation. Unionism has been the traditional bulwark. With Australian union density now at 25 per cent, down from 40 per cent in 1992, this is a weak or non-existent defence for many employees and stronger non-union protection is essential. This can only be established by government.

Second, the wage rates of low paid workers must increase so that the lowest paid do not make up a living wage through long and unsafe hours. For some workers on low wages, who are paid for their extra hours, overtime is their only means to a living wage. Increasing base rates will reduce unsafe levels of overtime in some areas. It is a vital part of a total strategy.

Employer, individual and collective responsibility: Refusing established norms

But change has to go beyond industrial machinery. Employers have a responsibility to manage work patterns to curb unsafe and anti-care long hours. While many will await a legal requirement to do so, others will not.

Individuals work long hours. In some cases they fight for them and the money they earn, or they drift into them. They may hate them – but workers *acquiesce* to them. This acquiescence is frequently shaped by pressure; it is far from a 'free' choice. But while we can increase the bulwarks around those who do not want to work long hours and, in some cases, penalise those who allow or work them, the refusal by the individual to work them is also important. We have seen that individual power to resist workplace cultures that entrench long hours is often very weak. The decline in union density has undermined resistance, especially in sectors where its traditions are weak (like the information technology industry). But only by both collective *and* individual refusal and organisation – underpinned by statutory rights – will long hours be stemmed in many locations, even with the firmest regime of industrial regulation. This means recording hours of work, making actual hours of work transparent and public, and *resisting* long hours.

For 'the overtime junkies' – as some workers call them – this will mean a cut in income. Higher base wages for the low paid will help those who make a basic living by working extra paid hours. But for others, less overtime and safer hours will affect consumption. This will be resisted, but with perhaps a quarter of Australians taking some voluntary action to 'downshift' in the past decade, this resistance may be weaker than supposed. As one electrician said of his reduced hours and money and his kids greater enthusiasm for him – running to him when he came home at night – 'that's worth any money or any amount of overtime, or anything'. When individuals make decisions that endanger the lives of themselves or others, we must prevent them so that they can neither be demanded – explicitly or implicitly – by an employer, or worked by employees. This requires change at the individual level: we must *refuse to work* long hours in the interests of happy households, healthy children and a robust community.

In the six years to 2000, productivity in Australia grew by over 10 per cent as hours of work increased for most full-timers.

If we took that productivity increase as reduced hours we could have reduced a 40 hour working week to 36, or taken an extra months annual leave. Instead we have seen productivity increases fund large increases in share values and managerial pay, and very little for those they manage. Time sovereignty is a key object for a decent working life and some European countries have recognised and moved towards this. Australia led the world in the 19th century on this important measure of social health: it does not now. However, there is no reason why, as a rich first world country, we should not do so again. Such change requires strong union initiative, a willingness by industrial tribunals and governments to take action, individual and household resolve around livable work and consumption standards, and a community environment that supports this kind of social and industrial reform. All of this is far from easy, but there can be no argument that it is not now pressing if we are to prevent the further intensification of the work/life collision.

CHAPTER 7

Short working hours:
Choice, careers, security

There are three main ways in which Australians reconcile care with paid work under the current Work/Care regime. The primary *combination* route is through combining paid work with care through part-time hours, well short of full-time jobs. These people limit their attachment to the paid labour market, in order to meet their care obligations; however, they tend to move between part-time and full-time work according to the intensity of care. A second route takes an *intermittent* approach to care and paid work: the two are interspersed either by means of leave from a paid tenured job to structure care and work around each other, or by means of serial jobs between, for example, children. A third and less used frequently used route over recent years exists by means of extended *absence or withdrawal* from the labour market: many primary carers with young children, or disabled or aged dependants do not take paid work for long periods while caring is intensive. Of course these alternative combination, intermittent or withdrawal approaches are not mutually exclusive over the life-cycle: some adopt combination and intermittent approaches at different points, with years out of paid work when their children arrive, followed by years of part-time then full-time work.

By international comparison, Australian carers are much more likely to adopt part-time work strategies than others, and they have increasingly turned away from leaving the labour force when they have children. This is hardly surprising in view of poor parental leave and the costs and uneven provision of long day child care.

In this chapter we consider the mechanism of shorter working hours through part-time work that so many Australians use to meet their dual work/care obligations. In Chapter 9 we consider the intermittent work/care arrangement, where blocks of leave are interwoven with paid jobs.

There are those who believe that the distinction between 'part-time' and 'full-time' work is artificial and outdated, and that the emphasis should shift to matching diverse employers' and employees' preferences, so that both are satisfied in jobs of any length. This debate signals an important issue: the gap between policy hope and workplace reality. While we might hold the policy *hope* that jobs have transformed themselves *from* a conception of 'proper jobs' as full-time and fully integrated into a labour market, *to* 'proper jobs' that are diverse in their hours and conditions and fully integrated into a labour market, the reality is somewhat different. While we might *hope* that our labour market is not divided into primary and secondary spheres, into mummy and daddy tracks, into core or periphery sectors, into male and female segments, into full-time or part-time jobs, the reality is otherwise. If policy makers operate from *hope* rather than *evidence*, they cannot make effective change. If 'jobs are to be jobs' – with equal chances of decent pay, security and labour market integration regardless of hours – then current realities must be understood and addressed. Policy makers, who work from hope and fond conception, rather than workplace reality, will be of limited effectiveness.

There is plenty of evidence that labour is segmented, and that different conditions attach to the jobs that fall within different segments. Shorter hours jobs are usually different from full-time jobs: they are more likely to be done by women or carers, and they are more likely to be lower paid, less integrated into workplace, occupational and industry labour markets, and to be less secure. Further, the transition between full-time and part-time work, and vice versa, is hazardous and poorly developed, so that part-time and full-time jobs are not well integrated into a single, seamless labour market. These are international characteristics, common in the OECD area (O'Reilly and Fagan 1998). However, some peculiar features characterise Australia.

Part-time jobs are increasingly significant in the Australian labour market. Just as jobs have been increasing at the long-hours end of the spectrum, they have been growing at the short-hours end, with a massive growth in part-time work. In the two decades since 1982, the proportion of jobs that are part-time has increased from 17 to 29 per cent of the total. Much of this growth has been among women: the proportion of women's jobs that are part-time has increased from 35 per cent to almost half. The growth has also affected men's employment, with a growth over 20 years from 6 per cent to 15 per cent of all men's jobs. Part-time workers work around 16 hours a week on average (ABS Cat No 6203.0). About a third of part-time employees would like to work more hours (49 per cent of men, and 31 per cent of women. ABS Cat No 6359.0).

Figure 7.1 Per cent of Part-time Employees, by Sex, Australia

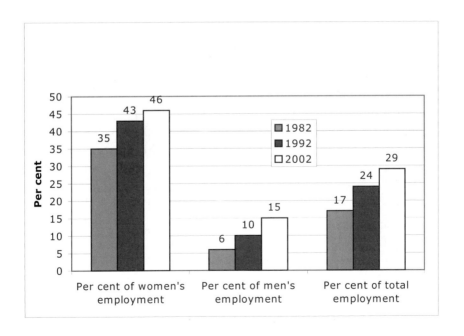

Source: ABS Cat No 6203.0.

Compared to full-time workers, many more part-timers find it easier to combine work with care. The 2001 HILDA survey shows that 48 per cent of full-time women agreed that 'because of the requirements of my job, I miss out on home or family activities that I would prefer to participate in', compared to a quarter of part-time women (the differences are less marked among men: Fisher 2002: 29). Similar differences exist with respect to the effect of work on 'time or energy to be the kind of parent I want to be' and missing out on the rewarding aspects of parenting, with fewer part-timers finding difficulties than full-timers, especially among women (Fisher 2002: 29).

Not all part-time workers are the same in terms of their preferences, situation or satisfaction with their part-time jobs. Nor are their preferences fixed over the life cycle. A study of 1000 Australian women bank employees in 1996 found that most were happy to work part-time but 20 per cent wanted to work full-time and almost one in two wanted to work full-time in the future (Walsh 1999).

Part-time work as it has emerged in Australia has some peculiar characteristics. First, it is widespread and growing quickly. The share of part-time work in the Australian economy is very high. Within the OECD area, only the Netherlands is higher at 33 per cent (OECD 2002a: 319). Since the early 1990s, the pace of part-time work growth has been faster than in most other OECD countries. Second, much Australian part-time work confers weak formal employment rights. A high proportion of it is insecure. Of the 2 million Australian part-time employees in late 2001, two thirds lack any entitlements to paid leave and most identify themselves as 'casuals' – with little job security or rights to control their working time although many have long years of service. The growth in casual employment has out-stripped the growth in permanent employment since the early 1980s. Casual employment is concentrated among part-timers with only 13 per cent of full-time Australian employees casual in late 2001 (ABS Cat 6310.0). The earnings of casual workers are very unpredictable: they varied for over half of the 1.8 million self-identified casuals in 2001.

In reality, many of the part-time jobs in Australia that are termed 'casual' are not genuinely casual (that is, short-term and unpredictable). Many are long lasting, with predictable earnings – or earnings that *could* be predictable. The peculiarly high level of casual employment in Australia has grown in 'the spaces left by gaps in the regulatory system' that created casual work as 'an officially sanctioned gap' in employment protection that has widened as the regulatory system has weakened (Campbell and Burgess 2001: 5). Other categories of insecure employment exist in the form of limited term contracts (about 6 per cent of the workforce (ABS Cat No 6359.0) and workers employed through labour hire agencies (around 2 per cent of the workforce (ABS Cat No 6359.0; Campbell et al 2002)).

Table 7.1 Employment Insecurity, by Sex, Full-time/ Part-time, Australia, November 2001 ('000)

	Full-time	*Part-time*	*Total*
Men			
Without paid leave entitlements	435.7	435.2	870.9
All Men	3276.8	542.6	3819.4
Per cent insecure	13%	80%	23%
Women			
Without paid leave entitlements	229.8	939.8	1169.6
All Women	1960.9	1520.9	3481.8
Per cent insecure	12%	62%	34%
Persons			
Without paid leave entitlements	665.6	1375	2040.6
All Persons	5237.8	2063.6	7301.4
Per cent insecure	13%	67%	28%

Source: ABS Cat No 6359.0.

Note: 'insecure' is defined to include those without any paid work leave entitlements (ie those that identify as casual, and those without paid leave entitlements who do not identify in this way; many of these are on limited term contracts). The data exclude owner/managers.

The growth in insecure employment places Australia behind just one or two other OECD countries with very high levels of insecure employment. The share of this employment has grown strongly since the early 1980s, contrary to the trend in many OECD countries. Australia represents 'an extreme case', both in terms of the level and accelerating growth in casual employment (OECD 2002b: 51; Campbell and Burgess 2001: 172), which has been boosted further by growth in limited term and temporary labour hire agency employment.

In Australia, being 'casual' is useful to employers seeking numerical flexibility. By employing on a casual basis they can hire and fire at will, on an hourly basis in many cases, and they can save on costs associated with employment conditions. Employees can sometimes gain some flexibility themselves – to say yes or no to hours. But this comes at the price of losing job predictability or security. A wage loading applies to many casual jobs which compensates for some of the lost conditions of annual leave, sick leave, long service leave and so on. But in many cases this loading is incomplete compensation in real terms, and the extent of its *actual* payment is unknown.

There are those who believe that casual work is a temporary life-cycle phenomenon for those combining study with earning 'pocket money' or supplementing other means of support. However, while insecurity is high among 15-24 year olds (54 per cent of whom are without paid leave entitlements), it remains a problem for more than a quarter of women *over* 25 years old (ABS Cat No 6359.0). It is not a problem that can be discounted as a temporary condition affecting only young students.

Figure 7.2 shows the massive growth in part-time work in Australia in the past 19 years. Most of it is concentrated among women in their childbearing and rearing years (25-50 years). It is directly related to family responsibilities. For men, however, part-time work is much smaller, and more evenly spread by age. It is slightly higher in the years in education (14-25 years) and has no obvious association with parenting. The gendered incidence of part-time work is very marked. Australian women

Figure 7.2 Part-time Employment by
Sex and Age, 1983 and 2002 ('000)

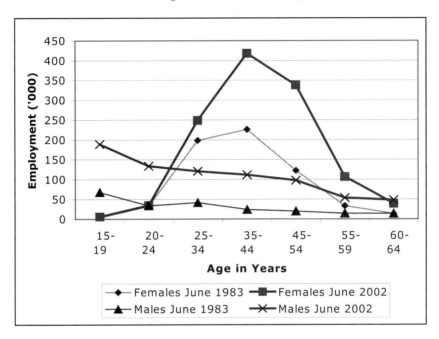

Source: ABS Cat No 6291.0.40.001

have turned to part-time work to cope with their dual roles as
earners and carers. They have essentially adapted the traditional
Worker-man/Carer-woman model by adding a half-time wage
earning role to the duties of women, while leaving men's participation largely in the full-time mode. However, this aggregation
conceals life-cycle changes: many women take time out of paid
work when their children are very young, and move to part-time
work while children are at school, and then into full-time work.
The tendency to *combine* care and work is dominant in Australia,
with more and more women – even those with children under
one year – in some form of work.

However, while many make use of part-time work, its terms
are degraded relative to full-time jobs. While only 13 per cent of
full-time jobs have no paid leave entitlements, 67 per cent of

part-time jobs lack these conditions. This means that while a third of *all* women employees lack job security and paid leave, a full *62 per cent* of women in part-time work lack these conditions. Thirty-eight per cent of single parents are in jobs that lack paid leave entitlements and are insecure.

Insecurity is especially evident in the retail trade, in accommodation cafes and restaurants, health and community services, property and business services, education and manufacturing. There are high proportions of casuals among elementary and intermediate clerical, sales and service workers, and labourers and related unskilled workers (ABS Cat No 6359.0)

The loss of security and paid leave are high prices indeed for shorter hours to permit carers and sole parents to combine their double day. These conditions are quite inferior to those in some other countries – though not all – where part-time work has developed as the road to worker/carer balance. They make a strong argument for improved part-time work conditions in Australia.

The 'choice' to work part-time

To what extent are patterns of part-time and casual work a reflection of worker choice? Neo-classical labour market economists understand labour market supply as the outcome of workers' preferences between paid work and leisure. But these preferences are in fact conditioned by institutional arrangements that shape the hours of jobs on offer. These include workplace conditions and traditions, and industrial awards and agreements, along with the social and family structures within which any worker is located. If child care is unavailable, then the work preferences of the worker with responsibility for children are irrelevant. If workers have part-time responsibility for dependent aged relatives, but no part-time jobs are on offer, then their preferences are irrelevant. If a worker wants to work part-time but also aims to be a partner in a legal practice, she may find she cannot do both; her preferences are irrelevant. Discussion of part-time work with part-time workers reveals several features. First, many part-time workers *must* trade-off career for part-time hours. Second, some choose part-time jobs in order to work full-time hours, rather than excessive hours. Third, the majority of part-time employees, regardless of their preferences, give up job security when they take a part-time job. Part-time work in Australia is saturated with insecurity. Finally, part-time work unhinges workers from core labour markets – whether internal to the firm, or external in occupational, industry or professional networks, so that the conditions of part-time in Australian are degraded in terms of wages, long-term career prospects, and access to many kinds of workplace benefits from basic communication through to promotion.

Many workers find that part-time work meets their needs: they want to be available for their families and avoid the stress of full-time jobs. They also understand the costs of working part-time: for job security, a career and higher earnings. Many – even those in permanent, secure part-time jobs – accept that they have 'a job not a career'. They see this 'choice' as between greedy, demanding, full-time, career jobs and being the peripheral part-timer. Many part-time workers feel they have limited access to a range of workplace conditions, including job security, training, information, development and promotion. They do not choose these conditions – indeed, many resent them – but they recognise them as the unarguable consequence of working part-time.

Is this then a 'pure' choice? Anne Junor has argued that several kinds of labour market choices exist, ranging from *free* choices to choices *restricted* by the limited options available, and choices, *constrained* by contextual factors (2000: 103, my emphasis). This leads her to argue that the language of *accommodation* is more appropriate to hours outcomes than the language of free choice. This approach finds support in the evidence we now consider.

Choosing between a career and 'just a job'

Many part-time workers are very clear about the direct trade-off of less than full-time hours, for a career. As Vera puts it:

> [Being both a worker and a carer] is very difficult especially when there are hospital visits. I spend a lot of time trying to organise things. I have taken a lower amount of hours in order to cope with my family and that meant giving up being a leader. I sometimes regret that I have had to make that decision. Being a team member (rather than a leader) is fine. But I only have a *job* now, instead of a career. (call centre, woman with dependants)

Vera has a deep sense of loss about making the decision to go part-time to care more for her dependent older relatives and her two sons with disabilities. This sense of loss is not about income; it is about the lost opportunity to make a leadership contribution in her workplace – a loss not only to her, but also to her employer:

> I have a sense of loss making my decision to give up a leadership position, even though I know I made the right decision. I am reluctant, however, to intervene any more at work and make a contribution as I am only a team member now. This is really hard because as a team member, if I intervene, it is seen to be interfering. But because I have until recently been in a leadership position there is a great sense of loss now that I can't do it – can't make that contribution.

Many women have 'chosen' not to take promotion, or to become casual part-timers, in order to be able to take time off, though their choices are clearly constrained. Both city-based and country women note a stark difference between 'the mother track' carved out through part-time work, and 'the career track':

> I think women on a part-time basis have to make that choice, which means a lot of women with young children – if you're on a farm as well – you are over-looked. (woman, part-time worker in country town)

> You have to work full-time to climb a ladder. In all occupations. (woman, part-time worker in country town)

Many part-time workers want to avoid higher stress and less flexible jobs, and the 'striving' and 'hassle' that they see full-time workers face. Choosing part-time work means avoiding 'hassle' at the cost of 'no progression', as Jesse puts it:

> Depends on whether you want a career. I've been doing virtually the same job for two and a half years. I'm quite happy doing that. I like my 20 hours. I don't want to have to strive to go somewhere else. Because nobody is going to really take me with 20 hours. (call centre worker, mother)

Jesse is happy and believes she will lose what she has – flexibility and part-time work – if she seeks change. She sees only 'hassle' and 'pressure' if she attempts to change her arrangements. Her full-time colleague, Margaret, agreed with her assessment, and was avoiding promotion, in order to avoid stress:

> I find the same with full-time. I would like to progress and get more money but I feel like if I progress I'll be put in a more stressful situation that would make me feel that I would not be able to cope so I stay at this level to the detriment of my career so that I can cope. (call centre worker, mother)

Margaret wants progression but sees that her 'choices' are limited. Progression will increase her stress so she chooses not to be promoted. While some express satisfaction about trade of career for part-time work, the contest between work and family forces a choice that many men simply do not face: the constraints are gendered. The gender pay gap – with Australian women earning around 84 per cent of men's full-time earnings at present – is one measure of some of the costs of this different set of work options and 'choices'. Professional women are particularly clear about the costs they incur through working part-time. They describe their co-workers' and business partners' views of part-timers as 'not serious' about their work:

> Part-time work makes you not very important. You are viewed as not serious. (doctor, mother)

You don't get the information, you don't know what's going on. You get the dummy jobs, the things others don't want to do. (lawyer, mother)

You are stifled. You can get so far and you reach that plateau, and that's it. I feel that I've reached a plateau. I haven't advanced because I'm part-time. (doctor, mother)

These workers have attempted to maintain their professional jobs, by adopting part-time work. However, they struggle with their own internal sense of how this diminishes them as 'proper doctors' and 'proper lawyers', and their discounted status in the eyes of their colleagues. Senior women in organisations with extensive part-time work opportunities agree:

There is a sense from some of your colleagues, too, that you should be satisfied with what you've got – that really you are not doing too badly 'for a woman'. (lawyer)

The dominant model of the professional worker – dedicated to the job – has implications for part-time work and undermines professional confidence:

I've been in full-time general practice, and part-time. It's the way others perceive you but it's even the way you see yourself. I felt that I was always there for everyone, and I felt a loss of professional satisfaction in going part-time. And people don't take you seriously if you're part-time because they think if you are a real GP, then you are there all the time … It can have an effect on your self-esteem and how you see yourself as a professional. I've had at least one peer question my attitude because I'm not prepared to participate in on-call work. I'm not obliged to – but he said 'I think that is an appalling attitude'. It made me angry, but it also nibbled away quietly at my self-esteem, and how seriously you take yourself. I had another peer say 'Well look, personally, I don't believe you can do what you are doing part-time'. I was angry but meanwhile my brain thought: maybe you're right! (woman, doctor)

For these employees, being part-time meant that career prospects are truncated. While some accept this, others resent its unfairness: if you are there half the time, why shouldn't you have access to half the chances – to train, travel, or be promoted? This discussion reveals the nature of the full-time 'proper' worker that shadows part-time workers who live in its shade. Some men are well aware of this shadow. A senior, long-hours, public sector worker and father of young children experienced a 'sense of danger' when he suggests during an interview for a new job that he work part-time. He felt this suggestion created the perception that he might become one of the 'stuck' employees, rather than 'a winner':

> I got an offer for a job – and so that really forced the question about would I go to a full-time job or could I go part-time? When I went for the initial discussion and when they described it as a full-time job I said, 'Look, I'm not entirely certain about this and I'd be quite interested in balancing things – [maybe] dropping down a level and going virtually part-time'. And it was very interesting. It was as if it didn't compute, they just brushed it aside and they said 'Ah ... well yes ... okay' and ploughed on with the description of this full-time position ... It put me in a fairly difficult position where there was a sense that I needed to be actually very, very delicate and discrete if I was going to keep open the option of this full-time – but also potentially a part-time – position. I ended up winning the position and saying would they be interested in taking me on as a part-time [equivalent] and the reaction was very cool, very cool and – well, first of all there was a sense of confusion about well 'why would you want to do that?' It got them thinking it was a very strange option to take.

In the end Bob decided not to pursue part-time work because of the reaction it created:

> I think that anyone who thinks of dropping a level ... there's a sense of danger about them, a sense of question marks about their competency ... There's a culture of people move up – so there's people who move up or there are people who are stuck

where they are, and that can have implications – sometimes
a bad thing. But the idea of someone going down [sends]
alarm bells.

He also felt that part-time work imposes constraints upon
managers who cannot expect employees to work long hours:
part-time work creates formal exit points in terms of hours.
Some workers take part-time jobs as a deliberate strategy to cut
down on the hours they work from 'more-than-full-time', to 'full-
time-but-paid-part-time'. As a manager of a community service
put it:

> And part-time work isn't *really* part-time work for women. You
> are only paid for those hours, but you probably work a lot more.
> Now I'm working full-time I can't do some of the things with
> my five year old that I'd like to do because I can't be reliable ...
> the demands of the job. You are actually a slave! You are owned
> by the organisation.

Casual workers: 'Choosing' to be insecure and low paid?

As long as part-time work positions those who do it as
secondary, 'family-centred' or not serious workers, it embeds a
'carers-track' in the labour market with significant penalties and
poor integration into the labour market as a whole. Perhaps its
greatest cost is insecurity which is a serious problem for many
part-time workers. This particularly affects women. Across Australia, casual workers are concentrated in the two occupations
where over half of all women are employed: basic and intermediate clerical, and sales and service workers. Over half of *all*
women in elementary clerical, sales and service jobs identify as
casual. In the retail trade, 45 per cent of all employees are self-
identified casuals, and 57 per cent of those in accommodation,
cafes and restaurants (ABS Cat No 6359.0). There is a significant
pay penalty for both women and men who work casually, because
in many cases the award provisions for higher hourly rates for
casual workers only partially compensate them for their loss of

sick, holiday leave and other conditions (Junor 2000, Smith and Ewer 1999, Pocock and Alexander 1999).

Very few casual workers say in interviews that *casual* work, in itself, is their preference. Many are seeking, primarily, less than full-time hours. They often assume – and find – that the only form of part-time work available to them is casual: these are the terms on offer. The preference against unpredictability is confirmed by an 2000 ABS survey which shows that while over 43 per cent of self-identified casuals worked 'casual or relief' patterns where their days were not set, this was the preference of only 23 per cent. In fact, two thirds of casuals want to work set days each week or month. (ABS Cat No 6361.0). For some whose casual employment is long standing and secure, this is less of a concern. However, others prefer permanency:

> I'd rather be permanent for the security. I do full-time work but I'm paid as a casual. (factory, casual, mother)

> It is very important for me to be a permanent part-time worker. I was a casual in the previous job and I hated not being paid adequately, not knowing how long the job was for. There is no security. You can't plan. It affects holidays, mortgages. You need to be there all the time. (office, woman, full-time worker)

The last comment undermines a conception of casual work as flexible on the employee's terms. Casual workers are more likely to view themselves as 'on tap' than 'in charge' of their working time. The flexibility is on their employers' terms, not their own. For those who are not full-time casuals or on a regular roster, there is a sense that they are at the beck and call of the employer:

> As a casual I don't get sickies, no holiday pay. At my old factory, the (labour hire company) would ring you up and say 'Go now!' I'd go, and then there is a machine breakdown and you have to go home. Or when you get there they want to know why you are there, and send you home! So you have travelled all the way there and back for no pay. (woman, factory casual, labour hire agency worker)

There is an expectation of many casuals that they are available at any time:

> They assume that casuals don't do other things when they are not working. (casual worker, mother)

The capacity to negotiate hours or shifts varies widely depending upon the stance and 'compassion' of management and supervisors, and the skills and resistance of employees:

> My rosters constantly change. The expectations are that I can drop everything and be available. The supervisor gets shitty if I can't be instantly available. But I feel guilty towards the kids. All the flexibility is on the supervisor's side. He has no compassion for my life. You work around the work. Your roster is without notice. It doesn't work both ways. It should. They manipulate your hours to keep you casual. You've got to be cunning – you have to conceal your plans. They know you have kids. Half of the staff have kids. School holidays are a nightmare … the span of hours that they can call you in for has increased. So for working mothers it's very hard. (casual, part-time cashier in security firm, mother)

The negotiation of hours and shifts is a very positive and valued condition for employees, and some employers actively ensure it. As one manager says:

> Our workers have the choice and none have chosen to go permanent part-time. Because they like the loading and their freedom. They can take leave whenever they want to. I have a very open attitude to people taking leave – they dictate what they do. But we have a very dedicated team who are dedicated to the clients. I understand the dangers of casual work but in this setting it works. And it's mostly women … It's very much a negotiated outcome … Being casual means they can ask for every school holiday off and they don't have to feel guilty. (manager, community based service for the aged)

This supervisor negotiates rather than dictates arrangements and her desire to keep her 'dedicated' team together gives the casual employees some bargaining security. They can avoid guilt when they ask for leave in school holidays – in exchange for being casual. In another example, the employee's willingness to 'stand up and organise' things – to actively advocate – has resulted in negotiations:

> The boss that I work for says 'let us know when you want to work' ... We workers got together and worked out what would work. It's worked really well. Because you've got people who will stand up and organise things and make things better. I'm an advocate. We have three shifts operating and we all do it together. (employee in contract cleaning company, woman)

Once again the idea of a negotiated outcome is critical to the satisfaction reported among employees. Others opt to become permanent when their jobs appear at risk:

> In the nursing home many of our casuals became permanent. We have some people who have been casual for ten years, and they have finally come onto permanent part-time, mainly when there is major change and uncertainty. (manager, nursing home, man)

The pay price for being casual

Alongside insecurity, part-time employees who are casual generally pay a sizeable pay penalty. This is compounded in relation to retirement savings and superannuation. Analysis of 1995 AWIRS data shows that casually employed men were paid 18 per cent less than men who are otherwise similar but not casual, while the penalty for women was 15 per cent (Pocock and Alexander 2001). This is despite the award provisions for greater hourly rates for many casual workers to compensate them for their loss of sick, holiday leave and so on. With so much casual work concentrated at the bottom end of the pay hierarchy, and further penalised in terms of pay relative to permanent employees, it is no surprise to find that some low paid casual workers are keen to retain access to the casual loading. However, significant numbers of casual employees are not motivated by the casual loading, recognising that it does not fully compensate for other conditions:

> You get loading as a casual but it is not a lot more. I look on it as getting your leave money paid in advance. (factory worker, casual)

Some assume that casual part-time work gives *employees* greater control over their hours of work. This is true for some. However, others report the opposite – that they must be readily available. Rather than facilitate their caring and household responsibilities, casual employment complicates them in its unpredictability and insecurity. It represents a poor 'choice' between limited options. Many employees feel that the current use of casual employment is inappropriate and that permanent part-time work should be available: as one put it 'Casual work should be just that. If a person is working in an ongoing part-time job they should get offered permanent part-time'.

Insecurity at work is not confined to casual employees. Limited term employees report that they 'usually can't take holidays, don't get holiday pay', along with a sense that a contract work system is growing in some fields, for example, in community services. In some cases the length of contract is shortening, and the pressure to perform is intense:

> I work on fixed term contracts that get shorter and shorter. This concerns me. I used to get three year contracts but now I get six months Even if the contract rolls over, there is a lot of pressure beforehand and loss of permanency, funding issues, annual leave. You can't take leave when you want and there is pressure not to take it and get paid out at the end. (community sector worker, woman)

> Any job now is stressful: performing to full capacity, proving yourself all the time because you are only on contract work. And until such time as you get permanency you will be stressed out. (community sector, Indigenous woman)

'Proper' jobs: The 'ideal-male', full-time standard

The ideal or proper worker in many Australian workplaces remains the full-time employee, who is increasingly likely to be working hours well in excess of 40 per week. As internal labour markets are built around this proper worker, the conditions and prospects of those who cannot meet its conditions, remain second rate. This second rate status applies to many part-time employees, whether men or women, and whether highly skilled and experienced or not. Many professional workers with caring responsibilities find that the model of the professional worker – the lawyer or doctor – is not easily reconcilable with choices like part-time work that accommodate care and work. 'Greedy' professional jobs require long hours and personal dedication to the job above all else: they do not fit with shorter hours, career breaks or extended leave. Carers who are professionals argue that this model is simply incompatible with serious parenting. As long as professional expectations are hostile to even minimal adoptions, like part-time work, talk of 'family friendly' flexibility is a distraction. In these professions the traditional male model – with expectation of a wife at home – remains strong, despite the increasing numbers of women who are becoming lawyers, doctors and managers. Management and leadership jobs have embedded expectations of a large commitment to the job. 'Family friendly' provisions (like rights to take family leave) are of little use to these workers, who see their commitment to the job as tested by their use, as Wajcman's research in large 'pro-family' multi-national companies reveals (1998). These 'commitment tester' conditions are often used to separate the 'proper worker', constructed within the male model of full-time worker without dependants, from the 'weakly committed' employee. They separate carers, from non-carers, and women from men. In some cases they create assumptions about *all* women, regardless of individual women's actual caring responsibilities.

It is therefore not surprising to find so many professionals with probable or actual primary responsibility for children, deferring child-bearing until they have some control at work –

control that ensures the flexibility they need. Others are avoiding children entirely:

> I wouldn't have had a child unless I was a partner in the firm because I wouldn't have been in control. I take time off because I am the boss. My partners cover or I have asked to adjourn a case. (lawyer, mother)

Her choice to have a child was only exercised after control over her hours was established. This is a form of choice, certainly, but between narrow, less than optimal possibilities, and means that other professionals who do not gain such control may not have children under these constraints. The inflexibility of work arrangements in many locations shapes decisions about the timing and number of children. A professional woman describes her working life at a large public sector organisation with exemplary family friendly policies, but no possibility of working part-time, avoiding unsocial overtime, or easily taking accumulated time-in-lieu:

> I got a job interview for my present job when I was eight months pregnant and they asked me how I was going to manage. The woman manager who asked, also had a child at home. I told them my husband was going to stay at home. I got the job. It was full-time and there was no negotiation. It was a 40 hour week with a rostered day off every three to four weeks, with a 'reasonable amount of overtime' not defined under the award. You can't say 'sorry I don't want to do any overtime' and there is supposed to be time-off-in-lieu of overtime worked. It is fairly rigid. There is no juggling of staff. It is probably the most inflexible job I have worked in. I have a lot of holiday pay owing, time off in lieu and so on – eight weeks owing – and I have asked if I can take Monday or Friday off and chip away at my leave. But the answer is 'No. That would be making a full-time job into a part-time job and it is an occupational health and safety issue'. So I said 'Okay, fine'. I didn't want to push it. They look upon family requests as if you are not being professional. Then they say, 'If you are not coping let us know and we will put a single

person in the job' – all this from a woman manager who has a small child also! (journalist, mother, city)

This journalist is very aware of the signals that are sent by those who want to put their family first – or even *alongside* their jobs: they are not serious about career, and risk losing their job to others assumed to be free of competitive commitments. As a result she had decided not continue working full-time if she had another child – though she did not plan to have a second:

> I don't plan on having another child. It's too much hard work, but if I did I would resign and go to casual. The shifts are offered and it is much more flexible. You can juggle this as long as when they call you don't say you can't work for family reasons but [say] you are at another venue. You mustn't mention the family. *Then* they will keep calling you back!

Women managers, lawyers, journalists and doctors talk about the incompatibility of their professions with maternity and caring. This incompatibility affects men, also, as their wives look for more help at home. But it particularly affects women's choices to have children, to stay in the profession, and their capacities to influence the reshaping of their professional practices and models:

> The model is too big. The history of these jobs is too big. The history of the job is that it is a *vocation* not a job. It is what you *are*. It's your life. You work all the hours that there are. You live in the hospital. You are perpetually there for everyone but yourself.

> It's very much a male model.

Younger women in the professions are choosing not to have children, or to have only one, or to have them later. Once again, a choice – but within constraints that firmly place the 'male model' at the centre of the choice, around which few options are available.

Ironically the impact of the double day on women and their continuing main responsibility for domestic work and care, means that their voice in professional, workplace and union bodies – to push for change to the established model – is inhibited precisely by their responsibility for care. 'Making it' to the professional pinnacle means making it to live and work the male model. The spectre of inflexible workplaces haunts many work lives, and stands in strong contradiction to the 'family friendly' workplace that has more mythical life than reality.

The male model continues to maintain a hold in all kinds of workplaces – from the factory floor to the professional business. The kinds of cultures and workplace practices confronting women in professional jobs are different from those facing women in lower skilled, operator jobs in factories and call centres, but both face serious limitations. While professionals criticise the demanding nature of the 'vocation', those in non-professional jobs point to rigid working time and leave arrangements. For example, employees working shift work in a factory describe unyielding inflexibility in relation to shift arrangements, changing their shifts and in attending to unexpected or even entirely predictable family events. A high level of unionisation does not appear to result in increased capacity to negotiate around 'set in cement' shift arrangements and rosters for some: as one factory workers and mother put it 'You don't get a say in the shifts you work'.

Secure, quality jobs with flexible, part-time hours

Part-time work is the means by which many Australians *individually* try to reconcile their responsibilities for home and caring. But part-time work means second-class citizenship in many Australian workplaces. It means less training, less communication and promotion, less work continuity, lower earnings, less recognition of skills, and unpaid extra hours of work to 'get the job done'. Many long-term, part-time employees are casual, with very restricted employment rights. This suggests that improved conditions for part-time work, and efforts to improve its integration within workplace structures (for example, by making

it permanent and improving access to promotion and training)
will assist those who both hold jobs and are carers. Jill Rubery
has argued, based on European experience, that without action
to raise labour standards around part-time work 'through the
incorporation of part-time work into the system of regulation' it
threatens standards of full-time work through 'leveling down
rather than leveling up' (1998: 151). A levelling up approach has
been adopted in the Netherlands and Scandinavia. Without such
levelling up, part-time work threatens to remain the Australian
second-rate, mother-track which particularly affects women for
many decades of their paid working lives.

Not every one wants promotion and a career. Some writers
have argued that carers are simply less committed to paid work,
and we should not be surprised at their secondary status. But
these choices are currently made in an extremely constrained
environment in Australia, where part-time work is read as a
signal of 'unreliable': as code for not serious, not promotable, not
trainable. Factory workers, clerical employees, para-professionals
and professionals, for example, must often choose between
decent jobs and desirable time with their children or other
dependants. It is the model of the 'proper worker' that is unrea-
lisable – at least not on the current terms that imply a devotion
to the job that places 'family' off the agenda. The contest for
commitment is perhaps most obvious in the case of the lawyer
partner who lightheartedly describes taking her decision about
becoming pregnant to a meeting of her professional partners.
What would have happened if they had not supported her?
Women with less workplace power must simply accept the terms
on offer: Vera must go part-time to look after her disabled sons
and aged parents, and she deeply resents the move from 'leader'
to 'mother-track'. Her choice is not between having children or
not, but between having the job she wants and meeting the
unpredicted demands of her disabled children and parents. She
fears that she is sidelined for the long-term. Factory workers
must accept the shifts they are allocated, in many instances, and
face rigid time regimes that they must carefully accommodate.

The cost is clearly evident in women's pay relative to men's. It is also recognised by even the most active advocates of part-time work: a human resources manager in one company who enthusiastically promotes part-time work reluctantly concedes that there are long-term costs of working part-time:

> I hope you don't pay a price for taking time out – for going part-time. It makes no difference, has been my belief. Certainly part-timers have different desires in their career. Many part-timers are prepared to put their career on hold. I'm pretty positive about this company and we have created opportunities for part-timers to do equally. All of our policies are equal, but they are not always *applied* equally. In the broader workforce is there is a price for being part-timer? Realistically I'd say it slows you down because you are not there as often … It shouldn't make any difference, but in reality it does.

Many part-time workers are happy to work less than full-time in order to meet other obligations and desires: they are glad to be part-time. But, given the option, many would prefer to have part-time work without degraded conditions of insecurity and marginality – and to have better transition arrangements into and out of part-time/full-time work over the life-cycle.

Why are the choices around career and work so narrow, and the price of working less than full-time, so high in the face of a massive expansion in part-time work in Australia? It is time to separate genuinely casual work from ongoing part-time work, and to find ways to better integrate the thousands of Australians who work, or want, shorter hours.

'Genuinely casual' work forms only a portion of the total number of jobs that are now casually paid. Many employees would prefer predictable permanent part-time work on decent terms. However, they pay the price of precariousness in order to be part-time – and in some cases to avoid guilt when they ask for time off. This is a big price, which is not necessarily a saving for their employers, though it does give them greater numerical control of their workforce, and it may increase their power over employees where they must stay 'on-side' to keep their shifts.

For some employees casual terms give greater control over their hours of work. However, a significant number report the opposite – that they are *on call* not *in control*. Rather than facilitate their caring and household responsibilities, it complicates them with unpredictability and insecurity. There are several steps that can be taken to make shorter hours jobs, a better fit with caring. Action by employers, unions and industrial tribunals will help, along with a change in Australian's overall regulatory treatment of short hours jobs.

Renovating the conditions of part time-work

Part-time work is an important means of labour market transition. The quality of transitionary bridge that it makes, varies, however. Cebrian et al distinguishes three grades of transition: part-time jobs can be *integrative* (integrating part-timers into the labour market), *maintenance* (maintaining participation at work) or *exclusionary* (leaving workers marginalised) (2000). In Australia, part-time work is an important means by which many women *maintain* their labour market participation but through a marginalised vehicle. Some women – both professional and lesser skilled – are reluctantly conscripted into poor quality part-time work with downward occupational mobility its consequence. A shift towards *integrated* part-time work, with conditions that both *formally and substantively* match those of full-time employees, is an important goal in the face of the work-life collision.

On the employer side, some changes with minimal cost make very important differences. Where carers have some flexibility in their hours, days, shifts and emergency leave, their working lives are immeasurably easier. The capacity to accumulate some time-in-lieu and use it flexibility to meet predictable or unpredictable family needs, is seen as very significant by those with dependants. In many cases the barriers to more employee-flexible arrangements appear more a matter of culture than cost. Workplaces that are in many respects similar, have very different arrangements with respect to flexibility and part-time work. And cultures vary not only between workplaces, but also between supervisors, suggesting that better training and policies make a difference within single organisations.

Given that so many Australians elect to meet their family needs by working part-time, employers can improve the conditions of part-time work, minimise turnover and retain skills. Coles Supermarkets, for example, set a goal of shifting from 40 per cent permanent employers in the mid-1990s, to 80 per cent in 2000, in pursuit of financial benefits from lower training costs and retention of skilled and informed workers. The full integration of part-time employees into internal labour markets is vital and requires change to the subtle procedures by which promotion, training, travel, information and other work benefits are allocated. A vital step in this, is a shift from casual to permanent jobs, where employment is not genuinely short-term and intermittent. The option for employees to convert from casual to permanent employment is necessary. Many employees also seek the opportunity to become part-time for agreed periods, with the right to negotiate a return to full-time work. All of these changes are relatively cheap and go a considerable distance in mediating the collision between work and household. But they depend upon benevolent and pro-active employers and supervisors. Many of these are men whose priorities and experience are otherwise. Models of 'best practice' are important beacons, but they will not be enough to make a difference to the working lives of most employees. The pace of change stimulated by recognition of 'best practice' has been glacial, after almost two decades of experience. To reach more workplaces we have to look to some regulatory stimulus.

Employment conditions in Australia are now set through individual employee contracts, collective agreements and awards that set minimal standards. Women and part-time employees are much more dependent upon awards than men or full-time employees, so that carers will be especially affected by changes in the award system (ABS Cat No 4102.0). Awards specify a (now limited) range of wages and conditions on an industry or occupational basis, and have traditionally been both friend and enemy of part-time workers. Awards have not stood in the way of a proliferation of part-time employment types over recent decades, allowing women to combine paid work with care. However, the strategies adopted in relation to casual work have affected its quality. The general response to the prospect of insecure, short-time employment has been to place a price on it (through award casual leave loadings) and thus a disincentive to its use, and in some cases numerical or proportional limits on it. With deregulation of the labour market and weaker enforcement, the later are generally uncommon, and the price disincentive of the loading has been eroded. Since 2000, clerical and manufacturing unions, have sought to restrict casual employment to genuinely casual work (that is short-term and/or unpredictable), to increase the loading to compensate casual workers for conditions they forego, and to permit them to convert to permanent work either after certain periods or when their work is predictable and ongoing.

Some important gains have been won. In 2000, clerks in the South Australian private sector won rights to choose to become permanent after a year of ongoing and regular employment. The Australian Manufacturing Workers Union won an increase in the casual loading in the federal metal industry award (to 25 per cent), rights to convert from casual to permanent work after six months regular systematic employment, and minimum shifts of four hours for full-timers and three for part-timers. The Queensland Council of Unions has won an increase in the casual loading in State awards (from 19 to 23 per cent).

Industrial relations tribunals have refused, however, to limit employers' use of casuals to short-term and emergency situations and backed away from union claims to limit by definition employer use of casuals to arrangements where employees are genuinely short-term and *ad hoc*. All of the measures won by unions have been vigorously resisted.

In the context of a proliferation of insecure part-time jobs, a six-pronged regulatory approach is now necessary: first, industrial regulation should distinguish between genuinely casual and permanent part-time work. Second, there should be trigger points (for example, more than six months' employment) that allow employees to choose permanent over casual employment. Third, the price disincentive for the employment of casuals should be increased to more accurately reflect the true costs of being casual and discourage inappropriate growth: loadings should be significantly increased. Fourth, enforcement machinery – which has traditionally relied upon unions (much diminished as union density has fallen) and industrial relations inspectorates, must be strengthened. Fifth, the 'wedge' conditions which make casual part-time employment more attractive to employers than permanent part-time jobs (like their weaker access to unfair dismissal remedies and redundancy compensation) need review so that non-price incentives in favour of casuals are reduced. Finally, workers needs better rights to shift between full-time and part-time jobs without having to break their labour market attachment and change jobs or workplaces or careers.

The institutional and cultural distain for part-time work needs to be shifted through public commitment to improve the conditions of short-hours work and increase its integration into existing internal and external labour markets. The European Commission has attempted this through its Directive on part-time work, concluded between private and public employer and union associations in 1997 (Council Directive 97/81/EC of 20 January 1998). This committed European member states to remove discrimination against part-timers and improve the quality of part-time work, and to facilitate the development of part-time work on a voluntary basis.

This Directive has been adopted with varying effects. Along with the ILO Convention on part-time work it is a 'weak equalising' approach to part-time work, rather than a more assertive 'promotional/positive action' approach which deals with the systemic problems of existing part-time work like its precariousness, low pay, or lack of promotional opportunities and training (Murray 2001). In the UK, for example, the eventual adoption of regulations has had relatively little effect, some argue, contributing little to the removal of substantive inequalities facing part-time employees (Busby 2001).

In reviewing action to improve the status of part-time work, it is useful to distinguish between *formal* and *substantive* action. Formal equality can be established, at a minimal level through laws (like those that came into effect in the UK in July 2000) that directly outlaw different rates of pay for these different categories of workers. However, this falls well short of substantive equality in many ways – for example if part-time workers are effectively excluded from accumulating training or experience that is critical to promotion, they are indirectly prevented from gaining promotion, and from substantive equality (Busby, 2001).

State and federal governments in Australia could adopt commitments and standards and publicly commend them through education programs to Australian workplaces. A strong national joint commitment of employer and union associations and governments would assist this, backed by regulatory change and clear, specific recommendations. But any such 'weakly equalising' exhortative action needs to be backed by regulatory award and/or legislative change that ensures the separation of short-term jobs from part-time work, *per se*, and creates rights to substantive equal treatment.

Professional associations are part of the machinery that creates the cultures and standards of practice and model workers. They have an important role to play, either replicating the terms under which current workers served their vocational apprenticeships (like long and unsafe hours as interns or new accountants and lawyers) or renovating these so that the changing population of new professionals can better accommodate their changing responsibilities outside their jobs. In many organisations, there must be more voice for carers and women to crack the male model.

Changes in the regulation of part-time work will not easily be agreed to, either by employers or conservative industrial relations advocates and ministers; they have been vigorously resisted at the international level (Murray 1998). Australia's trade unions – historically dominated by men and full-timers – have contributed to the second-rate status of part-time work and its casual nature. They are a vital part of its renovation. Many unions have long since moved on from a prohibition of part-time work (on the grounds that it sold out 'proper' jobs and undermined bread-winners), and have worked to improve the conditions and possibilities for both casual and permanent part-time work.

All of these organisations have an important role to play in securing a crucial renovation to meet the Work/Life Collision through improved terms of part-time work.

CHAPTER 8

Caring for those who depend on us

When Margaret Thatcher famously declared there is no such thing as society, she had forgotten about her childhood and she had not thought much about her old age. All of us depend on each other for some kind of basic care at some points in our lives. Human beings take decades to become fully independent and our increasing average life span means than many of us will experience years when some care from others will affect the quality of our old age. Much of this is reciprocal inter-household and within-family care. It is given out of love and/or blood connection – to friends, children, parents, neighbours. These reciprocal or one-way sinews of care are a vital part of our civilisation. Many of us give them priority – especially the care of young children, a disabled child or an aged parent – over many other things including our standard of living, the accumulation of money, paid work and ourselves. They both reward and demand. In 1998, a quarter of primary carers for people with a disability or older people said that they have lost touch with existing friends and many suffer sleep loss and depression; however, a third said they have been brought closer to the person they are caring for (ABS Cat No 4436.0).

Like other forms of work, care is highly gendered – both in the non-market and market spheres. Three quarters of most forms of unpaid care is done by women. They do most of the child care: in 1997, women spent 166 minutes a day, on average, caring for children compared to 68 minutes by men (ABS Cat No 4153.0). In 1998, women made up 70 per cent of the unpaid primary carers of the disabled and the aged (ABS Cat No 4436.0, 1998: 16). In the market sphere, most forms of care work are feminised, and have poor terms and conditions compared to similar male-dominated jobs. How else can we explain the fact that those who care for cars in car parks (mainly men) are often paid more than those who care for children in child care facilities (mainly women)?

Under the current Work/Care regime, the intersection between non-market care and paid work is *sore*. The two collide. In many places the articulation of the two kinds of work is primitive and awkward. Many carers contort themselves around jobs and workplaces – or give up on jobs. Forty per cent of primary carers for people with a disability or older people who are unemployed or not in the labour force would like to work but many have given up looking for suitable jobs (ABS Cat No 4436.0).

In February 2003, 38 per cent of the adult, non-student Australian labour force had dependants (ABS Cat No 6203.0). Over the life cycle a larger proportion of workers do so. These dependants include young children, those with a disability, or infirm relatives. This means that the combination of paid work and care of others is far from a marginal concern: it affects about four out of ten workers at any moment in time, and *most* of us over our lives. There are a number of points at which the collisions of care and paid work particularly hit worker/carers. Some of these affect health, self-care, emotional balance and, as we have seen, relationships and intimacy. Without doubt the issue of sick children or other dependants is a major point of pressure for households and especially women. It throws carers into crisis – repetitively. The concern carers feel about 'being there' is particularly acute around this issue. Feelings of being a little out of control, being stretched or torn, and at times chaotic, arise around unexpected events like sick children or sick aged parents. These problems affects a majority of working carers: the 2001 HILDA survey shows that more than 60 percent of those with children under five years who used or thought about using child care in the previous 12 months had some or significant difficulties finding care for sick children (HILDA 2001). Workplaces can facilitate or impede the intersection of jobs and care.

A second major issue for carers is the organisation of child care. Issues of access, cost, quality and hours preoccupy parents. Once again the HILDA survey confirms that this is widespread with over 70 per cent of those households with children under five years that used or thought about using child care in the previous 12 months having some or significant difficulties with the cost of child care and a similar proportion having some or significant difficulties with getting care for the hours needed (HILDA 2001). Costs of child care vary with the level of rebate based on household income, and by state: fees range from an average of $202 in the ACT to $170 in the Northern Territory (Jackman, *The Australian*, 14 February 2003: 4). The poor fit of such care to the hours of work, school and pre-school often means complex juggling – and many hours and kilometres of travel each week.

More families are becoming affected by these issues: whereas in 1984, 38 per cent of children used formal or informal child care, this rose to 52 per cent in 1990 and has remained at about this level since. The proportion of children in formal child care doubled from 12 to 24 per cent between 1984 and 1999, and the increase was greatest among those under two years (where it rose from 8 to 22 per cent) (ABS Cat No 4102.0). Population ageing makes the care of the elderly and infirm a parallel concern to an increasing number of households. In 1998, 158,200 employees between 15 and 64 years of age were primary carers for people with a disability or older people. Many more are secondary carers, so that 13 per cent of the total workforce in 1998 had caring responsibilities for someone with a disability or an older person (ABS Cat No 4436.0).

How should we look after those who depend on us for their care and quality of life? Various countries adopt different approaches to this issue. In Nordic countries, for example, quality care for young children is seen as a mainstream state responsibility, essential to underpin the workforce participation of women. At the other end of the spectrum, in the United States, the care of children is left to private solutions, with a low level of state support and very variable – and often poor – standards of care. Australia lies somewhere in the middle, with growth in the private provision of care over recent decades, and the costs shared between government and parents – and to a much lesser extent – some employers.

In this chapter we examine the dilemmas around caring for dependants, particularly children, first in relation to sick children, then child care. Despite the beacons of good practice – where working-carers have flexibility to suit their needs – many workers have trouble fitting care of their dependants around their jobs. Inflexible jobs shape care, like water flowing around rocks. And carers must often find better shaped rocks (by changing jobs or giving them up), to fit their care. The collision between work and life is nowhere more obvious than in the juggle of care to accommodate paid work, and the impact on workers, their families and their dependants is significant and costly.

Every worker/carer's nightmare: unpredicted sickness and accidents

Most workers with dependants identify the times when their dependants are sick as the moments when they feel the greatest collision of caring and work. This is often the first work/care issue mentioned, one that people feel strongly – whether living in the city or country, or high-paid or low-paid or in a white or blue collar job:

> If they are sick … Well, it's a huge drama and it's come to a head this week. When one of my kids is sick I can't go to work and someone has to cancel all my patients. He had conjunctivitis, so I went to work and took him with me – but it was not well received. And I've been pushed, so that now I won't come in when they are sick. (physiotherapist, mother of two, country town)

> Mine CAN'T be sick! (working mother of two)

A supervisor in a call-centre in the city describes similar dilemmas:

> The major crisis is when the kids are sick. You can't be in two places at once. My mother is minding mine at the moment! (supervisor, mother of two)

Some parents place younger children in the care of older ones while they work, which causes stress for parents and children, and compromises children's safety:

> More of a worry is when the kids ring up and say he's fallen down and hit his head. That's simply because they are at home unattended. Living a distance away and feeling the pressure. And it's a pressure on the kids as well. They are growing up too quick on that side of things too. (mother of four children under ten years).

Even years afterwards women wonder about their past decisions and the contest between commitment to their kids, and to their jobs. Did they do the right thing in going to work with sick children?

> Well, I look back now and what I went through. I used to try to get to work. And I wish I hadn't gone to work when the kids were sick . The bottom line is that you don't get any thanks for it. And the kids miss out. (women, call-centre, city)

Many feel guilt and anguish over their choices, and their children are aware of their parent's difficulty in coping with their sickness. They adapt around their parents. Louis takes his sick day when he knows his mother can 'fit him in':

> Last week Louis knew I had a day off and would be at home. He came in to me and he said 'I've been sick all week, and the teacher said to me, "Louis you should go home". And I said "But I can't. There's no-one to look after me. And I have a sore throat and a cough, and I think I should stay home!"' I said 'I think you should too!'. (country woman, worker)

Many employees are uncertain about their access to paid leave to look after family members and are unsure about whether they can use their own sick leave to look after sick children. Most employees make use of their own sick leave or annual leave to care for their unwell children (Morehead et al 1997). However, women – who do most of this care – are much more likely to take unpaid leave than men (43 per cent would usually do this, compared to 30 per cent of men). Access to paid family leave is very low in many industries where women's employment is high, including health and community services, retail trade and accommodation, cafes and restaurants (Morehead et al 1997: 447).

Many have used all their sick leave for this purpose: 'I always use my sick leave to look after her. If *I'm* a little bit sick I never take a sickie, because I might need it for her.' (mother, factory worker). In 1995, only 15 per cent of employees used paid family leave to care for their sick family members, while 36 per cent used leave without pay (Morehead et al 1997). Many employees thus go to work sick themselves, or make ad hoc arrangements – sometimes unsafe – for the care of their sick children. The lucky ones are grateful for the support of their employers, as these factory workers discuss:

> My daughter is a chronic asthmatic and when she is really, really sick if I can't find someone to look after her, and I can't leave her in the car, I have to let my son (14 years) stay home to look after her. He uses the nebuliser and all that so my son knows ... And I tell her if something is going wrong, just ring the factory and ask to speak to mum or dad and we'll come straight home. Because we don't have anyone to back us up. For three years now, he's been looking after her.

> I've been really lucky. Both of mine have not been on death's door, really sick. My son has juvenile arthritis. I have to take him to the specialist. They have been really good here. And they've let me take an hour or two off but we try and tee them up on [the days that I finish early] so that I don't have to take time off. Otherwise they look after themselves unless they are on death's door ... They are teenagers.

Like so many workers, this last mother works hard to juggle the demands of her children to minimise their impact on her employer. She is very grateful for the factory manager's recognition of her family's needs. Unless her teenagers are on 'death's door', they are on their own. Chronic conditions are not uncommon among Australia's children: in 1995, 16 per cent of Australian children had asthma as a recent or long-term condition, and 46 per cent reported a long-term medical condition (ABS 4119.0). Chronic illnesses pose particular problems for working parents – particularly in households that must often meet higher health costs and thus are very dependent upon two incomes. With the growing incidence of some forms of chronic illness, serious questions arise about the welfare of these children and their stressed parents and extended family. Many are very reliant upon supportive grandparents or friends:

> When my daughter was little, she was asthmatic. I've had very supportive parents. I had friends who didn't. They helped when she needed to have the nebuliser. When you think that one in four kids is asthmatic – and a lot of schools now will not administer medication. I'm concerned about kids that have asthma or diabetes, what happens to them?

Where they are available, grandparents and extended families are vitally important in these moments of crisis and some 'save up' their own parents for emergencies. But many want to be there themselves:

> My mother doesn't want to be involved, as she has had seven kids and spent over 40 years bringing them up. But over and above that, I want to be there when my daughter is sick, no one else. If I have to choose between the boss and my child, I choose my child. I take the time to get her well. (team supervisor, call centre)

Such 'choices' about how to deal with emergencies – that are frequent – create dilemmas and stress, with many wanting to put their children first. A contest for commitment is underway, and sometimes workers make arrangements that are less that ideal.

As a mother of two children, 11 and 13, in a senior supervisory position put it:

> It is difficult to just *get* there when you are called to a sick child. I am teaching them more responsibility. I sign them out (of school), take them home, and depending on how sick they are, I stay or go back to work.

Women without nearby extended family find emergency arrangements much more difficult, and this causes those contemplating children, and dislocated from their family, to pause:

> That half puts me off even starting a family. I have no family here. My mum works full-time and she's in Adelaide. Where would I leave my child? (married country woman, no children)

Some grandmothers surrender their own jobs or studies to help their children:

> My partner and I actually looked after my granddaughter when she was four and five, and I was at uni studying and working part-time. There was no support, no help if you're doing this as a grandparent. In the end I had to give up – I gave up Uni in my honours year because it was just too hard. (worker and student, grandmother, city)

While it might be expected that families on farms have more household options with respect to care, this is not always the case and sometimes carries safety hazards for children who spend the day around distracted fathers and moving machinery.

Issues around caring are not confined to young children: many women talk of the caring responsibilities they have for aging parents and grown up children with disabilities:

> We are faced now with sickness in my parents. So their role in helping look after the kids is being restricted and we are having to look at our options. One thing that is missing is a nurse in the child care industry, so that if you have to go to work, you can call upon a nurse or someone specialising in taking care of sick children. You are not allowed to take them to child care because of infection, and sure you'd like to be there but if you *can't* be

there and you are risking reputations, jobs, livelihoods, it would be good to have another option. (worker, mother of two, city)

School holidays and pupil free days were also points of pressure, with working mothers and fathers juggling their holidays and often taking them separately in order to cover school breaks.

Employees look for sympathetic responses from their employers and supervisors. They do not expect their needs always to be met, but comment that flexibility is often available on an arbitrary basis, or refused without good reason. One employee described a supervisor's lack of sympathy in one such situation:

> We had a lady, Mary, who had taken a week off when her husband had to elect to turn off his life support and they said 'you can have your two days bereavement' and she got to negotiate a few extra days. And she broke down about six months later. And they said 'you can't have any more time off – this bloke's on holidays'. That wasn't acceptable for her. They knew that she was severely depressed. She said 'I dragged myself to come to work [after he died]'. Her health suffered. She really hates them for what she did to her. And then her boss's father died, and everything changed! But it was so hard for her. (factory employee, woman)

Mary's story illustrates the importance of experience in changing responses to employee needs: when Mary's boss has his own bereavement, he becomes flexible. Perhaps in his next workplace crisis, he will be more understanding. As things stand, many carers try to find workplaces that they can fit around their lives.

Inflexibility imposes a high price on carers, making a strong case for more carer's leave and more flexible access to all forms of leave (including both paid and unpaid) to deal with family crisis. While those in higher paid, managerial or more senior positions might have more latitude to make informal, individual arrangements for themselves or their juniors, many at the bottom of workplace hierarchies lack that scope. While some carers 'choose' to stay at the bottom or avoid promotion because they think that will allow them to meet their family's needs, ironically it may keep them from positions where more latitude exists to do things more flexibly.

Child care: 'You have to be 110% happy'

One of the major care challenges and dilemmas identified by workers is child care: its quality, availability, hours and cost. The main forms of care are outside school hours care, long day care in centres (three quarters in private, for-profit centres), family day care (care provided by carers in their own homes) and – on a much smaller scale – employer-based and occasional care. The Federal Government has financially supported child care since 1972, and in 1999/2000, 443,400 formal child care places were offered in Australia (McIntosh et al 2002). Federal and State governments have contributed to the costs of constructing new facilities, while recurrent funding has generally remained a federal responsibility. The formal sector is subject to quality controls and standards of staffing and service provision. From 1990, federal fee-relief for families was extended by the Labor Government to those using private, for-profit care; it was previously only available to those using non-profit centres. From this point, the provision of care for those less than five years old entered the market in a concerted way, and it is now big business. ABC Learning Centres, Australia's largest child care company, listed on the stock exchange at $2 a share in May 2001 and was valued at $14 a share in October 2002. It doubled its profit to $6.9 million in 2001/02. Child Care Centres Australia, a new market entrant, forecast a net profit of $1.95 million on revenue of just under $15 million in the nine months to the end of 2002/03 (Reuters, 4 October 2002).

Under the Howard Government, further changes have been introduced so that families now receive a retitled Child Care Benefit to help reduce the costs of care, although less than half of those eligible claim their rebate (ABS 4402.0). Fee-relief is dependent upon family income (based on the income of both earners creating a disincentive for second earners (McDonald 2002)) and it is payable for up to 50 hours of approved care a week for each child. Operational subsidies to community-based centres have been eliminated, the level of fee-relief has been reduced for many, and it has been more tightly targeted (McIntosh et al 2002). Nonetheless, total federal support has grown from $546 million in 1992/93,to about $1.35 billion in 2000/01 (over $1 billion of it for fee-relief), and the States and Territories spent about $600 million in 2000/01. Child care now forms a sizeable slice of total expenditure on Australian families (McIntosh et al 2002).

Around half of children less than 12 years old use some form of care. The most commonly used arrangement is informal care, outside the government-funded sector, which 37 per cent of children use. Over half of this is provided by grandparents (57 per cent), 19 per cent by other relatives and 6 per cent by siblings. Unrelated people provided the remaining 25 per cent (ABS Cat No 4402.0).

Table 8.1 Percentage of Children in Child Care Arrangements, Australia, 1999

Types of care	Australia (%)
Formal Care	
Before and after school care	4.9
Long day care	7.7
Occasional care	1.4
Pre-school	7.4
Other formal care	0.9
Total children using formal care	**23.5**
Informal care	
Grandparents	21.2
Brother/sisters	2.4
Other relatives	7.1
Other person	9.4
Total children using informal care	**37.2**
Total children using formal or informal care	**61.2**

Source: ABS Cat No 4402.0, 1988: 11
Note: Some children use both formal and informal care.

About a quarter of children use some type of formal care, and this has been increasing steadily over the past decade. Most formal care before pre-school age is centre-based, with about 8 per cent of children in long day centre-based care and 2 or 3 per cent in family day care.

Middle income families are more likely to make use of formal centre-based care, though patterns of use depend on the availability of care. A recent report from the Department of Family and Community Services points out that about 70 per cent of all government child care payments go to households earning less than $50,000 a year (Jackman, *The Australian*, 14 February 2003: 4). This undermines the argument that it is the wealthy who benefit from public assistance for child care.

Formal care varies widely by age: only nine per cent of children under one year were in formal care in 1999; compared to almost three quarters (73 per cent) of those aged four, when many are in child care centres or pre-school. About half the parents using formal care do so because of work-related reasons, and 45 per cent of parents using informal care also do so for work-related reasons (ABS Cat No 4402.0). Many parents are very reliant upon their own parents for care, often in an ongoing way in many cases or occasionally in the event of sick children. It is hard to exaggerate the importance of many grandparents in assisting working parents.

In 1999, 242,000 children were in long day care. Many parents see this care as more educationally and resource rich than other options, providing valuable social skills: 'she will achieve so much more than some other kids'. They feel it is both reliable and accountable, and thus safe. They appreciate the visibility of their children and their carers. The fact that centres provided a place 'where you would know what was happening' was an important issue for many women in choosing centre-based care over family day care:

> I wanted a community-based centre that had eyes and ears and wasn't based in somebody's home where you didn't know what was going on. It was run by parents and there were always

enough passionate people whose hearts were in the right places. (full-time student, volunteer, mother)

While many express positive feelings about child care, and feel it offers something that they couldn't always get at home, there were still regrets, often expressed in relation to missing such milestones as the first steps or words:

> I still have days when I feel so much guilt and don't want to take her there. I really don't have any choice as we don't have any relatives here but I still feel really guilty. (casual worker, mother)

Women also feel that the quality of care in centres has been undermined by recent cuts in government funding. This led some women with higher incomes to feel ambivalent about centres and sometimes make use of nannies. Both Indigenous women and women from a non-English speaking background identified the absence of culturally appropriate care as a major concern, and in the case of Indigenous women, it was seen as a reason for the use of grannies and family care rather than mainstream centres:

> Rather than having our children going into mainstream, the grannies have to do it now. They don't want to lose their kids. So that is an added responsibility for grandmothers of Indigenous people. (Indigenous working mother, city)

Family day care was used by 87,100 children in 1999 (ABS Cat No 4402.0). Quality, reliable family day care is valued for its affordability and the fact that a specific carer exists. However, some are concerned about safety, and careful about their selection of carer:

> I used family day care for six months but found out that the woman used the neighbour to care for the child while she went out. Also my son was not allowed to play with the carer's children's toy and was put outside in the rain for three hours. I stopped using her and reported it. (woman in factory)

202 The Work/Life Collision

For most parents, informal care (including friends, grandparents and other family like older children) is used to cope with emergencies or to top up other care arrangements or as the main care. However, using friends or family to look after children before or after school is not without its dilemmas. Women not in paid work who are often asked to have an extra child, feel 'put upon'.

With 74,000 children under 12 in the care of their brothers and sisters, women are concerned about placing responsibility on older siblings to care for younger members of the family but many feel that they lack choices; as one put it 'I hated it when my older kids had to pick up my younger kids but I couldn't do anything else'.

Shiftwork as child care

In a range of occupations and workplaces including factories, offices, call centres and hospitals, workers choose to work at different times to their partners to avoid placing their children in child care. This strategy is used both because of the cost of child care and because it enables them to 'be there' for their child. For some this form of 'tag team' care was costly in terms of disturbed or inadequate sleep, and for intimate relationships:

> Doing different shifts, it is a big sacrifice. I do it for the kids because of child care – it can be expensive and you don't have the hassle of finding someone you trust. (factory worker, mother)

> I don't use child care – I work earlies so my husband gets the children to school and I race home to get them after school. (nurse, city)

One of the advantages of this strategy is that parents are available to care for sick children and for school holidays. But the choice was not without costs: 'the kids miss out on me ... There is always someone with them because my husband is home in the evening but they don't get me for five hours at night'. The 'alternative shifts' strategy sometimes leaves gaps where children are alone and at risk:

My daughter had to sit in the car in the factory car park for an hour waiting for my husband to finish his shift [He too works at the factory]. (factory worker)

There was also a cost to health and relationships as they passed each other 'like ships in the night':

We worked opposite shifts to look after kids, working 11 pm – 7 am then looking after the baby all day. I got three or four hours sleep. I looked like a ghost. (factory worker, mother)

Parents identify gaps in child care that create real stress for them and leave them juggling work and care and relying on informal care to fill the gaps. Many travel long distances to find solutions, placing more pressure on children and tired parents. School holidays are also seen as a time of great difficulty and stress for many:

School holidays are a problem – organising people to look after children. I feel guilt about where they are, are they happy, have you asked that person too often? It would be great not to have to worry about school holidays. (nurse, city)

The lack of fit between the hours of school, and the usual hours of work greatly complicates the lives of working parents. In many locations, out of school hours care is simply unavailable. In other cases, it sits out on the periphery of school in terms of its geography, management, facilities and funding. In some cases parents have fought hard to establish the service, and then for good facilities and staffing. The different funding and management systems of school, and out of school hours care, create complicated juggling. Others raise the issue of cost. This cost leads some parents to use older children to care for younger ones, or to leave children at home without care.

The provision of work-based child care affects workplace choices. Women at a call centre partly chose their workplace for its worksite child care. While most are not using it they feel it demonstrates a commitment to family. Women in both factories and hospitals cannot understand why there is no work-based child care at their large worksites. They can see that this would cut travelling time. The chance to be close to where children are cared for would greatly relieve the stress of juggling care and work.

The cost of child care is a major issue for many: 'a big bill every week'. For some it contributes to a decision not to return to the workforce: 'Going to work is not worth it with child care' as one put it. The inflexibility of formal child care, and the requirement that it be paid for even when a place is not used on a given day, contribute to concerns about cost: 'Child care could be more flexible – you have to pay even when you aren't using it'. Parents also recognise that quality child care is expensive to run:

> It is harder to maintain quality and price due to staffing costs. Parents don't want relief staff they want continuity through permanent staff. (management committee member, child care centre, mother, part-time worker)

There is, however, a view that government should play a greater role in ensuring the provision of affordable quality care. Those with higher incomes have greater child care choices and many choose more expensive, centre-based care that they believe to be more educationally rich and open to scrutiny. This pattern of income-based choice, suggests a hierarchical early childhood system, with wealthier households able to choose better quality, safer care with assured standards and educational programs. Lower income households are more likely to choose cheaper or informal care and to trade-off safety for affordability. This creates and reinforces disadvantage for children in lower-income households. That such a multi-tiered system exists in the early years – those most critical to children's development – must be a serious concern in terms of patterns of long-term inequality.

Being torn: Juggling, not balancing

Women in all kinds of positions talked about juggling care around work. As one senior team leader put it:

It's a matter of priority and we constantly have conversations about our involvement with the kids. My son is the most important thing in my life, but often work takes over and I'm still expected to do it all, so it's about juggling it all, and not feeling guilty.

This causes real stress, especially for sole parents who must manage the juggle alone. As the following exchange between supervisors and team leaders shows, this adds more pressure and complication especially for women in contrast to the men they work alongside:

If I don't leave dead on time at 4.45 pm and pick my daughter up, I get nervous. Then something else happens [at work] and then I am on the phone to find out who else can pick up by daughter, while I am working out a crisis.

Our male counterparts don't have to do this. Or pick up the kids and then cook dinner. Anyway they are so single minded – one thing at a time! – that they couldn't do it anyway. It's a boy-o thing. While the expectations for the woman is that you have to be good at everything!

Yes. We are many things to many people. I am a team leader, a mother, a wife, a sister, and people unload to you and you just can't walk away. If I do something for someone, someone else is going to miss out. There is nothing left for me!

We are constantly tired.

Better care for those who depend on us

At present caring responsibilities remain in the main with women, and most are done in the private sphere of the home, family and extended family. Like an invisible iceberg, around three quarters of care work is done outside the market and is hidden from public view. A great deal of informal care is undertaken by means of familial and neighbourhood reciprocity. These care reciprocities both arise from, and constitute, community. They are invaluable to society and its reproduction. But they often *conflict* with paid work and are a central component of the gendered inequities of both market and non-market work. The inadequacy of our current Work/Care regime, and the clash between the two, provide a strong argument for change – in workplaces, in industrial regulation, and government supports for care.

Employers and supervisors make a very important difference to the nature of the collision between care and work. Those who ensure the negotiated flexibility of hours, start and finish time, days of work, shifts, and flexibility in the face of family emergencies – with a real voice for employees – reap high rewards in terms of lower stress for employees, higher commitment, lower turnover, and less lost investment in human capital. Ensuring this requires action both at the regulatory and policy levels, but also in the attitudes and actions of supervisors. Great diversity of outcomes is obvious in single workplaces, depending upon local cultures and individuals, so that attention to the training and capacities of supervisors is essential. Many of these changes are not costly; they are significant departures from established workplace cultures and practices, however, and it is these that require attention.

Australia's workplaces are located within a regime of legal arrangements that specify leave. Many industrial awards now provide for the limited use of employees' own sick leave to deal with family emergencies. However, many workers do not understand this right or do not yet have access to it.

What is more, existing provisions are insufficient to many needs, and result in employees saving their own leave for the family and coming to work sick. An education program around existing rights would help, but access to more paid leave is also essential.

It is vital that the regulatory regime around work allows the normal events of family and household life to occur alongside normal patterns of paid work. Provision of family leave in addition to, and quarantined from, existing employee sick leave would help recognise the sea-change that has occurred in the Australian workplaces as more parents and carers enter it.

A universal system of integrated care and education

Child care in Australia has evolved rapidly since 1972. It has overtaken the pre-existing preschool system which catered to children three or four years old, and now sits awkwardly alongside it. Our evolving system is increasingly for-profit, less based in the community and public sector, and offers very different outcomes depending upon income and proximity of services. Those with more money can buy better early childhood care and pre-school education, embedding social disadvantage/ advantage in a new, pre-school hierarchy of care. The cost of care, and its mismatch with paid work, creates stress for parents and children, creating strong arguments for a general overhaul.

Peter McDonald has pointed out that the largest share of non-parental care for Australian children is provided by schools. However, care of young children has been a casualty of the Federal/State division of responsibility between child care/ schooling (including preschool), creating 'care territory' and 'education territory'. The defence of these territories 'has been the main obstacle to the development of early child education and care policy in Australia' (2002: 1).

Preschool was largely established as a means of education for children three or – more often – four years old before they entered school. Many parents find it difficult to make use of preschool care where it ends mid-way through the normal working day. Generally, such State-provided care is free, but it has failed to adapt to the growth in paid work among mothers, and so sits awkwardly in relation to working life, so that many pay for family day care or centre-based care to secure continuity of care over the working day, rather than make use of free pre-schools. This poor articulation of preschool with child care serves many parents badly and discriminates against working mothers. It also serves young children badly, given the importance of these early years to child development. This has led McDonald to argue for the provision of universal fee-free early childhood education for all three and four year olds for 20 hours a week (2002, 2001b). The key issue for carers, however, is the articulation of this care/education with other forms of care where it is needed, and with the work patterns of parents. A national system of free pre-school education for all three and four year olds, which recognises and responds to (but does not discriminate on the basis of) the work status of their carers, will greatly increase the welfare of children, parents and employers. It is long over due and its universal provision would meet many of the care, cost, access and safety concerns of parents. Articulation of such care/education with care for younger children under three years would reduce the disruption and resettling that children and parents experience with early childhood institutional or carer change.

Given that many women spend extended periods at home with young or dependent family members, a fair, flexible support system for those who undertake such care is also vital. One approach is to pay carers while they are at home. European experience with payments to home carers raises some important issues. It is important that carers are not locked into dependency or poverty, especially given rising rates of divorce, and that they do not lose access to paid work. It is also important to ensure that public resources are allocated in ways that assist those most in need, as opposed to subsidising the existing choices of the relatively well off. We return to these issues in the following chapters.

The lack of fit between the hours of work and the hours of normal school creates dilemmas for parents, many of whom deal with the issue through part-time work. Perhaps other more radical solutions are possible. While calls for a longer school day and the further institutionalisation of children often meet opposition in the community, perhaps more flexible, innovative solutions are possible, including a four day school week. At the very least, the provision of out-of-school hours care is essential in many locations.

The cost and regulation of child care

Changes to centre-based child care over the past decade have increasingly pulled the provision of care into the private, for-profit market, and marginalised community-based and community-managed non-profit care. Brennan argues that the share of community-based child care will continue to fall to reach 15 per cent of total centre-based provision, weakening their contribution to 'neighbourhood links, the building of support networks, the task of working together in a common enterprise' (Brennan 1999: 97). It will also, she points out, contribute to industry pressure to lower standards of care. Parents feel very strongly about the standards of staffing and care in whatever forms of care they use. They rely upon the surveillance and monitoring of centres by the state along with their own obser-vations, to assure themselves about the safety of their children. Not all children in care are safe at present; but any moves to weaken regulatory standards will cause great anguish to carers. Instead, standards of care and staff/children ratios should be increased in recognition of the concerns expressed by many mothers about changes they are now witnessing as centres deal with a fee/cost squeeze and market instability in the face of highly price-sensitive demand.

The cost of centre-based care is now beyond the pockets of many Australian families. This should not be so. If true choice is to be the motif of our Work/Care regime then the real costs of child care, net of rebates, should not be eroded. Indeed, the reverse is essential: over time the true net cost to carers must fall. Social policy analysts have often argued against the tax-deductibility of child care, given that this confers a much greater benefit on higher income families. However, there is a basic inequity in the right to claim work-related food and clothing expenses, but not expenses like work-related child care. This treatment indirectly discriminates against women.

The terms and conditions of child care workers in the paid formal sphere also deserve attention, and unions have acted on these issues over many years. The situation of family day care workers is especially poor, with their status as employees or independent contractors unclear in many locations, and their low hourly return remarkable: in 1999 most family day carers earned $13,000-$15,000 per year and could only reach $20,000 by working long hours and having the maximum allowable children in their care (Brennan, 1999: 91). As a result, many family day care workers work very long days. The pay of child care workers generally is very low relative to similarly skilled workers in other occupations. It presents a pressing case for work-value increases.

Finally, there is the issue of getting appropriate care to those who need it. Many pockets of Australia lack enough places in care for children under two, and private sector centres have proved themselves much less inclined to provide this form of care, relative to less labour intensive and more profitable care for children two to five years old: Brennan estimates that only 10 per cent of places in private centres are for children under two years compared to 16 per cent in community-based centres and 21 per cent of those in family day care (1999: 91). Further, parents in the country often find child care difficult to secure. This might be addressed by better rewards for family day care workers, and there are also arguments for seasonally-based services that meet predictable seasonal needs, and for flexible or mobile services that assist parents of sick children.

The small number of places in Australia that are provided through employer-based services should be redressed. Many carers would like to see care closer to, or in, their workplaces and wonder why this is not possible. Greater support for employer initiative on this front, in cooperation with local communities, would be very beneficial for many. Finally, parents from non-English speaking and Indigenous communities see great value in services that are attentive to their cultural backgrounds.

Given the costs, patchy availability, and poor articulation between forms of public and private care, Australia's child care provision is a very long way from a universal, low cost, high quality system. Such a system is essential if all those parents and carers who undertake paid work are to truly have 'choice'.

Current arrangements depend upon a great deal of informal care – ranging from the voluntary, loving care of extended family through to conscripted grandparents, and children who are simply uncared for as their anxious parents race between shifts or cross their fingers and used the telephone from work to 'check on the kids'. An essential component of an improved work/life regime is a better national approach to the care of those who depend on us – including young children, the infirm, the disabled and the aged – and it requires better institutional care arrangements along with better arrangements in workplaces. It also requires more support for those who spend extended periods at home caring, as we discuss in the next chapter.

CHAPTER 9

Combining work and life:
The role of leave

For the century to the 1970s, Australia was at once an international pioneer of working time and paid leave advances, *and* an
international delinquent. It led the world on the eight-hour day
in the mid-1800s and pioneered long service leave; however, two
thirds of Australian women still await paid maternity leave, more
than 80 years after the ILO adopted its first maternity leave
convention. The causes of this uneven development lie in Australia's Work/Care regime and its gender system with the male
bread-winner at the centre of the paid workforce and carers at
home – and sometimes paid allowances to be there. The first
government payment to new mothers was introduced in 1912:
five pounds was paid on the birth of a child except where the
mother was 'Asiatic or an Aboriginal of Australia, Papua or the
Pacific islands' (*Maternity Allowance Act* 1912).

A male-dominated employing class, eager to minimise labour
costs, governments willing to subsidise motherhood by means of
allowances to mothers-at-home but opposed to recognition of
them as workers, and a union movement dominated by men and
their preoccupations, all contributed to an industrial regime that
saw a three month break after ten years' work (Long Service
Leave) and annual leave bonuses, as more important than a paid
break for workers who have just had a baby. Surely only those
who have never experienced the physicality of birth, followed by
the combination of caring for a new-born *and* paid work, could
make such strategic choices? These outcomes emerged out of
haphazard historical circumstance where unionists built opportu-
nistically on platforms that existed – like colonial administrators'
access to leave to return to Britain in the case of LSL – rather
than carefully prioritised needs. The historic male-domination of

representative interests, and the Australian gender system, impose a high cost on women even today.

In this chapter we review the current leave arrangements in Australian workplaces. Despite the significant changes underway in the workforce and the shape of the family, there has been no real increase in the statutory amount of paid leave for Australian workers for decades, although the flexibility and reach of existing leave has changed. This discussion highlights the importance of leave to *all* workers to reproduce themselves, and their families, households and community. It also highlights the value of leave as a means of managing and cushioning the transition from one Work/Care state to another, for example, from worker to carer. We also consider some innovative ways in which such leave can be extended and made more widely available to meet work/life demands. The case of leave provides a prime example of how institutional arrangements and structures frustrate new patterns of behaviour and activity and people's preferences.

For the last quarter century general advances in the quantum of leave for Australian employees have been negligible: there have been no significant advances in the days of leave available through the legislative system for the bulk of employees since the unpaid maternity leave decision of 1979. Advances have been made in terms of broader *eligibility* for some leave (with fathers and ongoing casual employees now eligible for unpaid parental leave for example), the *gradual diffusion* of existing standards like unpaid maternity leave, and the use of leave for more broadly defined *purposes* (bereavement leave to care for sick family members for example). Against these, growth in the proportion of Australians who are employed on casual or precarious terms, has resulted in a contraction in eligibility for significant forms of leave including sick and holiday leave. Overall, the advances are in terms of eligibility, spread and flexible use more than in actual amounts of leave. The shift to enterprise bargaining and individual contracts underway since 1991 has seen some leave improvements through enterprise agreements and individual agreements – mostly in the public sector – but most of these do not offer improvements in family friendly provisions and many work to the contrary, by extending the normal span of hours and limiting employee co-determination of hours. Positive advances have reached only a small slice of the workforce. Only 14 per cent of enterprise agreements registered between 1995 and 2000, and 12 per cent of Australian Workplace Agreements, had any work family provisions within them (including those related to leave, child care, job sharing, career breaks, elder care and work from home) and the incidence of these provisions has been falling in the last few years (Whitehouse 2001: 113).

The lack of change in leave arrangements in Australia, in a quarter century of remarkable change in the demographics and caring responsibilities of Australian workers, give us a leave system calcified around the male worker of 150 years ago, not the working-carer of today. The gap is measured in a loss to the quality of work and life for Australians. This is a largely privatised cost, external to the labour market: it is felt by carers who cannot care, workers who are made anxious by the squeeze on their capacity to care *and* to do their jobs, and it affects the quality of lives more broadly. It also has an economic cost to the public purse through health costs, welfare payments, workers compensation, sickness benefits – to name a few of the socialised costs of an inadequate leave regime.

Most of the significant changes in leave for Australian workers have been achieved by unions through test cases publicly argued before the Australian Industrial Relations Commission (AIRC), or won in specific sectors and transmitted by means of the award system across the larger workforce over time. The reduced powers and scope of these since 1991, and especially since 1996 under the conservative government, do not encourage optimism about leave advances through these mechanisms without legislative change. However, enterprise and individual bargaining have delivered very little for worker/carers in the past decade. A new agenda for leave is urgently needed to meet the reshaped Australian workforce and household.

Weekends, holiday leave, sick leave and public holidays

The most common forms of leave from paid work are weekends, annual leave, sick leave and public holidays. Overall, access to these as quarantined forms of common, community, non-work time has declined in recent years and there have been no new advances in their quantum. Enterprise agreements and award changes over recent years have eroded the weekend, along with the payment of penalty rates, which compensate for the unsociability of working on weekends.

In 2000, only 59 per cent of Australian workers usually worked Monday to Friday and had the weekend off (52 per cent of women, compared to 64 per cent of men). This had fallen from 62 per cent in 1995 (ABS Cat No 6342.0). A quarter of all enterprise agreements current in late 2002 extend ordinary hours into the weekend (ACIRRT 2002). The loss of penalty rates encourages employers to use workers at these times, while removing compensation to employees for their loss of premium family and community time.

Australians enjoy a number of public holidays most of which result in long weekends. These are important opportunities for families, friends and community groups to spend time together and for recreational and sporting activities and general rest. These are often occasions when extended families get together. There are eight national Australian public holidays each year and between one and four State public holidays, so that most Australians have some access to between nine and 11 long weekends each year. These have been fixed for many years in most States, and nationally. This quantum of public holidays compares with 11 public holidays in New Zealand and the Netherlands, 12 in Canada and the US (with some additional State holidays), nine in the UK and 15 in France. The long weekend has suffered from the same encroachments as weekends more generally, as a growing number of employees work on them. The deregulation of bargaining and growth in individual employment contracts has accompanied an increase in work on public holidays in some industries, with less access for some workers to extended weekend breaks.

Sick leave is available to most workers in Australia. Casual workers generally do not have access to this form of leave, and so must refuse work when they are ill, or go to work sick. As we have seen in Chapter 8, the most common way carers deal with sick dependants is by using their own sick leave: women report 'saving' their own sick leave so that they can look after sick children. The lack of paid family leave makes this their best option, one not available to almost a third of women who lack any paid sick leave.

Most permanent workers in Australia have access to four weeks paid annual leave, and two weeks paid sick leave although this varies from award to award. Many employees also have access to two or three days bereavement leave. However, this leaves a third of women (most of whom are casual employees) without paid annual leave (Table 9.1); a third also lack sick leave. A quarter of male employees are without paid annual leave and a quarter without paid sick leave. While the casual loading that many casually employed workers (though not all) receive is intended to compensate for this loss, it is inadequate compensation for many (Smith and Ewer 1999).

The rapid growth in the proportion of Australians who are paid casually has resulted in the significant erosion of the basic leave rights of holiday and sick leave, especially for women who – ironically – are most likely to need them to meet the demands of their own sick children and dependants, to care for children on school holidays, and to recover from the double working day. Twenty-seven per cent of women employees aged 25-54 years, when caring responsibilities are most intense, lack any paid leave entitlements (ABS Cat No 6359.0), and the proportion who are excluded from even this basic form of leave is rising. In 1991, 80 per cent of all employees were entitled to paid holiday leave *or* paid sick leave but this fell to 73 per cent in 2001 (ABS Cat No 6310.0).

Table 9.1 Access to Leave from
Paid Work, 2001 (per cent)

	Women	*Men*	*All*
Holiday leave	67	75	72
Sick Leave	68	75	72
Long Service Leave	59	65	62

Source, ABS Cat No. 6310.0 Employee earnings, Benefits and Trade Union Membership, August 2001

Paid holiday leave is commonly accompanied by a bonus payment of around 17.5 per cent of base salary ('holiday leave loading'), which grew out of recognition that annual leave often meant extra costs for the worker and their family or the loss of shift and overtime payments when annual holiday pay fell back to the base rate. In some cases, with the rise in enterprise bargaining since 1991, this loading has been 'cashed out' and rolled into a general wage rate.

In terms of the timing of holidays, not all employees have control over when these can be taken: in 2000 only 70 per cent of employees could choose when to take holidays and men have more chance to choose than women.

With 20 days annual leave a year for most permanent employees, Australia is ahead of US workers (around 16 days a year), but behind Sweden, Denmark, France, Austria, Spain and Germany with at least 30. Annual holiday leave is an important means of personal regeneration and recovery from paid work, and a vital opportunity for friends, families and communities to spend time together. However, many adults in couple households with children do not take simultaneous holidays in order to 'cover' school holidays.

Overall, the steady erosion of access to sick and holiday leave for Australian employees, inadequately compensated for in some cases, has been little remarked in Australia. The erosion is especially marked for women, who do most care and are in need of leave. It represents a long-term slide in basic leave conditions, at a time when much work and life attention has focused on other forms of leave – special family leave, maternity leave and so on. This discussion might more appropriately address *both* access to established forms of basic leave *alongside* promotion of new innovations and standards. The growing proportion of Australian workers who lack paid sick and holiday leave creates a strong argument for reducing casual and precarious work.

Long Service Leave

Long Service Leave (LSL) is an almost uniquely Australian form of extended leave which is currently available to 62 per cent of Australian employees, *provided* they accumulate qualifying levels of continuous service with their employer (usually about ten years to earn about 13 weeks paid leave at full pay, although there are many variations around this). For those who are eligible and manage to accumulate the necessary years of service, LSL is a very significant benefit – among the most valuable available to Australian employees. However, over the past ten years the proportion of eligible employees has fallen.

LSL provides valuable income support while undertaking unpaid work activities – whether holidaying, studying, having a baby, or caring for an aged parent. It also provides a form of income support to search for another job when employees are retrenched, provided employers have made adequate financial provision. Many corporate collapses result in the loss of entitlements like LSL, so employees making difficult labour market transitions are robbed of a vital, earned entitlement at the moment when they most need it. A 'bank' of paid leave, while maintaining job tenure, can underwrite personal regeneration after many years of paid work. It is also an important source of help in significant labour market/care transitions, whether into parenting/care, into education, or into a new job. Long service leave provides an important basis on which to build further leave related to better work/life and facilitate transitions.

In 1984, 67 per cent of all employees were eligible for LSL (that is, they were eligible to *accumulate* the service and receive the leave; however, many eligible employees fail to receive such leave because they leave their employer). In 1984, three quarters of men were eligible compared to 56 per cent of women. Only a quarter of part-time employees were eligible, compared to three quarters of full-timers (Burgess, Sullivan and Strachan 2002: 24). Over the past 20 years, access to LSL has gradually eroded until in 2001 only 62 per cent of employees were eligible. The decline has been especially sharp among men: 65 per cent of men are now eligible, compared to 59 per cent of women. While the eligibility of full-timers has not changed, it has increased for part-time employees (ABS Cat No 6310.0).

LSL first became available in 1862 as a consequence of colonial government and its distance from the English homeland of administrators. The first LSL rewarded South Australian and Victorian civil service workers with ten years service, with an extended return to Britain (Selby 1983, Burgess et al 2002: 21). LSL was gradually extended to most public servants and is now a more generally available statutory provision (Burgess et al 2002). The rationale for LSL is reward for continuity of service to a single employer and recovery from a long stint in paid work.

LSL is rarely mentioned in relation to parental responsibilities although the *Workplace Relations Act* 1996 allows eligible parents to take it in connection with unpaid parental leave. Some women use their LSL for maternity and family responsibilities. Protection of the existing entitlement and greater flexibility in its use are important issues. Many employees would benefit from a portable benefit that allowed them to gradually accumulate LSL across jobs. While such rights have been achieved in male-dominated industries like building and construction, they have not flowed to service and hospitality sectors where so many carers would benefit. The absence of such a benefit for long-term workers who are termed 'casuals' has provoked change in at least one State: the Queensland Government has increased the access of these employees to entitlements subject to some conditions (Burgess et al 2002: 36).

Rostered days off

Rostered days off (RDOs) were won by a number of unions in 1982 as part of a campaign in support of a shorter working week. This shorter week was to be achieved by taking rostered days off (weekly, fortnightly or – most commonly – monthly) in exchange for extra minutes of work each day. For example, in the paint industry many workers worked an additional 45 minutes on regular work-days to accumulate fortnightly paid rostered days and work a nine-day fortnight.

By 1995 just over a quarter of workers had RDOs. However, access to RDOs fell from 27 per cent in 1995 to 20 per cent in 2000 (ABS Cat No 6342.0). As in the case of LSL, the fall in access has been greatest among full-time men. Men have greater access to RDOs than women: 24 per cent of men, compared to 16 per cent of women had RDOs in their main jobs in 2000. Only 5 per cent of part-time employees have access to an RDO. Just as hours of work have been increasing for full-time workers in particular, their entitlements to leave for recuperation, social and family time has been eroded.

Unpaid parental and maternity leave

Many Australian women work when they are pregnant, and others with less than 12 months tenure in their jobs return to work out of economic necessity within weeks of having a baby. This is barbaric. Many women have a strong commitment to keep up their paid work while pregnant – even against great odds, and their motivations are not just economic:

> I just carried my bucket with me. I was a vomiter. All the way through. I'd go to hospital and be re-hydrated ... Life goes on. I was so busy. It wasn't good. I had to keep working – to get everything done. It wasn't money. It's the way I was bought up – to just keep going. I've always worked. I don't know any different. It's my fault I guess for needing to work. It was boring at home. It's what you have to get done. (worker in family-owned small business, city)

Unpaid maternity leave has been a legal award right for Australian women with 12 months continuous service since 1979. Given that eligibility is dependent upon at least 12 months continuous employment with the one employer, the proportion of Australian women eligible for unpaid maternity leave has fallen as women's job mobility has risen in recent years. In 1992, about a fifth of women had changed jobs in the previous year and in 2002 it reached 24 per cent (ABS Cat No 6209.0).

The 1979 decision of the AIRC, supported by the ACTU, secured a right for women to take 12 months unpaid leave and return to their previous jobs, or their equivalent provided that they had 12 months continuous employment. In 1985, this right was extended to those adopting children and, in 1990, to allow fathers to share unpaid parental leave with mothers provided they had 12 months continuous service. This standard of unpaid parental leave has been embedded in workplace relations law since 1994. In May 2001, regular casual workers (both part-time and full-time) covered by federal awards who had been in their jobs for periods equivalent to 12 months were also granted access to 12 months unpaid parental leave. However, union claims for extended unpaid leave − of two years − have been rejected. The ACTU plans to make another attempt to increase unpaid leave to three years in 2003 and some retail industry agreements now include unpaid leave of up to two years.

In making a claim for extended unpaid leave for two years for working parents in 1999, the ACTU also sought general rights for employees to return to paid work on a part-time basis, and to revert to full-time work after a period of part-time work. This was not granted; however, employees can do so *if* their employer agrees and the ACTU has embarked upon a new work and family test case in 2003.

As discussed in Chapter 4, many Australian parents, especially women, take extended periods away from paid work when their children are small, though this proportion has fallen dramatically in the past 25 years. Those in paid work before their children are born value job tenure while parenting. Unfortunately, at present very few have it. Most who take extended leave lose their labour market foothold, and the price for lost skills, productivity and lifetime earnings is very high. A policy of extended unpaid leave alongside periods of paid maternity and parental leave, should be a high policy priority. It will extend the meaningful choices of women and men, increase productivity and reduce the lifetime costs of parenting.

Paid maternity leave

Paid maternity leave (PML) has long been an objective of many in Australia. However, it has been a long time coming except for most in the public sector. Australia has a PML regime which is less a *system* and more a lottery. Our arrangements give general access to 12 months *unpaid* parental leave to the three quarters of women with a year of service with their current employers, but arbitrary and patchy access to *paid* maternity leave, leaving the majority of women without it. The fact that PML exists for only a third of Australian women, 80 years after the ILO recommended it, makes debate about its universal provision, passé. Nonetheless, a lively debate has been underway with some members of the Federal Government actively opposing it. The key policy challenge now, however, is how to best provide paid leave equitably. The creation of a national solution is an essential *remedial* measure to redress an historical oversight and persistent inequity which leaves Australia, with the US, among the last OECD countries to implement a national provision. While the survey evidence is limited, recent polls suggest that most Australians support paid maternity leave. Seventy-five per cent of those surveyed in 2001 supported PML (Sun Herald Taverner, *Sydney Morning Herald*, 5 May 2002: 4).

Women working in the Commonwealth Public Service, universities and some individual workplaces enjoy some access to paid leave, but even this is well short of the standards that apply in many other countries, including some in the Third World. In addition, some seek greater access to general paid leave across the life cycle – for study, care of elders, long service, personal development and so on:

> What I'd like to see is all your leave lumped into one and you take it as you want – for study, to look after older parents or whatever. (country woman, worker, mother)

If the circumstances of early mothering and parenting are to improve, and support for working mothers is to apply fairly, then PML is essential. Thirty-eight per cent of Australian women have access to some level of paid maternity leave, leaving 62 per cent without any (ABS 6361.0). Only six of the top 100 federal awards (by coverage of employees) provide some level of paid leave (HREOC, 2002b: 19) and only 7 per cent of all current federal enterprise agreements include such provisions (Department of Employment and Workplace Relations et al 2002: 7). The duration of paid leave varies widely from a few days to fourteen weeks, or – exceptionally – 52 weeks at the Australian Catholic University. Most commonly it is around six weeks. Enterprise bargaining has not provided a route to paid leave for most women, and awaiting enterprise level developments would be a long wait (Baird, Brennan and Cutcher 2002). Highly skilled women, public sector women, full-time permanents, and those in larger companies have better access to paid leave than others. Sixty-five per cent of managers and administrators have some PML, compared to only 13 per cent of those employed in accommodation, cafes and restaurants, and 20 per cent of those in the retail industry (HREOC 2002a: 21). Women in the public sector enjoy varying levels of paid leave ranging from 12 weeks in the federal public sector and universities, for example, to only four in South Australia.

Paid maternity leave is supported by the Australian Labor Party and the Greens (though the details of their approaches are unknown) and PML has been long standing Democrat policy. Senator Natasha Stott Despoja introduced a Private Members Bill into the Senate in 2002, to provide 14 weeks PML for most working women by means of a government payment at the level of the minimum wage, topped up where possible by local bargaining (Parliament of the Commonwealth of Australia, Workplace Relations Amendment (Paid Maternity Leave) Bill 2002 and its Explanatory Memorandum).

However, the Liberal Government remains divided on the issue and has not supported PML. Instead the Government has introduced a 'Baby Bonus' scheme which must be one of the least supported public policies ever to put money into the pockets of Australian families. The Baby Bonus provides a tax-benefit to mothers of first babies, with a payment ranging from $500 to $2500 per year for up to five years depending upon labour force participation before and after birth. Higher paid working women who reduce their post-baby labour force participation, earn most. The bonus has been roundly criticised for its expense ($510 million in its fourth year), poor targeting, failure to make much real difference, lack of benefit to women who are not in paid work prior to birth, disincentive to return to paid work and regressiveness.

The arguments in favour of PML include the positive impact on the welfare of mother and child; the contribution it would make to removing a discriminatory barrier to women's employment; the savings to employers who face lower rehire costs, training, and higher morale, retention and productivity; the creation of equity between working women; and its potentially positive impact upon Australia's declining birth rate. The provision of PML would also meet long established international labour standards (HREOC 2002a, b).

There appears to be widespread support for a scheme like that recommended by the Human Rights and Equal Opportunity Commission and the Australian Democrats which delivers the ILO standard of 14 weeks paid leave by means of a federal government minimum payment, topped up by local bargaining. Paid at the minimum wage ($431 per week in 2003) or pre-maternity earnings whichever is the lower, this means a sum of around $6000 – or replacement earnings for between 35 and 48 per cent of all working women – while a payment at average weekly earnings would replace earnings for over three quarters of working women (NPEC 2002). Existing supports like the Maternity Allowance could be replaced by PML. A publicly-funded basic payment would ensure that small businesses and employers with many women employees of child-bearing age are not disproportionately affected by an employer payment.

PML recognises that paid maternity leave is an *employment* issue. But this is not to say that *any* woman having a baby is not deserving of support. Around 28 per cent of births occur to women outside the paid labour market. The community benefit that arises from well-nurtured babies and healthy families, and the important contribution, work and care of women outside the labour market who have a baby also deserves public assistance. About 72 per cent of women in the 20–45 year age range are in paid work, so many will receive PML. Fortunately, mothers at home already receive some assistance, including tax benefits, a flat rate Maternity Payment ($780 in 2003) and the Maternity Immunisation Payment ($209). Many will also be eligible for the Government's 'Baby Bonus' (at the minimum annual level of $500 for five years). A taxable maternity payment close to the basic government PML (around $6000) less the above payments for mothers outside the paid labour market would address this issue. This will amount to a relatively small new payment given that, for example, a woman married to a retail worker receiving the base shop assistant rate is already receiving over $4300 on the birth of a child out of existing payments and tax benefits.

The estimated cost of a government payment is sensitive to the nature of exclusions and payment levels. The minimalist HREOC proposal is costed at $213 million in 2003/04 net of tax and the payments it will replace (HREOC 2002b). This is much less than the Baby Bonus scheme and a very small proportion of overall government spending on Australian families, now esti-mated at more than $18 billion a year. Paid maternity leave at minimum wages for 14 weeks is a minimalist scheme. It is inferior to many other countries and over time should be exten-ded in terms of length of paid leave, and increased to ordinary earnings. If our economy and society is to rely upon the paid work of women and mothers – as it presently does, and at an increasing rates – then it must recognise these physical facts and protect the welfare of new mothers who work and their babies. Without it, too many households face financial pressure at birth, too many women are back at work too quickly, and too many babies are in very early child care against parents' wishes. The arguments on the basis of welfare, equity and efficiency are per-suasive. It is simply uncivilised to allow a labour market comprised of 43 per cent women to function without paid rest and recovery for working mothers.

Paternity leave

Maternity leave recognises that carrying a baby in late preg-nancy, giving birth, recovering from birth and early mothering and, where possible, to establish breast feeding, are physical acts that affect the body and being of the mother. PML distinguishes this physical phase of maternity from paternity and general parenting, which can involve either fathers or mothers. The active participation of men in parenting is extremely important, and deserves strong practical support. Some countries provide paid parenting leave for parents and leave it to them to decide how to share it, although most is taken by women even when conditions are very favourable to men. A low male take up rate led Sweden to quarantine a proportion of paid parenting leave for men, with the loss of this leave by the family if fathers do not use it (instituting 'fatherhood by gentle force', as Leira describes it (2002: 93)). Despite this, only 14 per cent of all paid parental leave is taken by Swedish men and less than half make use of parental leave (Swedish Ministry of Health and Social Affairs, 2002: 2; Leira 2002: 86). Results have been more positive, however, in Norway where most fathers make use of their four weeks quarantined leave, and it has achieved widespread acceptance. New Zealand recently implemented new parental leave which gives parents the right to share up to 12 weeks paid parental leave; specific rights exist for two weeks unpaid paternity leave. (New Zealand Department of Labour 2002). The New Zealand Prime Minister has indicated that further improvements are also being considered (*Workplace Express*, 18 February 2003).

Paid paternity leave is not generally available in Australia. In the AWIRS 1995 survey in workplaces with 20 or more employees, employee relations managers said that paid paternity leave was available in 18 per cent of workplaces (31 per cent public, 13 per cent private; and more commonly in medium sized workplaces than very large) (Morehead et al 1997). Paternity leave has hardly been a lively subject of enterprise or individual bargaining, with provisions in less than 2 per cent of enterprise agreements registered between 1995 and 2000, and less than 4 per cent of Australian Workplace Agreements between 1997 and 1999 (Whitehouse 2001: 115). Paid paternity leave would greatly assist men in the early days after the arrival of a new baby and many women say that this early experience with a new baby encourages fathers to be more active parents.

Paid parental leave

Australian employees have no general statutory rights to paid parental leave, unlike many other countries where extended periods of paid leave are available to carers. A number of countries have improved parental leave arrangements in recent years both as a labour market policy and family policy. Arrangements across Europe vary widely, ranging from two years in Austria and Germany, and until the child reaches 36 months in France (but only for the second and third children), up to 52 weeks in Norway, and almost a year in Italy (Leira 2002: 79). Sweden famously offers parental cash benefits in connection with childbirth and adoption for up to 480 days (390 at 80 per cent of the parent's qualifying income and 90 days at universal flat rate). In France, parents with two or more children (one under three years) and appropriate levels of employment before birth, are eligible for a flat rate benefit where one parent reduces hours or gives up work until the youngest child is three (Leira 2002: 83).

Levels of payment and eligibility vary widely, with close to normal income replacement in the Nordic countries and much lower levels elsewhere in Europe. Levels of take-up also vary widely: they are low in France and the Netherlands, perhaps reflecting the low rate of payment, but high in Germany and Austria where the rate of payment is also low; Leira suggests that this may reflect the absence of child care alternatives in the latter two countries. Low rates of compensation contribute to segmented patterns of use, with low-income households unable to make much use of unpaid leave.

While many countries adopt parental leave arrangements that allow both parents to use them, overwhelmingly it is women who take parental leave, leading some to raise the question of how much paid parental leave contributes to gender equality. However, while it may be highly gendered in its use, and highly sensitive to income level and eligibility thresholds, there can be no doubt that the chance to take extended parenting leave while maintaining employment tenure and some level of income replacement provides a superior quality of life for many women who are the main carers of children. Without parental leave, most must surrender their work and labour market footing and lose an income, or reluctantly return to work before they want to and juggle work and young children, or accept a precarious labour market position. Paid parental leave may entrench gendered caring roles, with women making most use of it, but without such leave, it is women who largely manage the work/care juggle in the shadow of the male-model of jobs – and bear its privatised costs, and it is women who lose an income in the absence of a paid benefit.

Cash benefits in place of childcare: Paying women to stay at home?

Parental Leave is part of a larger package of supports in some countries especially Denmark, Norway and Sweden which provide high compensation for long periods of paid leave, extra leave for care of sick children and publicly funded child care. In

Finland, a cash benefit is available (instituted in 1990) in place of a publicly funded child care place after the end of paid parental leave and up to when the child turns three:

> This cash transfer gives parents the opportunity to extend their leave of absence. A considerable proportion of parents have claimed the cash benefit, and the accommodation of Finnish children under 3 in publicly sponsored daycare has decreased (Leira 2002: 89).

For previously employed parents, job security is maintained. This scheme is used by a large majority of eligible mothers especially those on lower incomes: 'the majority taking a shorter period, ie until the child was 12-18 months, while 15% used the full period until the child reached the age of 3' (Leira 2002: 117). This scheme has led to debate about its impact upon gender segregation in both paid and unpaid work and its entrenchment of the traditional male worker/female carer model with the risks it creates for both sexes in the event of divorce. However, it gives greater care choice – *but only* where publicly funded child care places are readily available, and jobs are available. The high initial rate of take up in Finland occurred in a period when jobs were scarce. (Leira 2002).

After much controversy, a cash benefit in place of use of publicly funded childcare was introduced in Norway in 1999, with a non-taxable flat rate, low payment (relative to wages) to parents at home not using a public child care place with children 12-36 months. In effect, given the low rate of payment the arrangement relies upon a primary earner in the household and has been described by some 'as the state's gift to the traditional husband/father' (Leira 2002). Early assessment of the Norwegian experience suggests that it has resulted in little change in the choices made by women (while its take up rate is high, many women would have chosen to be at home anyway), and virtually none to men's. Some suggest that the lack of quality, affordable child care in many locations has led to women staying home (Leira 2002).

Different regimes of care and income support result in different outcomes: for example, Leira points out that Sweden's superior levels of paid leave at high pay, mean that women are drawn out of paid work (decommodified) and child care becomes 'familised', while in Denmark leave is shorter, child care widely available and women's labour is commodified along with care. In all of these cases, *true choice* is dependent upon several factors:

- the availability of paid work on decent terms for women and men;

- The availability of paid parental leave on decent terms so that it is attractive to low and middle income households, and to single parents;

- and availability of affordable, quality child care so that decisions about care/work are genuine and parents are not conscripted to home through lack of choice, or new parents conscripted to the workplace through fear of losing their jobs and labour market foothold.

The implementation of a cash benefit in place of child care, without accompanying reforms of Australia's Work/Care regime and better transition points into and out of care and work, is likely to further embed sex-segmentation of both domestic/care work and paid jobs, with long-term costs to productivity, women's incomes, and men's relationships with their families. This traditional model leaves women dependent upon men's earnings or assigned to poverty or low incomes where they live alone and have a poor labour market foothold. It also carries hazards for men who maintain their primary bread-winning status sometimes at the cost of deep relationships with dependants. Both risk significant losses in the event of relationship breakdown.

Carers leave and other family-friendly provisions

Family emergencies and sick dependants are a key concern for working carers. Many countries have specific paid or unpaid leave for parents to care for sick children, including Belgium,

Germany, Greece, Spain, Italy, Austria, Portugal, Finland, Sweden, and Norway (Leira 2002: 81). Parents in Sweden have access to generous paid leave to care for sick children up to aged 12 (and in some circumstances up to age 16): they can access 120 days of leave per year at 80 per cent of qualifying income. However, only seven days per child are used on average each year (Swedish Ministry of Health and Social Affairs 2002: 2).

There has only been limited recognition of this need in Australia, at least within the formal regulatory regime, beyond loosening the purposes for which employee's own sick and bereavement leave (usually two or three days) can be used, and allowing a limited portion to be available for family purposes. In 1994 and in 1995, the AIRC recognised the need for carers to take leave to care for sick family and household members by adopting a two-stage process which allows employees to use up to five days of their own sick leave to care for a member of their family who is ill, and to aggregate sick and bereavement leave for this purpose (ACTU 2000). However, the AIRC refused union claims for five days *additional* days of special family leave. In addition to these minimal legal rights, some employees – mostly in larger companies and the public sector – have been granted or bargained additional rights to carers leave and other family friendly provisions.

Table 9.2 shows the low incidence of a wide range of family-friendly provisions in registered enterprise agreements in December 2001, with only a small slice having paid paternity or paid maternity leave, and the most common provisions already generally available through awards (like access to single days annual leave, access to other existing leave for family purposes, and family carers leave through the use of employee's own sick leave). Enterprise bargaining has hardly resulted in widespread innovation or even the wide dissemination of existing rights to support working carers.

There are many examples of family friendly steps being taken in individual firms, including through paid maternity leave, extra leave to care for families, flexible work arrangements, permanent

Table 9.2 Family Friendly Provisions
in Enterprise Agreements, 2001

	Per cent of Agreements
Access to single days annual leave	13
48/52 career break/purchased days	3
Sick leave unlimited	1
Family carers leave	27
Extended unpaid parental leave	2
Regular hours/days rostered for part-time work	7
Home based work	1
Family responsibility provisions	3
Childcare provisions	1
Access to other leave for family caring purposes	18
Paid family leave	3
Paid maternity leave	7
Paid paternity leave	4
Paid adoption leave	2
Job sharing	3

Source Workplace Agreements Database, Department of Employment and Workplace Relations

part-time work and other measures. They have been widely celebrated, documented and critiqued (see national annual awards by DEWR for family friendly exemplars, ACTU 2000, Whitehouse and Zetlin 1999, Breakspear 1998, Strachan and Jamieson 1999 for examples). Many of these steps have assisted employees in significant ways. However, they are islands of enterprise-based exemplary good practice, afloat in a sea of poor provision. They do not do Australian working/carers justice and they represent a patchy and uneven set of developments with all too little impact on the majority of employees, especially those who rely on minimum statutory standards for their rights, particularly those in small and medium sized businesses.

Perhaps worse, these exemplars and their publication have provided useful cover for the true deterioration in access to many established leave standards like the weekend, sick leave, annual leave, RDOs, Long Service Leave and unpaid parental leave. Renovation of the terms of paid work in light of the reshaping of employment and households, requires both the creation of new leave standards and protection and repair of those that have deteriorated.

More leave

Overall, Australian leave arrangements are skewed away from those that specifically assist households dealing with work and care, in favour of those that assist sick, tired, male or loyal workers. Recent innovations favour those who wish to participate in our volunteer defence force. While over the past century countries like France, New Zealand, Germany, Sweden, Norway, and most recently the United Kingdom, have been improving leave to support working carers, Australia – which *began* behind the pack – has lagged further. The past quarter century has seen declining access, on average, to many long established standard forms of leave. This deterioration has given momentum to the Work/Life collision. It is time for action to repair the erosion, remediate the gaps, and implement innovative approaches on a general basis.

Current discussion about paid maternity leave has provoked a number of divisive debates, with government ministers encouraging a wedge between 'ordinary battlers' and a 'middle class on welfare' (ie receiving paid maternity leave); between mothers at home and mothers also in paid work; and between those who have children and those who do not. Part of the means to diffuse these unproductive debates – which do nothing but ensure inaction – may lie in new approaches including the creation of general leave banks for employees. But new possibilities are secondary to the need to provide better underpinnings to those who currently care and work: support for carers at home, leave to care for sick dependants and extended paid parental leave.

A general leave bank

Australia has the basis for a general leave provision to assist with labour market transitions, intensive care, and the rebalancing of work and life, in the form of long service leave. A general leave bank built on the LSL tradition would give greater flexibility to employees in terms of the timing of leave to meet diverse needs: to meet caring responsibilities, to have holidays, retrain, pursue non-work interests or adjust to work changes or new jobs. Many workers use their long-serve leave for these purposes, but almost forty per cent of workers lack any entitlement and many more cannot accumulate enough service to collect it. A general leave bank, portable between employers, could build upon this uniquely Australian provision, extend it to a broader slice of the workforce and allow employees to increase it. This could be achieved by:

- creating a national bank that makes existing long service leave portable between employers,

- foregoing national wage rises arising from productivity changes to accumulate more leave rather than higher pay (an employee contribution),

- accumulation of overtime into a general leave bank,

- additional negotiated contributions from employers and employees,

- new statutory rights to increased long service leave (effectively an employer contribution),

- a generally available 48/52 scheme that allows employees to be paid for 48 of the 52 weeks they work in a year and take extra leave,

- more flexible use of existing leave (so that, for example, employees can go into leave deficit, on the understanding that they work off the deficit, or pay it out if they leave employment).

To be useful to the majority of employees such a leave bank would need several features:

- First, employees would need to be assured that their leave 'savings' were protected and 'real' rather than in danger of disappearing in the event of corporate collapse,

- Second, that they are portable to protect those who change jobs or interrupt their working lives,

- Third, they should be available on a *pro rata* basis to all employees (including part-time and precarious employees) so that a further disincentive to the employment of such employees is averted,

- Finally, such a bank should not replace basic rights like holiday, sick, maternity and parental leave, but facilitate the accumulation and use of additional periods of leave.

Juliet Schor proposed the trading of income for time in her 1992 book, *The Overworked American,* arguing that taking a 2 per cent pay rise as *time* instead of *money* would reduce the annual US working week by two months over ten years, or give a six and a half hour day (1992: 147). At a time of declining real incomes among US workers, it is not surprising that the idea has had little practical effect, especially given the US state and employer hostility to the general improvement in regulatory or leave regimes. However, for several reasons the idea may have better prospects in Australia. First, Australian workers, employers, government and industrial tribunals now have extensive experience with trading money for social wages (for example, through superannuation). Second, the high priority that many Australian employees now place on time over money provides a strong basis for developing support for such an approach. Third, the survival of centralised federal machinery in the form of the AIRC – weakened though it is – through which time-based test cases can be run, provides an important statutory vehicle to spread local gains more broadly. Fourth, the long established tradition of minimum Living Wage increases, that lift the wages of the low paid, could continue to protect them while general productivity increases were distributed through reduced time for all.

Innovative mechanisms to retrieve time from paid work, and give more time sovereignty to Australians will help to restore the slowly eroded quality of life for many.

Conclusion

Overall, paid and unpaid leave represents a critical and essential support for workers with caring responsibilities who want a life. It is a powerful cushion against Work/Life collision. Emergency family leave can relieve the greatest stress points faced by carers. Just as importantly, blocks of paid leave facilitate transitions from one state to another as workers and their families and employers deal with intensive non-work demands (like a new baby or a dying relative) or adjust to changes in circumstances. Blocks of paid leave are important to all workers – regardless of their caring responsibilities – who want to live a full life, through study, travel, rest, recreation, recuperation, voluntary work and the pursuit of both work and non-work activities. Access to blocks of leave, beyond sick and holiday leave, is rudimentary for many Australians, and eligibility for them is in decline. An increase in the quantum of leave, with flexible access, would make a very important positive contribution to the lives of working Australians. Such an increase should be seen as additional to the essential, remedial implementation of paid maternity, paternity and parental leave and leave to care for sick family members. Historically, reductions in working time and increases in paid leave have been vigorous resisted by Australian employers and many governments. However, a staged approach towards clear goals may be achievable. These goals should include:

Remedial and repair action

- national extension of paid maternity leave to all working women, in specific recognition of the sex-based physicality of pregnancy, birth and any attempt to establish breast-feeding;
- Containment of precarious working conditions to genuinely casual, short-term, or peak requirements, and prevention of

phantom 'independent contractor' arrangements which substitute for genuinely self-employed arrangements, under-mining general access to established leave;

New Leave Entitlements

- Paid paternity leave of two weeks on the birth of a child;
- Paid parental leave of up to a year to be shared by parents;
- Two weeks of paid emergency family leave to deal with sick dependants, in addition to recreation and own sick leave;
- Extended unpaid leave for workers;
- Flexibility in taking leave (either full-time or part-time);
- General leave banks available for multiple purposes, drawn down at employee convenience subject to agreement with employers.

Current arrangements for leave illustrate all too well the disjunction between the institutions of our Work/Care regime and the working carer's needs. In real life, workers make ad hoc adjustments around inadequate maternity, sick, parental and carers leave in workplace institutions, while facing reduced rights as employment insecurity undermines access to existing standards. Improvements to better fit institutional arrangements like leave to the real demands of work and life are an essential component of a better Work/Care regime in Australia.

CHAPTER 10

Countering the collision:
What we can do now

Australians are not an unhappy lot as a whole. Most are satisfied with much of their lives: 85 per cent of respondents in the 2001 HILDA survey were satisfied with 'life as a whole' (Melbourne Institute 2002: 20). This places Australians at the more satisfied end of the industrialised world. Satisfaction with life is not, however, evenly spread in relation to different aspects of life, or across the population. Many Australians have financial worries (just under half are satisfied with their financial situation) and while most feel safe and most are satisfied 'in their homes', only 57 per cent feel 'part of the local community'. Well-being could be significantly improved through measures that cushion the collision between work and life. These measures are likely to have effects well beyond the personal satisfaction of Australians and even their health and welfare: they will strengthen the sinews of community, improve social capital and are likely to improve broader economic and social health. Not all Australians feel the direct effects of this collision, most notably the thousands of unemployed, but its effects reach well beyond the individuals and households that are directly affected. The situation of the unemployed is partly shaped by a Work/Care regime that loads up paid working hours onto full-time workers at one end of the spectrum, while at the other 600,000 cannot find any paid hours at all.

Regime misalignment: Institutions and culture lag behind behaviour

The Work/Care regime modelled in Chapter 2 is the outcome of cultures, institutions, and behaviours. The model suggests that Work/Care regimes are the unstable and changing outcome of the intersection, mutual effects and contradictions between institutions, culture and actual behaviour. Institutions and government policy do not always move in tandem with people's behaviour and wishes. Sometimes policy runs ahead of behaviour (like anti-discrimination law) while at other times it lags (for example, when child care provision runs behind the work patterns of parents). The work and family behaviours and preferences of Australians have changed at a pace well ahead of policy reform and much faster than many workplaces and services have been able to accommodate. Women have moved into paid jobs ahead of even basic accommodations like leave when they have a baby. Such disequilibriums are not uncommon in human history. Leira describes the Nordic experience:

> More often than not, mothers have started the entry into employment with marginal support from state-sponsored services for childcare. In the Nordic region, where the welfare state has often been considered women's 'best friend', the first generation of mothers joined the labour force without waiting for the welfare state, employers, or fathers to share the responsibility for the care of children. Access to publicly sponsored childcare was not readily available, and for a relatively long time, demand exceeded supply. For the second and third generations of working mothers, however, in the late 1990s, access to publicly sponsored childcare is close to universal in Denmark and Sweden, and is established as an unconditional right of the parents in Finland (2002: 137).

Beyond Australia's current institutional disequilibriums, however, there is strong cultural and attitudinal *resistance* to some changing behaviours. Surveys of general attitudes about what women with children *should* do, for example, suggest that attitudes run well behind what women *actually* do (Evans and Kelley 2001). These lagged values and norms create cultural resistance to living in new ways — including in this example within mothers themselves, their children, their partners, governments, workplaces, and in broader society. Mothers particularly feel the dissonance between traditional values and what they do as mothers. The gap between values and behaviour is at least as marked for fathers: over 80 per cent of Australians think that a father should 'be as heavily involved in the care of his children as the mother' (HILDA 2001). Very few are. However, this dissonance between beliefs and behaviour in relation to *fatherhood* has little bite: it is not generally experienced by fathers as a conflict of culture with personal behaviour, or accompanied by the epidemic of guilt that so many women name. The cultural constructions of 'proper motherhood', and deviations from them, are much more potent than those that surround around 'proper fatherhood'.

What is more, the fit of *institutions* to mothers – or carers in general – with jobs is characterised by dissonance, with leave arrangements, industrial regulation and the supply of care lagging well behind demand. The reverse can sometimes be said of the institutional response to fatherhood where some policies, like paternity leave, have moved well ahead of behaviour. Fathers, as some interviewees have said through this book, are much more likely to receive praise when they provide care above the 'going rate', rather than criticism when they do not. This is not true for mothers.

Dominant cultures – along with institutions – exert a pull on behaviours. This pull can go in either of two directions. They can pull *with* the direction of current behaviour change – for example by supporting the life-cycle work participation patterns of carers and the leave of those for whom caring is intensive. Or these policies can pull *against* current change to 'change back' to what was: for example policies that pay mothers to stay at home *where they are not accompanied by policies and institutions that adequately support the choice to be a carer/worker* are effectively policies that remove choice. They amount to a 'change back' policy. Without the possibility of living a decent life as a worker/carer, paying carers to stay at home amounts to an attempt to re-privilege the breadwinner/carer model of relationship and household, and to remove choice. Without quality, affordable care options across the years of dependency, leave that gives employment security, and supports care and flexible jobs, then paying carers to care at home will constrain the choices of the majority. Swimming so hard against the direction of actual change, such an approach will not necessarily broaden the menu of options, but – as some have described the Norwegian payment to carers at home – may amount to the 'state's gift to the traditional husband/carer'.

There are many reasons why men and women undertake paid work: money, identity, pleasure in exercising skill and contributing, loneliness at home, the low valuation of caring work in our culture, and minimising the risk of long-term poverty and labour market exclusion if the breadwinner/carer household breaks down. Despite these pulls, many governments – whether conservative, liberal or social democratic – have resisted women's entry to paid work, and men have resisted the erosion of the male breadwinner. This resistance has been especially strong in Australia where the male breadwinner has stood for so long at the centre of the workplace and social welfare systems, and at the heart of the definition of masculinity itself. The Australian gender order is more masculinist than many other industrialised countries, and the Work/Care regime, which is partially shaped by this gender order, reflects the masculinist legacy. These are powerful forces to contest. In the Nordic environment (where women's right to work is generally uncontested, long parental leaves exist and the debate has moved onto *paternal* responsibilities) there are now also initiatives to make payments to carers at home, most of whom will be mothers. This is not without controversy, but they occur in countries that have well established public provision of child care, good part-time work opportunities and Work/Care regimes that are supportive of women's – and men's – contributions as workers and carers in a 'joint venture of the state and the family' (Leira 2002: 140).

Australia's Work/Care regime is two generations behind these examples. Resistance to worker/mothers exists and is still mobilised to undermine even basic provisions like paid maternity leave, and to separate 'working mothers' from 'mothers at home' as if the two are separate populations, which – over time – they often are not. Child care is far from universally available, it is often expensive and more than half of Australians with young children who use it or think about using it have difficulties with finding care, with its quality, getting care for the right hours, and its costs. Notwithstanding 20 years of anti-discrimination legislation, women's right to work is not uncontested in a society where very traditional conceptions of 'workers as men', run deep and leave their legacy. In the mid-1990s, Paul Keating felt that the 'really big problem' facing Australia was 'all the women in the workforce. And all the children in care, or being brought up by their fathers when they should be at home with their mothers.' (Watson 2002: 505). Keating was 'agitated' that his Government's child care benefit encouraged women to work. When a progressive Labor Prime Minister's attitudes to working mothers are such, then mothers with jobs are in trouble. Until recently, Keating's successor, John Howard, was known for his 'white picket fence' approach to household life, with the bread-winner/carer couple firmly at centre. A private venture of women carers with too little help from the state *and* from men – in public or private – is a long distance from a 'joint venture of state and family', to use Leira's description of the Nordic approach. This is not to suggest that any other country's model of 'joint venture' is appropriate to Australia (where are emp-loyers in this model?), or that institutional care of children is ideal for all. Shifting care to the state in a 'state-family' venture that commodifies women's labour on the same basis as men's, while institutionalising children, is not an option favoured by most Australians. The experiences of many women who attempt a commodification on these terms is writ large through this book. It amounts to the right to add an exhausting and leng-thening paid day to care of dependants and home, and its fall-out is widespread in both public and private spheres. It affects men, women, children and community. However, we can learn from international experiences. Key lessons include ensuring contri-butions from employers, the state, employees, men and women; and ensuring that the needs of worker/carers over the life cycle are met, including the needs of those who are full-time carers for shorter or longer periods as well as carers with jobs.

Under our current Australian Work/Care regime – generations behind others – the behaviour of Australians is running well ahead of culture and institutions – and way in front of some recent Prime Ministerial attitudes in both major parties. Institutions are 80 years behind on paid maternity leave, and this is but one minor measure among many others. On top of this are several peculiar deteriorations that are making our Work/Care regime more hazardous to family life: the intensification of paid jobs, the growth in hours of travel and paid work, the poor terms of part-time work and the growing proportion of precarious jobs with eroded leave and other rights. Access to even long-established forms of family-facilitating leave (like holiday and sick leave) is deteriorating. The slide is real, and it occurs in a labour/household constellation where more – not less – carers are working. The collision is increasingly hazardous as neighbourhood communities are thinned by the exit to the office and factory. A new joint venture of women, men, households, the state and workplaces is necessary. What should be its guiding principles and main ingredients?

Guiding principles for a New Work/Care regime

The evidence and argument of this book suggest six key principles that should guide reform of Australia's current work/care arrangements. These are summarised in Figure 10.1:

Less collision: An integrated/life-cycle approach

A guiding object of reform in Australia should be to shift current arrangements away from a collision between work and care towards those that foster integration of care with paid work, interspersion of the two, and opportunities for intensive care without penalty over the life cycle. This means taking a life-cycle approach to labour and to care, with policies which enhance genuine options rather than narrow them. An integrated,

Figure 10.1 Guiding principles for a New Work/Care Regime

Principle	Features
Less Collision: An Integrated/ Life-cycle Approach	Fosters integration of work and care across life-cycle and minimises labour market exclusion arising from care. Facilitates transitions between states.
Real Choice: A Menu of Options that Accommodates Diverse Situations	Ensures substantive options: to combine work and care, intermit them, or care full-time. Underwrites full-time care and work/care combination through job opportunities, public care, flexible jobs. Must be gender neutral (ie equivalent benefits available to men and women unless physical differences relevant (ie around birth)), and provide equivalent benefits to those in paid work or providing care.
Transparent, Straightforward, Administratively Simple and Easily Understood	Simple and transparent to users.
Quality, Affordable Care	Ensures quality affordable care to meet diverse needs.
Shared Costs and Benefits: Governments, Employers, Employees and Households	Governments, employers, employees, men and women all contribute with more from each of the former groups and less from women.
More Support for Those Who Need it More	Ensure that lower income, less wealthy households and those with greater need get more support than those who need it less.

life-cycle approach means ensuring good transitions between states of care, paid work, education, recuperation and so on.

Real choice: a menu of options that accommodates diverse situations

The fact that individuals have different preferences, that these change over time (often in unpredicted ways), and that many work and care events arise not from preferences but circumstances beyond individual control, means that policy should provide *a menu of options that accommodates diverse situations*.

These options should be genuine. They should be substantive (that is, have real life) rather than be merely formal (that is, real in name or law only – rather than *used* or *effective*). For example, a payment to carers at home, without real choice to do paid work (through job opportunities, child care, supportive leave and flexible workplaces), is not in support of genuine choice. Of course all options should be equally available to men and women (except where physical differences are in play, for example, breast feeding and birth). They should offer genuine options to both carers in paid work or outside it. They must recognise forms of care beyond children, including the aged, disabled, frail and others who depend on us.

Transparent, straightforward, administratively simple and easily understood

Lack of time is a critical factor for many households. Time pressures may well explain some of the low take up of the child care rebate (less than half of those eligible claim it at present). For this reason, and to ensure that access to any new regime is fair across a range of household types, it is important that all elements of a reformed Work/Care regime are straightforward and as simple as possible. Complex, multiple benefits are expensive to administer, difficult to use and the risk of making a mistake (and having to pay it back) is a disincentive to apply.

Quality, affordable care

This is a prime requirement of any regime that has as its primary goal the welfare of those who depend on us – whether sick, aged, frail, disabled or young. Child are needs to be cheaper, with increasing overall quality, and available to meet diverse needs.

Shared costs and benefits: governments, employers, employees and households

A better Work/Care regime requires large contributions from all of these. At present many of the costs of reproduction and care of those who depend on us are privately born, and their externality costs are hidden from view. However, many of the benefits – like reproduction of the labour force and maintenance of its capacity – are publicly shared or the basis of private profit. A *greater* contribution from governments and from employers is essential to a new and better regime in Australia, with a *lesser* contribution from those who take on most of the care and bear its costs, especially women, private households, dependants and the non-market community.

More support for those who need it more

Some Australian households need more support than others, depending upon income, education, unemployment and employment, and regional location. A good Work/Care regime will ensure that enough support reaches those most in need.

Key elements of a New Australian Work/Care regime: Reformed institutions and culture to support what we actually do

With these guiding principles in mind, we can consider the key elements that would contribute to a more effective Work/Care regime, arising from the previous chapters. The following ten areas of change refer to key institutional and cultural changes that are implicated through this book. They are summarised in Table 10.2 and are considered in turn.

Reduced hours of work

Australia's current Work/Care regime has particular characteristics which are hostile to the easy combination of jobs and care, and this regime is being set backwards by the intensification of jobs and their growing hours. 'Proper workers' are re-made in a more, not less, care-unfriendly 'ideal worker' image. Carers cannot easily meet standards that make it *harder* to accommodate behaviours like a shared household practice of work and care. It is harder to be a carer when your partner works long hours. And it is harder to be a worker when that is the growing expectation. For these reasons, change in the hours of paid work, as set out in Table 10.2 are vital if we are to achieve a better Work/Care regime. These include reduced full-time working weeks, control of overtime, the eradication of unpaid overtime, staffing levels that do not drive a tendency to overwork, and challenges to the long hours cultures that pervade too many workplaces now. The benefits of these changes will be felt in workplaces, households and neighbourhood communities. They will benefit our dependants and – especially if the low pay problem that drives some to work excessive hours is met through wage increases for the low paid – they will enhance the lives we live.

Secure part-time jobs

Part-time work is one of the main Australian means of attempting to reconcile work and care. It contrasts with other possible approaches: taking extended paid leave to care (through paid leave as in Sweden or payment to carers), or having high levels of state support for care so that carers can work full-time and be confident their dependants are well cared for (as in Finland).

However, in Australia, workplace institutions – and the gaps in their regulatory machinery – mean that part-time work is undertaken on poor terms: it is concentrated among low paid jobs, it has poor security and it lacks many basic conditions (including things essential to carers, like holiday, sick and paid maternity leave). This might be called the 'degraded work/care combination track'. Its renovation is critical to a better work/care system and several changes are essential. Table 10.2 sets out a plan to 'de-casualise' part-time work that is not genuinely short term and restore rights to holiday and sick leave along with many other conditions, rights and workplace benefits. These require legislative, award and workplace action.

Leave

Australia's work leave regime is in need of both significant repair and extension. Deteriorating access to long established leave rights like sick and holiday leave, makes repair of these provisions essential, along with access for all women to paid maternity leave, and improved rights for men and women to paid parental leave, paid leave to care for sick dependants and more flexibility in leave taking.

Care

Concern about cost, quality and access exists among those who use paid care. Each of these is central to ensuring that a universal right to publicly provided care is meaningful for all workers. Not all will make use of it, but its lack of provision removes *substantive effective choice* for worker/carers about their key decisions. The absence of affordable, quality care, conscripts women to home or forces their use of informal care. While informal care is successfully used by many Australians – either through mother's own care, or extended family or community – without the option of quality public options, its use is forced. The outcomes for women, children, other dependants and the community can be sub-optimal and sometimes tragic.

Workplaces

Workplace arrangements can either facilitate worker/carers or frustrate them. Many measures can be taken in workplaces that are cost-neutral, involving some reorganisation of established practices. They mean changes in culture and the valuation of workers and their larger lives. Employees value the efforts of employers and supervisors to make work more care-friendly. Other measures like paid leave to care for sick dependants require real expenditures by employers. These are a significant impost. But as one of the main long-term beneficiaries of the reproduction of consumers and employees, workplaces have a great deal to reap from a better Work/Care regime.

Government payments to families

There can be no doubt that Australia is in need of an overhaul of work/family payments, one of the largest areas of government spending in the nation. The Federal Government currently spends over $18 billion a year on family supports like child care, family tax breaks, baby bonuses and so on. With so much spent, why are so many families and households reporting continuing pressure? There are many better ways we could allocate resources, including through a simplified system of payments that are made directly to carers (rather than to their working partners through the tax system), with support especially targeted at the years of intensive caring (that is, under three years in the case of children). Payments should be restructured to provide government funding for paid maternity leave for all women in paid work, and to provide payments to carers with children at home (which those carers can then elect to take as income, or use to buy care).

Domestic work and unpaid care

The fairer redistribution of housework and care of those who depend on us is one of the most obvious ways in which our current arrangements need to change. Yet this redistribution is among the hardest to make. Women and men in this study associate men's definition of themselves 'as men' with their refusal of housework. This cultural mud has serious consequences – it costs marriages and destroys intimate relationships – and without change it threatens to perpetuate itself through successive generations. Mere hope that men will change, that boys will grow up differently, that fairness will gradually prevail, has proved a weak force in the face of masculine culture. Nonetheless, this area of work and care reallocation between the sexes remains a pressing need. Women's turn to the market for assistance has limitations: only those with disposable income can get this help, and it has its limits as many forms of care are better done by intimate relations than strangers. This redistribution also raises issues for women, many of whom are attached to the domestic sphere and define themselves through care, domestic work and 'their standards'.

The cultures of motherhood, fatherhood and care

Motherhood is undergoing a paradigm shift with new work patterns. In practice it is shifting away from a model that placed the woman/mother at the centre of the domestic sphere. Now, mothers sit on unstable terrain. What should they be? What are they? The fact that there are so many ways, now, to be a mother has made society uncertain about mothers, and a profound anxiety frequently attaches to the business of being a mother. This anxiety is expressed through criticism (and self-criticism) of many forms of mothering and mother's decisions – even where these decisions are clearly household and community decisions, with partners, employers, government all ghosts at the table, effectively shaping outcomes. This critique and the 'mother wars' it provokes, is visited upon women in many ways, on many issues. This is most obviously evident in competing discourses about mothers – whether 'proper' mothers, welfare mothers, working mothers, at-home mothers, super mothers. The self sacrificing ideal of traditional motherhood has given away to a much more diverse set of possibilities in practice, but the cultural hangover of the intensive, self-sacrificial mother means that most of these possibilities are lived out by women amidst an epidemic of guilt, persistent adjustment and readjustment, and internal and external conflict. Among other indicators, we can read the costs of these outcomes in divorce statistics. Many of these experiences are privately felt. But some find social expression in community conflict and controversy – over child care (to use, or not to use), over paid work (to do, or not to do), and over voluntary work in the community ('I'm doing yours'). An important component of a new Work/Care regime is liberation from the cultures of intensive mothering, greater expectations of fathers, and greater valuation of care itself.

Revitalising community

Our communities are being reconfigured. Whereas 20 or 30 years ago many Australians experienced and recreated their communities at the local street or regional level, now community is increasingly located and created through our workplaces. Our streetscapes have been de-populated by day, and this has implications for those who remain there – mothers, carers and the unemployed. If the workplace is increasingly a place where social webs are created, what are the implications for those outside the web? People increasingly define themselves through work and their jobs. They gain considerable pleasure from these identities. But many are then shaken when they leave the workplace or are outside it for any lengthy period of time – to do unpaid work at home, for example – and this has important implications for the quality of home life and for social capital. For these reasons, more deliberate strengthening of local communities is important, through support for those doing unpaid work, voluntary work, and improved neighbourhood facilities to support those who live there.

Rethinking consumption

Working parents talk about using their income to compensate their children for their hours at work and many pay for the care of their parents. Parents of young children talk of ameliorating guilt about hours in paid work and away from children, through buying things. As we have seen, the level of comfort with this compensation fluctuates. It represents a new degree of marketisation: trading money for love. Where money has long been used to buy many forms of care, the shift of paid work to centre stage in the social organisation of our lives has created new exchanges, and some ambivalence. Its effect on our overall welfare and happiness is unclear. The relationship between money and happiness has attracted growing research interest recent years, revealing a weak relationship between the two. This is surprising in view of the centrality of money and its pursuit in the lives of so many. These quandaries suggest a rethinking of consumption patterns which drive hours of work and household work patterns. The growth of competitive consumption is very strong, as individuals work hard to keep up with the new things and standards acquired by friends and neighbours. Many acquisitions have perhaps a limited impact on quality of happiness, especially when their time cost is weighed. For these reasons, a rethink about consumption is timely; indeed it is underway in many households with one in four Australians downshifting in the past decade, as they re-evaluate their work and spending habits (Hamilton and Mail 2003). Downshifting the expectations of children seems to be an important part of this picture.

The program of reform set out in Table 10.2 is large and expensive. It challenges deep cultures and so cannot be quickly implemented. It sets out goals for the long term. But such a long-term plan is essential if progress is to be made and measured. Governments approach such areas of reform with much shorter term timeframes: a few years at most. Even within such shorter frames, however, important changes can be accomplished and some priorities stand out: notably change with respect to hours, part-time work and leave. Even within these areas, some issues are more pressing that others, while in the remaining seven areas other priorities are also pressing (not least support for carers at home and for improved child care provision). Without change in cultural factors, like attitudes and behaviours around domestic work, care, motherhood, fatherhood and consumption, change is likely to be slow and hesitant. Each of the ten key areas needs reform if Australia's Work/Care regime is to achieve a more comfortable alignment of behaviour, institutions and culture.

Conclusion: love, life, care and work

Australia's current Work/Care regime is characterised by dissonance and instability. In Australia at present many experience the misalignment of culture, institutions and behaviour, as the old 'breadwinner man/carer woman' household attempts to make the shift to new relationships in the context of a Work/Care regime and its culture and institutions that cannot easily accommodate these new behaviours. The Work/Care misalignments, and their implications for our lives, are many. Many people speak positively of their relationships and rewards through their jobs.

Table 10.2 Ten Key Measures for a New Australian Work/Care Regime

Ten Key Measures for a New Australian Work/Care Regime	Nature of Specific Changes	Benefits
Hours of Paid Work	• Reduce ordinary hours of full-time working week • Cap overtime • Phase out unpaid overtime • Give greater rights to workers to avoid carer-unfriendly working hours • Staffing agreements that ensure adequate staffing • Increase wages of low paid who use overtime to earn living wage • Increase compliance machinery to ensure regulations are implemented • Increase means of reducing hours through leave banks, 48/52 or related schemes • Measures to modify prevailing 'long hours' cultures through management initiatives and modelling	• More productive and healthier workplaces and workers • Hours that support worker/carers, rather than make their juggle more difficult • Better welfare for mothers, fathers, children and other dependents • Healthier and stronger communities, underwriting greater social capital • Better health outcomes • More intensive fathering, less intensive mothering • Increased equality between women and men • Redistribution of work from over-worked to under-employed and unemployed
Part-time Work	• Increase the status, security and conditions of part-time work by national and state legislative change, award amendment and enterprise initiatives • Give casual employees rights to convert to permanent work after six months employment • Establish rights to part-time work for all employees, with rights of reversal to full-time • Confine casual employment to the genuinely casual • Fully compensate for casual's lost benefits by increasing casual loading	• Greater permanency and better conditions for part-time work • Less discrimination against part-timers • More stability for households and individuals dependent on part-time work • Retention and development of part-time skilled employees

Ten Key Measures for a New Australian Work/Care Regime	Nature of Specific Changes	Benefits
Part-time Work (cont)	• Eliminate any differences in conditions between full-timers and part-timers that create an employer incentive to casualise (eg weak rights to unfair dismissal, redundancy, consultation, representation) • Strengthen and enforce anti-discrimination measures to prevent direct or indirect discrimination between classes of employees based on hours of work alone • Create portable rights for shorter term workers to carry forward entitlements including leave • Modifying objects of workplace relations law to make secure, quality part-time work an object of the industrial system • Strengthen institutions that facilitate 'integrative transitions' between care/full-time/part-time work (eg labour exchanges, group employment schemes) • Adoption of protocols and directives for quality part-time work	• Greater productivity in workplaces • Greater gender pay equity
Leave	• Reinstate access to holiday and sick leave for all workers who are not genuinely casual (and who should be fully compensated for their loss) • Improve access to long service leave and build upon this scheme to create portable leave banks • Implement three months paid maternity leave for all working mothers at close to ordinary earnings • Phase in paid parental leave for one year to be shared by parents • Implement paid paternity leave of two weeks • Implement two weeks of paid emergency family leave to care for sick dependents and household care emergencies	• Greater productivity in workplaces • Retention and development of skilled employees • Better welfare for mothers, fathers, children and other dependents • Healthier communities and stronger communities, underwriting greater social capital • More father involvement in care of dependents, more equity for mothers and female carers

Ten Key Measures for a New Australian Work/Care Regime	Nature of Specific Changes	Benefits
Leave (cont)	• Provide extended unpaid leave for workers where they retain job security and tenure while undertaking non-work activity • Give greater flexibility in leave taking through award and enterprise agreements • Establish general leave banks to facilitate the accumulation of leave to meet variety of needs	
Care	• Extension of quality, affordable universal child care within reasonable distance of children of all working Australians • Extend out of school hours care to all potential users • Improved respite and other forms of public care to support full-time carers • Implement access to free, government-funded pre-school education/care for all three and four years olds in Australia, integrated with (ie co-located and end-on-to) child care • Integrated state/federal system of pre-school/child care education for 3–4 year olds • Higher pay for those who provide care • Strong regulation of formal care, with effective enforcement and support for providers • Better public funding of formal care	• Real choice for parents between work/care and home/care combinations • Reduced child care imposts on parents which create disincentive to work • Safer children and dependents with better educational and care outcomes • Less parental worry • Fewer institutional transitions for children between forms of care • More administrative efficiency • Greater gender pay equity
Workplace	• Provision of more flexible working hours at workers' discretion, subject to negotiation • Tax and other supports for carer-friendly initiatives by employers • Provision of new leave to care for sick dependents and emergencies	• More productive workplaces • Retention of skilled and experienced employees • Better reproduction of next generation of workers

Ten Key Measures for a New Australian Work/Care Regime	Nature of Specific Changes	Benefits
Workplace (cont)	• Supervisor and management training about work/care combination • Initiatives to reduce long hours and break long hours cultures, including through management example • Implementation of part-time work arrangements with both formal and substantive equality between full-timers and part-timers • De-casualisation of part-time work	• Better workplace relations and environments • Fairer workplaces
Payments to Families	• Financial support for full-time carers through payment directly to carers, especially when caring is most intensive (ie higher payments to carers of children 0–3 years). Payments can be used as carers see fit (eg as payment while caring at home, or for public care fees)	• More choice for parents between work/care and home/care combinations • More financial support for carers • Better opportunities for parents to provide care • More support for informal carers • Greater capacity for volunteering and formal and informal community activity
Domestic Work and Unpaid Care	• Men do more unpaid care work • Men do more housework • Women lower standards, exercise less control, and do less care and unpaid domestic work • Children trained, especially boys, to do domestic and care work • Better provision of household support and care services	• Fewer divorces • Less marital discord • Fairer sharing between women and men • A more equal workplace for women • Stronger relationships between men and dependents

Ten Key Measures for a New Australian Work/Care Regime	Nature of Specific Changes	Benefits
Cultures of Motherhood Fatherhood and The Value of Care	• Higher value placed on care, carers and dependents across society • Liberation of women from cultures of 'intensive' mothering, and greater sharing of care with men • Greater valuation, and expectation, of men as carers • Greater public benefits, including payments, to full-time carers • Higher pay to workers in caring occupations and to caring institutions	• Less guilt for women and mothers • Fairer measures of guilt between the sexes • More sex • Higher pay for feminised occupations and industries (where most public care is done) • More validation of women who choose not to mother • More men modelling care to their children
Revitalising Community	• Improved neighbourhood facilities and organisations that *enable* local community and counter the shift of community to workplaces • Greater support for carers so that unpaid work is shared more among more carers, and their local communities are more densely populated	• Healthier neighbourhood communities • Greater social capital • Less isolated carers and dependents
Rethinking Consumption	• Wanting less stuff beyond a decent living standard • Less competitive consumption (ie seeking what others have regardless of real need) • Educating children to want less stuff • Recognising that money is no substitute for life and love	• More non-work time in households • More care-rich, materially-realistic dependents, less parental harassment in pursuit of material wealth • Less unproductive consumption • Better environmental outcomes

But these rewards are not without complications – for raising children; running homes and schools; for health and well being; and for our most intimate relationships. A great number enjoy their paid work, but they also talk of growing pressures to *do* more and *be* more. As paid work has become more intense, and employees have extended their hours and skills, these pressures have increased. The tensions between the different spheres of our lives – and the shifting boundaries between them – are unsettling for relationships, families and community.

Our institutions and cultures lag behind the changes in our lives. The fit is now poor – in terms of the ways that workplaces and community institutions fit with parenting, pregnancy, care of elders and the disabled, responsibility for households, and the career and income aspirations of women and men. This poor fit affects those in paid work as well as those who want to stay home when their children are small or beyond, making it difficult for them to re-enter work later, imposing a burden of social isolation and an unfair degree of voluntary work on some. The workplace and family vectors of change collide with lagging institutions and culture, and the casualty is life and its quality.

The public policy discussion about the 'family friendly' workplace and about men's changing roles, is revealed as more rhetorical than real. It is an important 'cover story'. The iceberg tip of work and family 'good practice' – as modelled in Chapter 1 – is contradicted by the great bulk of dangerous berg that lies beneath the surface. Workplace, domestic and personal rigidities stand unchanged in many locations. Common assumptions about greater 'family friendliness' in our institutions and society are quite out of step with many of the experiences revealed in this book. Indeed, growing demands in many workplaces, and employment insecurity and unpredictability are making it more difficult for many. Not all are directly caught in the collision, but many feel its consequences, including the unemployed and under-employed, the one in four Australian women who are likely to remain childless, and the larger society which is affected by both.

Community expectations are out of kilter with the changing reality of many lives, so that some women at home feel criticised for being there while some women in paid work also feel criticised. It is time for greater genuine acceptance of the diversity of options that people live – women, but also men – and for better public policy to support these and other options. It is time for our institutions to catch up with the realities that are now our lives. The sticky mud of culturally constructed 'intensive' mothering and its 'going rate' remains a mirror held up – one way or another – to real mothers, and the gap between the image and reality is painful. Women constitute most of the growth in the paid labour market at present, and most of it predictably into the future. Men's participation in paid work is in long-term decline; their greater participation in the work of care and domestic production is long overdue. Fathering has remained unintensive for most. The issue of a collision between our lives and institutions and sticky cultures, is likely to get bigger not smaller. The squeeze on care and community by paid work is likely to intensify rather than naturally abate.

There is a significant shift underway in Australian society. At present this shift is being met, largely, by the marginal adaptations that women and men make as individuals (working part-time or shiftwork, for example) and by anxiety or overwork at home when these are inadequate. It is time that the adaptive mechanisms moved to the community's centre-stage, through more widespread and fundamental changes – by men, workplaces, governments and the larger community. A failure to recognise the shift that is underway, and to allow adaptation to it to be privately born by individuals – particularly carers – weakens the fabric of community, and affects the quality of life – not only of women, but also children, the aged and infirm, the unemployed and men. It certainly affects workplaces, productivity and the labour market, and it costs governments money, not least when families disintegrate under pressure. Perhaps one of the most obvious effects of this shift, and the collision between our institutions and the circumstances of our lives, is the declining birth rate in Australia. Environmental concerns aside, this decline (with its multiple causes) has important implications for the future of Australian society, its workforce, the dependence of retirees on the future working population, and our standard of living. Many arguments about a 'birth strike' miss a key point: wombs are connected to brains. Women are not fools, and neither are their partners. Nor are they selfish, self-interested and absconding from a responsibility to nation. As the ones who, in the main, end up with main care of children and other dependants, women – having achieved control of their fertility – are thoughtful about their decisions. Many of their grandmothers and great-grandmothers did not want to have eight or six or even four children. But they had no choice. The long-term, secular decline in the birth rate is a slow effect of the exercise of choice about fertility and its changing social and work circumstances.

Now that women largely have a choice about reproduction (though far from all forms of care), they think carefully about their own options, and the experiences they observe around them, including in their own families where so many of their mothers entered paid work but were offered no relief on the home front and faced inflexible terms at work. Many of their mothers won the dubious right to the exhausting double day. And work/family supports have shown too little change in the past few decades, rhetoric aside. So a major obstacle to the exhortation to go forth and produce is the inconvenient link between womb and brain. The poor circumstances for the combination of caring and paid work in Australia particularly affect women who are the principle decision makers when it comes to reproduction. They are contributing to women having – whether by choice or fact – smaller numbers of children, later pregnancies, or no children at all. Exhortations to marry, to have more children, or to have them earlier, will fall upon deaf ears until the practical business of leading a full life – with realistic choices, less guilt, more gender equity, better and fairer rewards at work, and more societal support for their decisions – is improved.

There are many priorities. 'Too many priorities' can become a convenient shield in the face of a specific demand like more leave for carers with jobs. Those who oppose such changes, generate the list of alternatives, not because they want to *give* other things, but to derail specific demands. This is the device of 'too many alternatives, let's do nothing'.

The challenge we face is to modify our Work/Care regime to meet diverse needs and catch up with behavioural realities. These needs are not always the result of choice: no-one chooses a disabled child or a dependant parent. As long as policy makers or governments believe the issue is one of 'choice' they are ascribing too much power to individual agency. Policy makers in this frame are easily satisfied that enough choice exists. Or they may decide to expand choices at the margin. Either way, this framework does not encourage a focus on the constraints that shape or determine choices, and it keeps the cultures and habits that construct and limit choices, out of view. As long as the emphasis is on choice, it keeps a deeper renovation and broader menu of options, conventions and habits, off the agenda. At present in most places there is simply *no* option to choose, for example, decently paid permanent part-time work or income support while caring for a child for a year or two. Payment to stay at home and care for children is more conscription than choice unless decent employment opportunities underpinned by affordable care options exist. Second, the 'choice' framework encourages a *mildly incremental* policy approach, rather than a deeper renovation that examines the social, economic and institutional basis of current patterns. The core ideals of the ideal-male market worker – with his carefree habits of full-time work, long hours and skill or career – are not reformed, any more than the idea that of the ideal-female domestic and care worker.

How freely is choice truly exercised in any given set of institutions or culture? What constraints exist? Are all the penalties and rewards of these choices and constraints known in advance? These remain key issues for policy and theory in relation to work, care and life. Without a focus on constraints –

in all their social, cultural, economic and institutional reality – the presumption of choice is mistaken. It is a cover story for the true situation. As Joan Williams puts it 'Choice rhetoric serves to veil the powerful mandates of domesticity in the language of self-fulfilment' (2000: 39).

Without romanticising the lives of women and men who have gone before, some of the boundaries and fixities we now live with are inconsistent and inequitable. The implications of the growing marketisation of care, food and social life – even sex – have important effects on our lives and their quality. Money cannot replace love or time. The market sale of our time, love and care also has important implications for those other major aims in life: the creation of community, family, friendship and intimacy.

The current boundaries and the roles that women, men and children adopt in relation to them – between paid and unpaid work, home and workplace, kitchen and office, public and private – and the increasing reach of the market into care, affects the quality of our lives, our families and our relationships. The frontiers of these boundaries are changing. We are seeing a strong expansion of the market boundary in relation to care and the domestic sphere. We are also seeing a shift in the boundary between volunteer work and the paid labour market, with government policies that – in the name of 'deinstitutionalisation', 'mutual obligation' or of cost-cutting – put caring for the sick, disabled or aged back into the community. Some current patterns of paid work, undermine both the conservative and 'New Labor' calls for a return to reliance upon community – a community made frailer by some current changes.

A rhetorical valorisation of the unpaid carer accompanies this call. However, money, training and good institutional support for the unpaid worker is slower to follow. At the same time, with a growing intrusion of paid work into our lives – with more and more hours of both women's and men's time sucked into the vortex of paid work – those who do unpaid work struggle for enough time to do unpaid work, whether it is formal in schools, service and sports clubs or informal through 'street-care' of neighbours, parents and friends.

Intergenerational shifts like those experienced over the last half century are so gradual that they are rarely mapped, so that societies fall into unconscious choices and privatised costs and benefits. It is not clear that they are always for the better. With powerful interests making significant profits from our consumption of particular services (fast food, aged and health care for the wealthy) and little profit from others (community managed child care of babies or care of the mentally ill), there are powerful motors driving the shape of market patterns. And these are being imposed on a landscape that is inscribed with ancient patterns of gender that promise women and men different outcomes. We need to be more conscious as a community about the true public and private costs and benefits of how we live and work now, and how we make and remake the larger landscape within which we all live.

This is not an argument for a return to some golden age when we all cared for each other, made our own butter, and women stayed home. This was no golden age, as many stories of private misery and violence remind us. Women's 'choices' in this age did not include control of their own fertility, entry to education and political voice, or access to an income of their own. Care for the vulnerable or dependant was poor. Many men found themselves on a long-term treadmill of dangerous or hard work with limited relationships with their children. It is, however, an argument for a deeper and a more deliberate community conversation about our values, actions, and options in a world that is increasingly dominated by paid work and where we use money to buy all kinds of goods and care, and sometimes, even – we hope – love. And there is a strong argument for action to provide better options that support the reality that will confront most of the current and next generation of Australians: how to – over the life-cycle – combine paid work with care of oneself, one's loved ones and dependants, nested in an enabling community, and to make better lives.

Appendix: Data sources

This book makes use of two main sources of qualitative data – interviews and focus groups – and sets them in the context of various sources of quantitative data – mostly large surveys. Many of the latter are time series collected and available from the Australian Bureau of Statistics; these are listed in the bibliography. Two other large surveys are referred to:

The Australian Workplace Industrial Relations Survey (AWIRS) Survey

This survey, conducted in 1990 and 1995, collected information in a broad range of over 2000 workplaces with 20 or more employees. It involved collection of data about workplace characteristics, and surveys of general managers, employee relations managers, some workplace delegates and, in the 1995 study, a random survey of over 19,000 employees. This provides information about a wide range of workplace and employment-related issues, as well as detailed information about employee views on a wide range of issues (Callus et al 1991, Morehead et al 1997).

The Household, Income and Labour Dynamics in Australian (HILDA) Survey

This longitudinal survey is described in the 2002 HILDA Annual Report (Melbourne Institute 2002). It is based on similar international studies and collects data from a large, nationally representative sample of households about income, labour market and family dynamics. The initial sample of households was conducted in 2001 and these households will be re-surveyed in subsequent surveys. The 2001 study collected data by means of an initial personal interview of at least one adult member of the household, a personal questionnaire of all household members aged 15 years or over, and a self-completion questionnaire provided to all those adults personally interviewed. In the first round, successful first interviews were undertaken in 7,682 of the 11,693 randomly selected 'in scope' households and personal interviews were conducted with 13,965 adults. Most of these also completed the self-completion questionnaire.

The first wave of HILDA was conducted in the second half of 2001, and is referred to as 2001 HILDA throughout the book, though most references are drawn from secondary sources. The survey is run by the Melbourne Institute for Applied Economics and Social Research at the University of Melbourne.

Qualitative data

Two main sources of qualitative evidence are drawn on through the book and both have been discussed in more detail elsewhere (Pocock 2001a; Pocock, van Wanrooy, Strazzari and Bridge 2001). The first data arises from focus groups and interviews among 163 mainly women living in South Australia. These investigated how work – broadly defined – is affecting people. The second source is a set of interviews of workers in 12 industries or occupations across Australia, and their partners, investigating the effects of long hours of work on individuals, families and the community. These qualitative materials draw on relatively small, non-random samples. They are used to give voice to individuals about their social experiences. They have several limitations, for example the first study is over-reliant upon women. This problem is not uncommon in social and labour market research – more commonly through an over-reliance on men, or the failure to distinguish the sexes at all. Sennett relies, for example, almost exclusively upon male accounts and experiences in his 1998 book, and this is not unusual. As Bittman and Mahmud Rice observe 'Traditionally the study of labour market behaviour has been the study of the behaviour of men' (2002: 13). In my first source of qualitative data only six of the 163 subjects are men. This means that the issues affecting fathers and men are under-attended. But this does not negate the analysis, which draws only in part on these qualitative materials; it does mean, however, that it is incomplete. I hope this gap will be filled in further research.

The South Australian location of the first set of subjects is also an issue. However, it is unlikely that the pressures on workers and carers in South Australia are *less* than those experienced in the much larger states of New South Wales and Victoria, for example, which are dominated by large cities where the pace of lives, and problems of housing and travel are widely recognised as much more intensive that in smaller States like South Australia.

Focus groups are useful for investigating issues that require self-appraisal, an exchange of views, and reflection (Probert and MacDonald 1996). They allow a conversation about complex issues. Fifteen focus groups were conducted, along with 28 additional interviews. The focus groups were selected to represent a diverse range of work/home situations including carers at home, volunteers and paid workers in a variety of situations including call centres, factories, hospitals, nursing homes and farms. The focus groups included a variety of occupations across the employment hierarchy from factory and call centre operatives, to professionals like lawyers and doctors. At least one focus group was held for each of these groups. Supplementary interviews were conducted with those who could not easily participate in focus groups (these included those running small business, managers, supervisors, volunteers, journalists and nurses on shift work). 'Work' was defined to include paid and unpaid work, so the group of subjects included carers at home with dependants, those in paid work, and volunteers. The subjects received widely varying incomes, and included residents in cities, towns and on farms, and individuals with a diverse range of caring responsibilities (children, grand-children, aged relatives, dependants with disabilities) and in full-time, part-time, casual and self-employment. Their ages ranged from 17 to 70, with the most common participant being a woman of between 25 and 60 years old, with caring responsibilities, in some form of paid or voluntary work. The focus groups and interviews were established by invitation through workplaces, community organisations, unions, small business networks, women's organisations, child care centres and preschools. The research set out to examine in open-ended conversation, the relationships between paid work and personal and family life, particularly as these affected women. Focus groups and interviews were audio taped.

Participants were found by several methods: approaching employers who called for volunteers from their workplaces; approaching individuals from particular occupational or representative groups (like mothers or fathers at home, doctors, lawyers) who were then interviewed or organised focus groups of other similar people; approaching community, health, and child care centres and preschools to organise focus groups and interviews, approaching unions and local representatives on regional bodies in country towns to find points of contact from which to organise focus groups and interviews. People in middle and senior management and small businesses from both the public and private sectors were also interviewed.

The second source of qualitative data is provided by a set of interviews with 54 workers who worked long hours, and further interviews with 35 of their partners. These interviews were collected in 2001 as part of the ACTU test case to reduce unreasonable hours. With the help of unions, lists of long hours workers were generated from which a subset were randomly selected and interviewed for around an hour. The interviews were audio taped. These employees worked in 13 industries and included doctors, public service workers, strappers in the racing industry, supervisors, teachers, postal workers, electricians, technicians, engineers, miners, flight attendants and paramedics. Many of the partners of these workers held jobs in other industries and occupations while others worked at home caring for the household. Once again, open-ended interviews were conducted and recorded around a range of themes: general information about hours and type of work, the effects of working hours on individuals, families and communities, and their ideas about ideal hours of work in their households. Interviews recorded an open-ended conversation, and in most cases long hours employees and their partners were interviewed separately. Sixty-nine per cent of the 54 employees interviewed were men, and three quarters of the partners were women. Two thirds lived in households with dependent children, 15 per cent in couple-only households and nine per cent lived alone.

Bibliography

ABS (1995) *Working Arrangements, Australia*, Cat No 6342.0, Canberra, ABS.

ABS (1998) *Caring in the Community*, Australia, Cat No 4436.0, Canberra, ABS.

ABS (1999) *Balancing Work and Caring Responsibilities*, Tasmania, Cat No 4903.6, Canberra, ABS.

ABS (1999) *Children, Australia: A Social Report*, Cat No 4119.0, Canberra, ABS.

ABS (1999) *Household and Family Projections, Australia, 1996-2021*, Cat No 3236.0, Canberra, ABS.

ABS (1999) *How Australians Use Their Time*, Cat No 4153.0, Canberra, ABS.

ABS (1999) *Measuring Australia's Progress*, Cat No 1370.0, Canberra, ABS.

ABS (2000) *Occasional Paper: Unpaid Work and the Australian Economy* Cat No 5240, Canberra, ABS.

ABS (2001) *Managing Caring Responsibilities and Paid Employment, New South Wales: Summary of Findings*, Cat No 4903.1, Canberra, ABS.

ABS (June 2000) *Survey of Employment Arrangements and Superannuation April-June 2000*, Cat No 6361.0, Canberra, ABS.

ABS (Various years) *Australian Social Trends*, Cat No 4102.0, Canberra, Australian Bureau of Statistics.

ABS (Various years) *Births, Australia*, Cat No 3301.0, Canberra, Australian Bureau of Statistics.

ABS (Various years) *Forms of Employment, Australia*, Cat No 6359.0, Canberra, ABS.

ABS (Various years) *Labour Force, Australia*, Cat No 6203.0, Canberra, ABS.

ABS (Various years) *Labour Force, Australia, Preliminary*, Cat No 6202.0, Canberra, ABS.

ABS (Various years) *Labour Force, Selected Summary Tables, Australia*, Cat No 6291.0.40.001, Canberra, ABS.

ABS (Various years) *Labour Force Status and Other Characteristics of Families, Australia*, Cat No 6224.0, Canberra, ABS.

ABS (Various years) *Marriages and Divorces, Australia*, Cat No 3310.0, Canberra, ABS.

ABS (Various years) *Population by Age and Sex, Australian States and Territories*, Cat No 3201.0, Canberra, ABS.

ABS (Various years) *Working Arrangements, Australia*, Cat No 6342.0, Canberra, ABS.

ABS (Various years) *Childcare, Australia*, Cat No 4402.0, Canberra, ABS.

ABS (Various years) *Employee Earnings, Benefits and Trade Union Membership, Australia*, Cat No 6310.0, Canberra, ABS.

ABS (Various years) *Household Expenditure Survey, Australia: Detailed Expenditure Items*, Cat No 6535.0, Canberra, ABS.

ABS (Various years) *Labour Mobility, Australia*, Cat No 6209.0, Canberra, ABS.

ABS (Various years) *Voluntary work, Australia*, Cat No 4441.0, Canberra, ABS.

ACIRRT (1999) *Australia at Work: Just Managing?* Sydney, Prentice Hall.

ACIRRT (2001) *Working Time Arrangements In Australia: A Statistical Overview*, Sydney, ACIRRT.

ACIRRT (2002) *September ADAM Report*, Sydney, ACCIRT.

ACTU (1999) *Employment Security & Working Hours – A National Survey of Current Workplace Issues*, Melbourne, ACTU.

ACTU (1999) *A Report on the 1997 ACTU National Survey on Stress at Work*, Melbourne, Occupational Health and Safety Unit.

ACTU (2000) *Working Families in the New Millennium, An ACTU Action Plan for Balancing Work and Family Life*, Melbourne, ACTU.

AIRC (2002) Full Bench Decision, *Working Hours Case*, 23 July 2002, PR072002, Melbourne, AIRC.

Allan, C (1997) 'The Elasticity of Endurance; Work Intensification and Workplace Flexibility in the Queensland Public Hospital System', *New Zealand Journal of Industrial Relations* 23(3): 133-151.

Allen, C, O'Donnell, M and Peetz, D (1999) 'More tasks, Less Secure, Working Harder: Three Dimensions of Labour Utilisation', *Journal of Industrial Relations* 41(4).

Appelbaum, E, Bailey, T, Berg, P and Kalleberg, A (2001) *Shared Work/Valued Care: new Norms for Organizing Market Work and Unpaid Care Work*, Washington, Economic Policy Institute.

Australian Education Union (1999) *Building on the Foundations of our Future: A National Research Project Exploring the Context of Women Teachers' Work in the Late 1990s*, Southbank, Australian Education Union.

Australian Institute of Family Studies (1997) *Australian Family Profiles, Social and Demographic Profiles*, Melbourne, AIFS.

Australian Institute of Family Studies (1999) 'Costs of Children Update', *Family Matters* No 53: 60-64.

Baird, M, Brennan, D and Cutcher, L (2002) 'A Pregnant Pause: Paid Maternity Leave in Australia', *Labour & Industry* 13(1): 1-21.

Baxter, J (2000) 'Barriers to Equality: Men's and Women's Attitudes to Workplace Entitlements in Australia', *Journal of Sociology* 36 (March)(1): 12-24.

Baxter, J (2002) 'Patterns of Change and Stability in the Gender Division of Labour in Australia, 1986-1997', *Journal of Sociology* 38(4): 399-424.

Belkin, L (2002) *Life's Work: Confessions of an Unbalanced Mom*, New York, Simon and Schuster.

Bell, M and Hugo, G (2000) *Internal Migration in Australia, 1991-1996*, Canberra, AGPS.

Biddulph, S and Biddulph, S (1999) *The Making of Love, The Nuts, Bolts and Roses of Staying in Love as a Couple Even with Kids!* Sydney, Doubleday.

Bittman, M (1998a) 'Changing Family Responsibilities, The Role of Social Attitudes, Markets and the State', *Family Matters* Winter(50): 31-38.

Bittman, M (1998b) *The Land of the Lost Long Weekend?: Trends in Free Time, Among Working Age Australians, 1974-1992*, Sydney, Social Policy Research Centre, UNSW.

Bittman, M (1999) 'Parenthood without Penalty: Time Use and Public Policy in Australia and Finland', *Feminist Economics* 5(3): 27-42.

Bittman, M and Mahmud Rice, J (2002) 'The Spectre of Overwork: An Analysis of Trends Between 1974 and 1997 Using Australian Time-use Diaries', *Labour & Industry* 12(3): 5-21.

Bittman, M and Pixley, J (1997) *The Double Life of the Family: Myth, Hope and Experience*, Sydney, Allen & Unwin.

Bittman, M and J, Wajcman (2000) 'The Rush Hour: The Character of Leisure Time and Gender Equity', *Social Forces* 79(1): 165-177.

Bourdieu, P (1980) *The Logic of Practice*, Cambridge, Polity Press.

Breakspear, C (1998) *From Juggling to Managing/ The Evolution of Work and Family Policies in Three Australian Organisations*, Sydney, UNSW Studies in Organisational Analysis and Innovation, No 14, Industrial Relations Research Centre, UNSW.

Brennan, D (1999) *Childcare: Choice or Charade? Women, Public Policy and the State*, L Hancock, Melbourne, Macmillan: 85-98.

Buchanan, J and Thornthwaite, L (2001) *Paid work and parenting: Charting a new course for Australian families*, Sydney, ACCIRT.

Burgess, J, Sullivan, A and Strachan, G (2002) 'Long Service Leave in Australia: Rationale Application and Policy Issues', *Labour & Industry* 13(1): 21-38.

Busby, N (2001) 'The Part-time Workers (Prevention of Less Favourable Treatment) Regulations 2000: Righting a Wrong or Out of Proportion?' *Journal of Business Law* July: 344-356.

Callus, R, Morehead, A, Cully, M and Buchanan, J (1991) *Industrial Relations at Work, The Australian Workplace Industrial Relations Survey*, Canberra, AGPS.

Campbell, I (2001) *Cross National Comparisons, Submission to the AIRCs Test Case on Unreasonable Hours*, Melbourne, ACTU.

Campbell, I (2002a) 'Extended Working Hours in Australia', *Labour & Industry* 13(1): 73-90.

Campbell, I (2002b) 'Snatching at the Wind? Unpaid Overtime and Trade Unions in Australia', *International Journal of Employment Studies* 10(2): 109-156.

Campbell, I and Burgess, J (2001) 'Casual Employment in Australia and Temporary Employment in Europe: Developing a Cross-National Comparison', *Work, Employment and Society* 15(1): 171-184.

Campbell, I, Watson, I and Buchanan, J (2002) Temporary Agency Work in Australia: Towards an Analysis, Paper for a Conference on 'International Perspectives on Temporary Work and Workers', Newcastle, 28 February-1 March 2002, Newcastle.

Cebrian, I, Lallement, M and O'Reilly, J (2000) Introduction in J O'Reilly, I Cebrian and M Lallement, Cheltenham (eds) *Working-Time Changes, Social Integration Through Transitional Labour Markets*, Cheltenham: 1-24.

Cebrian, I, Lallement, M and O'Reilly, J (2000) *Working-time Changes, Social Integration Through Transitional Labour Markets* Cheltenham, Edward Elgar: 25-60.

Chapman, B, Dunlop, Y, Gray, M, Liu, A and Mitchell, D (1999) *The foregone earnings from childrearing revisited: Discussion paper No 47*, Canberra, Centre for Economic Policy Research, Australian National University.

Charlesworth, S, Campbell, I and Probert, B (2002) *Balancing Work and Family Responsibilities: Policy Implementation Options*, Melbourne, Centre for Applied Social Research, RMIT.

Connell, RW (1987) *Gender and Power: Society, the Person and Sexual Politics*, Cambridge, Polity Press.

Connell, RW (2002) *Gender*, Cambridge, Blackwell Publishers.

Considine, G and Buchanan, J (2000) *The Hidden Costs of Understaffing, An Analysis of Contemporary Nurses' Working Conditions in Victoria*, Sydney, ACIRRT.

Dawson, D, McCulloch, K and Baker, A (2001) *Extended Working Hours in Australia: Counting the Costs*, Adelaide, The Centre for Sleep Research, University of South Australia.

de Vaus, D and Wolcott, I (1997) *Australian Family Profiles: Social and Demographic Patterns*, Melbourne, Australian Institute of Family Studies.

Demsey, K (1990) *Smalltown: a study of social inequality, cohesion and belonging*, Melbourne, OUP.

Department of Employment and Industrial Relations Women's Bureau (1985) *Maternity and Parental Leave*, Canberra, AGPS.

Department of Employment and Workplace Relations (2001) *Workplace Agreements Database*, Canberra, Department of Employment and Workplace Relations.

Department of Employment and Workplace Relations (2002) *ACCI National Work and Family Awards 2002*, Canberra, Department of Employment and Workplace Relations.

Department of Employment and Workplace Relations (2002) *Trends in Federal Enterprise Bargaining, December Quarter, 2001*, Canberra, Department of Employment and Workplace Relations.

Department of Employment and Workplace Relations, Department of the Prime Minister and Cabinet and Department of Community Services (2002) *Submission to the Senate Employment, Workplace Relations and Education Legislation Committee*, Canberra, The Senate Employment, Workplace Relations and Education Legislation Committee.

Eckersley, R (1999) *Quality of Life in Australia: An Analysis of Public Perceptions*, Canberra, The Australia Institute.

Evans, MDR and Kelley, J (2001) 'Employment for Mothers of Pre-school Children; Evidence from Australia and 23 Other Nations', *People and Place* 9(3): 28-40.

Evans, MDR and Kelley, J (2002) 'Changes in Public Attitudes to Maternal Employment: Australia, 1984 to 2001', *People and Place* 10(1).

Fagan, C and Lallement, M (2000) Working Time, Social Integration and Transitional Labour Markets, in I Cebrian, M Lallement and J O'Reilly, *Working-time Changes, Social Integration Through Transitional Labour Markets* Cheltenham, Edward Elgar: 25-60.

Fagan, C and O'Reilly, J (1998) Conceptualising Part-time Work: The Value of an Integrated Comparative Perspective in J O'Reilly and C Fagan (eds) *Part-time Prospects, An International Comparison of Part-time Work in Europe*, North America and the Pacific Rim, London, Routledge: 1-33.

Fagan, C and Rubery, J (1996) Transitions Between Family Formation and Paid Employment, in G Schmid, J O'Reilly and K Schomann, *International Handbook of Labour Market Policy and Evaluation*, Cheltenham, UK, Edward Elgar: 348-378.

Fisher, K (2002) *Fertility Pathways in Australia: Relationships, Opportunities, Work and Parenting*, Canberra, Commonwealth Department of Family and Community Services.

Folbre, N (2001a) *The Invisible Heart, Economics and Family Values*, New York, The New Press.

Folbre, N (2001b) *The Distribution of the Costs of Children, International Perspectives on Low Fertility: Trends, Theories and Policies*, Tokyo, Paper presented to Conference in International Perspectives on Low Fertility, 21-23 March.

Frank, R (1999) *Luxury Fever: Money and Happiness in an Era of Excess*, Princeton, Princeton University Press.

Galinsky, E (1999) *Ask the Children: What America's Children Really Think About Working Parents*, New York, William Morrow and Company.

Galinsky, E, Kim, S and Bond, J (2001) *Feeling overworked: when work becomes too much*, New York, Families and Work Institute.

Giddens, A (1992) *Transformation of Intimacy : Sexuality, Love and Eroticism in Modern Societies*, Cambridge, Polity Press.

Gilligan, C (1982) *In a Different Voice: Psychological Theory and Women's Development*, Cambridge, Harvard University Press.

Glezer, H and Wolcott, I (2000) Conflicting Commitments: Working Mothers and Fathers in Australia in L Haas, P Hwang and G Russell *Organizational Change and Gender Equity*, London, Sage: 43-56.

Glucksmann, M (1995) 'Why Work? Gender and the "Total Social Organisation of Labour"', *Gender, Work and Society* 2(2): 63-75.

Hakim, C (2000) *Work-lifestyle Choices in the 21st Century*, Preference Theory, Oxford, Oxford University Press.

Hamilton, C (2002) *Overconsumption in Australia: The Rise of the Middle Class Battler*, Canberra, The Australia Institute.

Hamilton, C and Mail, E (2003) *Downshifting in Australia, A Sea-Change in the Pursuit of Happiness*, Canberra, The Australia Institute.

Hancock, L (ed) (1999) *Women, Public Policy and the State*, Melbourne, Macmillan.

Hays, S (1994) 'Structure and Agency and the Sticky Problem of Culture', *Sociological Theory* 12(1): 57-72.

Hays, S (1996) *The Cultural Contradictions of Motherhood*, New Haven, Yale University Press.

Heiler, K (2001) *How Effectively Do We Regulate Excessive Hours of Work in Australia?* Discussion paper Prepared for the Victorian Government, Sydney, ACIRRT.

Hewitt, P (1993) *About Time: The Revolution in Work and Family Life*, London, IPPR/Rivers Oram.

Hochschild, A (1997) *The Time Bind, When Work Becomes Home and Home Becomes Work*, New York, Metropolitan Books.

Hochschild, AR (1983) *The Managed Heart, Commercialization of Human Feeling*, Berkeley, University of California Press.

Hochschild, AR (1989) *The Second Shift: Working Parents and the Revolution at Home*, New York, Avon.

Human Rights and Equal Opportunity Commission (2002a) *Valuing Parenthood, Options for Paid Maternity Leave: Interim Paper*, Sydney, Human Rights and Equal Opportunity Commission.

Human Rights and Equal Opportunity Commission (2002b) *A Time to Value, Proposal for a National Paid Maternity Leave Scheme*, Sydney, Human Rights and Equal Opportunity Commission.

International Labour Office (2002) *A Future Without Child Labour, Global Report under the Follow-up to the ILO Declaration on Fundamental Principles and Rights at Work 2002*, Geneva, ILO.

Jackman, C (2003) Low Paid Use Most Child Care, *The Australian*, 14 February, p 4.

Jansen, D, Newman, M and Carmichael, WC (1998 (revised edition)) *Really Relating: How to Build an Enduring Relationship*, Sydney, Random House.

Junor, A (2000) 'Permanent Part-time Work: Rewriting the Family Wage Settlement?' *Journal of Interdisciplinary Gender Studies* 5(2): 94-113.

Kinnear, P (2002) *New Families for Changing Times*, Canberra, The Australia Institute.

Lane, RE (2000) *The Loss of Happiness in Market Democracies*, New Haven, Yale University Press.

Lash, S (1994) *Reflexivity and its Doubles: Structure, Aesthetics, Community, Reflexive Modernisation, Politics, Tradition and Aesthetics in the Modern Social Order*, Cambridge, Polity Press: 110-173.

Leach, P (1999) *Your Baby & Child: From Birth To Age Five*, Melbourne, Penguin.

Leira, A (2002) *Working Parents and the Welfare State, Family Change and Policy Reform in Scandinavia*, Cambridge, Cambridge University Press.

Lewis, V (2001) *Family and Work: The Family's Perspective*, Melbourne, Australian Institute of Family Studies.

Mackay, H (1993) *Reinventing Australia*, Sydney, Angus & Robertson.

Mackay, H (2001) Ever-changing Us: No Surprise At All, *Sydney Morning Herald*, 19 May, p 7.

Managing the Work/Life Balance 2003 (2002) *Work/Life Initiatives – The Way Ahead, 5th Annual Benchmarking Survey, Executive Summary for 2002*, Sydney, Managing Work/Life Balance.

Manne, A (2001) How to Breed Australians (It's not as simple as you think) *The Age*, 15 December.

McDonald, P (2001a) *Theory Pertaining to Low Fertility, International Perspectives on Low Fertility: Trends, Theories and Policies*, Tokyo, Paper presented to Conference in International Perspectives on Low Fertility, 21-23 March 2001.

McDonald, P (2001b) 'Work-Family Policies are the Right Approach to the Prevention of Very Low Fertility', *People and Place* 9(3): 17-27.

McDonald, P (2002) *Issues in Child Care Policy In Australia*, Canberra, Demography and Sociology Program, ANU.

McIntosh, G, Phillips, J and King, M (2002) *Commonwealth Support for Childcare*, Canberra, Parliamentary Library, Social Policy Group, e-brief, Parliament of Australia.

Meagher, G (2000) 'A Struggle for Recognition: Work Life Reform in the Domestic Services Industry', *Economic and Industrial Democracy* 21: 9-27.

Melbourne Institute of Applied Economic and Social Research (2002) HILDA Survey Annual Report 2002, Melbourne, Melbourne Institute of Applied Economic and Social Research.

Morehead, A, Steele, M, Alexander, M, Stephen, K and Duffin, L (1997) *Changes at work: the 1995 Australian Workplace Industrial Relations Survey*, Canberra, DEWSRB.

Murray, J (2001) *Transnational Labour Regulation: The ILO and EC Compared*, The Hague, Kluwer Law International.

National Pay Equity Coalition (2002) *Submission to the Senate Employment, Workplace Relations and Education Legislation Committee*, Canberra, The Senate Employment, Workplace Relations and Education Legislation Committee.

New Zealand Department of Labour (2002) *Parental Leave General Entitlements*, Fact Sheet, Wellington, New Zealand Department of Labour.

O'Farrell, P (1994) Introduction in P O'Farrell and L McCarthy, *Community in Australia*, Sydney, University of New South Wales: 7-11.

O'Farrell, P and McCarthy, L (eds) (1994) *Community in Australia*, Sydney, University of New South Wales.

O'Reilly, J, Cebrian, I and Lallement, M (eds) (2000) *Working-Time Changes, Social Integration Through Transitional Labour Markets*, Cheltenham, Edward Elgar.

O'Reilly, J and Fagan, C (eds) (1998) *Part-time Prospects: An International Comparison of part-time work in Europe*, North America and the Pacific Rim, London, Routledge.

OECD (1998) *A Caring World: An Analysis*, Paris, OECD.

OECD (2002a) *OECD Employment Outlook,* Geneva, OECD.

OECD (2002b) *Babies and Bosses, Reconciling Work and Family Life, Volume 1, Australia, Denmark and the Netherlands,* Paris, OECD.

Parliament of Australia (2002) Workplace Relations Amendment (Paid Maternity Leave) Bill 2002, Explanatory Memorandum, Canberra, The Parliament of Australia.

Parliament of the Commonwealth of Australia (2002) Workplace Relations Amendment (Paid Maternity Leave) Bill 2002.

Peel, M (1995) *Good Times, Hard Times, The Past and the Future in Elizabeth,* Melbourne University Press, Melbourne.

Pfau-Effinger, B (1998) Culture or structure as Explanations for Differences in Part-time Work in Germany, Finland and the Netherlands? in J O'Reilly and C Fagan (eds) (1998*) Part-time prospects; An international comparison of part-time work in Europe,* North America and the Pacific Rim, London, Routledge: 177-198.

Pocock, B (2001a) *Having A Life: Work, Family, Fairness and Community in Australia 2000,* Adelaide, Centre for Labour Research.

Pocock, B (2001b) *The Effect of Long Hours on Family and Community Life, A Survey of Existing Literature,* Brisbane, Queensland Department of Industrial Relations.

Pocock, B and Alexander, M (1999) 'The Price of Feminised Jobs: New Evidence on the Gender Pay Gap in Australia', *Labour & Industry* 10(2): 75-100.

Pocock, B, van Wanrooy, B, Strazzari, S and Bridge, K (2001c) *Fifty families: What Unreasonable Hours are Doing to Australians, Their Families and Their Communities,* Melbourne, ACTU.

Probert, B (2001) *'Grateful Slaves' or 'Self-made Women': A Matter of Choice or Policy?* Melbourne, Clare Burton Memorial Lecture 2001.

Probert, B, Ewer, P and Whiting, K (2000) 'Work versus Life: Union Strategies Reconsidered', *Labour & Industry* 11(1): 23-47.

Probert, B and MacDonald, F (1996) *The Work Generation: Work and Identity in the 1990s,* Melbourne, Brotherhood of St Lawrence.

Probert, B and Murphy, J (2001) 'Majority Opinion or Divided Selves? Researching Work and Family Experience', *People and Place* 9(4): 25-33.

Probert, B, Whiting, K and Ewer, P (1999) Pressure From All Sides, Life and Work in the Finance Sector, Melbourne, Finance Sector Union.

Probert, B, Whiting, K, Ewer, P and Segall, WP (1999) *Building the Foundations of Our Future: A National Research Project Exploring the Context of Women Teachers' Work in the Late 1990s,* South Bank, Australian Education Union.

Pusey, M (2003) *The Experience of Middle Australia, The Dark Side of Economic Reform,* Cambridge, Cambridge University Press.

Putnam, R (2000) *Bowling Alone, The Collapse and Revival of American Community,* New York, Simon and Schuster.

Richardson, L (1990) *Nobody's Home, Dreams and Realities in a New Suburb,* Melbourne, Oxford University Press.

Rubery, J (1998) Part-time Work, A Threat to Labour Standards? in J O'Reilly and C Fagan (eds) (1998*) Part-time prospects; An international comparison of part-time work in Europe,* North America and the Pacific Rim, London, Routledge: 137-155.

Russell, G, Hwang, P and Haas, L (2000) *Gender equity and organisational change: International perspectives on fathers and mothers at the workplace,* Sydney, Thousand Oaks, Sage.

Russell, G, Savage, G and Durkin, K (1992) *Balancing Work and Family: An Emerging Issue for Private and Public Sector Organisations*, Unpublished Paper.

Schmid, G (1995) 'A New Contribution to Labour Market Policy: A Contribution to the Current Debate on Efficient Employment Policies', *Economic and Industrial Democracy* 16: 429-456.

Schor, J (1992) *The Overworked American: The Unexpected Decline of Leisure*, New York, Basic Books.

Schor, J (1998) *The Overspent American: Why We Want What We Don't Need*, New York, Basic Books.

Schwartz, F (1989) 'Management Women and the New Facts of Life', *Harvard Business Review* 67(1): 65-77.

Selby, H (1983) *Long Service Leave*, Sydney, Law Book Company.

Sennett, R (1998) *The Corrosion of Character, The Personal Consequences of Work in the New Capitalism*, New York, WW Norton and Company.

Sennett, R and Cobb, J (1972) *The Hidden Injuries of Class*, Cambridge, Cambridge University Press.

Smith, A (1952 [1776]) *An Inquiry into the Nature and Causes of the Wealth of Nations*, Chicago, Encyclopedia Britannica, Inc.

Smith, M and Ewer, P (1999) *Choice and Coercion: Women's Experiences of Casual Work*, Sydney, Evatt Foundation.

Spearritt, K and Edgar, D (1994) *The Family Friendly Front: A Review of Australian and International Work and Family Research*, Melbourne, National Key Centre in Industrial Relations.

Stewart, C (2003) The Incredible Shrinking Childhood – Growing up Fast in the 21st Century – 21st Century Child, *Australian Magazine*, 25 January, pp 1-3.

Strachan, G and Burgess, J (1998) 'The `family friendly' workplace', *International Journal of Manpower* 19(4): 250-65.

Strachan, G and Jamieson, S (1999) 'Equal Opportunity in Australia in the 1990s', *New Zealand Journal of Industrial Relations* 24(3): 319-341.

Swedish Ministry of Health and Social Affairs (2002) *Swedish Family Policy: Fact Sheet*, No 5, April 2002, Stockholm, Ministry of Health and Social Affairs.

Taksa, L (1994) Definitions and Disjunctions, P O'Farrell and L McCarthy, *Community in Australia*, Sydney, University of New South Wales: 22-26.

The Weekend Australian Magazine (no author) (2002) The Weekend Australian Magazine, 14-15 September.

Tonnies, F (1957 [1887]) *Community and Society*, [Gemeinschaft and Gesellschaft) trans, CP Loomis, East Lansing, Michigan State University Press.

Wajcman, J (1998) *Managing like a man*, St, Leonards, Allen and Unwin.

Walsh, J (1999) 'Myths and Counter-Myths: An Analysis of Part-time Female Employees and their Orientations to Work and Working Hours', *Work, Employment and Society* 13(2): 179-203.

Waring, M (1988) *Counting for Nothing, What Men Value and What Women are Worth*, Wellington, Allen & Unwin.

Watson, D (2002) *Recollections of a Bleeding Heart, A Portrait of Paul Keating PM*, Sydney, Knopf.

Whitehouse, G (2001) 'Industrial Agreements and Work/Family Provisions: Trends and Prospects Under Enterprise Bargaining', *Labour & Industry* 12(1): 109-130.

Whitehouse, G and Zetlin, D (1999) "Family friendly' Policies: Distribution and Implementation in Australian Workplaces', *Economic and Labour Relations Review* 10(2): 221-239.

Williams, J (2000) *Unbending gender, Why family and work conflict and what to do about it,* New York, OUP.

Wolcott, I and Glezer, H (1995) 'Impact of the work environment on workers with family responsibilities', *Family Matters* 15(Winter): 15-19.

Wooden, M (2002) Conference Paper, ACIRRT Conference ' Working Time Today', 16 August 2002, Sydney, ACIRRT.

Workplace Express (Various years) <www.workplaceexpress.com.au>.

Wright Mills, C (1970 [1959]) *The Sociological Imagination*, Harmondsworth, Penguin Books.

Index

Also available from The Federation Press:

Fragmented Futures
New challenges in working life

accirt – Ian Watson, John Buchanan, Iain Campbell, and Chris Briggs

Fragmented Futures examines how working life has become more 'fragmented' as a result of significant social and economic change in Australia in the last quarter of the twentieth century. It asks how we should address such fragmentation in pursuit of a society in which prosperity is shared, diversity, choice and opportunity are increased, and exclusion and inequality are minimised.

The book begins by examining the dominant model for Australian working life throughout most of the twentieth century (known as 'Harvester man'), its breakdown and the response to date. It then explores the specific fragmentation processes that have occurred, using a combination of surveys, statistics and other qualitative and quantitative research. Trends and issues covered include:

- our aspirations
- opportunities for work, unemployment and underemployment
- industry restructuring and the disappearance of jobs and occupations
- the growth of non-standard forms of employment
- longer and more intense working hours
- wage trends and the rising gap between rich and poor
- the work/life balance
- skills, training and education
- retirement and superannuation
- how international factors such as increased competition, consumption and investment have contributed to the above changes.

Fragmented Futures provides a foundation on which to begin addressing the real social problems faced in work and life today. Its themes are at the core of everyday Australian experience; our response to its challenges will determine every Australian's future.

2003 • 1 86287 471 9 • paperback • 256pp • $49.50

The Hidden Gender of Law (2nd edn)

Regina Graycar and Jenny Morgan

[A]n understanding of the problems posed by Graycar and Morgan is a most important step along the road to equal justice for women and, ultimately, to equal justice for all.

Justice Mary Gaudron, High Court of Australia

This innovative book ... has much to say to anyone seeking to use the law to pursue equality and eradicate disadvantage, in Canada and elsewhere. The Hidden Gender of Law makes a wonderful contribution to reconceptualising law in the twenty-first century.

The Hon Madame Justice Claire L'Héureux-Dube,
Supreme Court of Canada

[T]he level of scholarship and analysis on the part of Graycar and Morgan is very high. ... strongly recommended.

Peter Barr, Balance (Law Society NT)

This is *a good book. For anyone with questions about feminism, or about law, or the seductive power of rhetoric and doctrine, this book has value.*

Sydney Law Review

[Q]uite simply, a tour de force.

Canadian Journal of Women and the Law

A starting point for becoming a new sort of practitioner.

New Zealand Universities Law Review

The contents is an easy-to-use look-up guide covering sub-topics as diverse as women's unpaid work, nervous shock, abortion, breast implant surgery, child custody, violence against women and pornography. ... Each topic is discussed within the context of current Australian statistics and attitudes.

Michaela Ryan, Law Institute of Victoria Journal

2002 • 1 86287 340 2 • paperback • 512pp • $66.00

The Black Grapevine

Aboriginal Activism and the Stolen Generation

Linda Briskman

The Black Grapevine tells the extraordinary story of Indigenous efforts to stop children becoming part of the 'stolen generation' and to end the government policies and practices which destroyed their families.

Linda Briskman uses the story of SNAICC to centre her book. Indigenous people involved tell how they came together to form a national organisation for child care, how they found similar experiences from one end of Australia to the other, how they pooled experience and emotion to provide support for one another, how they lobbied for a national inquiry.

And how they campaigned. Indigenous activists fought with astonishing resilience for recognition of past and present practices, for the right to have Indigenous viewpoints to the forefront, and for resources.

Briskman's story goes beyond the contest with the state to give a convincing portrait of the ways in which Indigenous groups work. There are connections with international action, educational projects, and the much-vaunted annual Aboriginal and Islander Children's Day.

She concludes by reflecting on the successes of campaigns and actions to date, and the extent of 'unfinished business' – the ongoing removal of Indigenous children from their families and the trauma still faced by those who are part of the stolen generations. Briskman's strong academic background combines with the oral testimony of the activists to produce a fast-moving book that is both entertaining and rigorous.

2003 • ISBN 1 86287 449 2 • paperback • 224 pages • $22.95

What Are Human Rights?

Thomas Fleiner

This is extraordinarily clear and simple account of what human rights are and why they are so important ... Each of the 35 chapters begins with a little story having human rights implications, and around that story Fleiner weaves his arguments. ... In an age when human rights are on the top of the global agenda, this excellent book written in simple prose appears as a 'Bible' of human rights.

West Bengal Political Science Review

This fascinating little book ... an easy-to read-style using simple language and many stories ... Almost anywhere one dips into the book one finds reference to topical issues ... most useful and stimulating

Panorama

A clearly-written book that engages the reader through practical examples and thought-provoking anecdotes

Journal of Family Studies

Fleiner successfully presents a realistic appraisal of human rights, one that acknowledges and highlights rather than avoids the difficulties inherent in the protection of human rights.

Australian International Law Journal

Thomas Fleiner is a leading Swiss constitutional lawyer who has practical understanding of government in countries as diverse as South Africa, the USA, Russia, China & Columbia. He was for over a decade a member of the International Committee of the Red Cross and has been involved in attempts to resolve some of the most terrible modern human rights problems, most notably in the former Yugoslavia. His book has previously been published in German, Russian, French and Spanish.

1999 • ISBN • 1 86287 328 3 • paperback • 176pp • $25.00